The Spiritual Formation of Leaders

Integrating Spiritual Formation and Leadership Development

Chuck Miller, Ed.D.

Endorsements for *The Spiritual Formation of Leaders*

Chuck Miller has not just written this book; more importantly, he has lived it. Chuck's impact on countless leaders comes from his life of integrity, his commitment to prayer, and his genuine godliness. There is no doubt in my mind that you will be a better leader by putting into practice the insights you find in *The Spiritual Formation of Leaders*. —*Jim Burns, Ph.D., President, HomeWord*

No one knows more about church leadership and building disciples than Chuck Miller. His insights always energize us. —*Rev. John Yates, pastor of The Falls Church (Anglican), Falls Church, Virginia, author; Susan Yates, author, speaker, Family Life Speaking Team, Campus Crusade for Christ*

There is a crisis of leadership in all areas of life today. One reason is that we are not doing a very good job shaping the character of potential leaders. Chuck Miller not only calls us to enjoy God's life-transforming grace, but he also provides life-shaping tools for both our inner lives and the roles of influence to which God calls us. This book is a practical guide which can be used by emerging leaders and experienced leaders alike. —*Dr. Stephen A. Hayner, Peachtree Associate Professor of Evangelism and Church Growth at Columbia Theological Seminary, Decatur, GA and President of InterVarsity Christian Fellowship (1988–2001)*

For all of us average, tired, productivity-driven ministry leaders who feel disconnected from Jesus, Chuck's clear vision of a leader's core passion as abiding with Jesus sweeps away all the debilitating debris of how-to leadership that so strangles the leader's soul. Pitcher/Cup...Saucer/Plate—brilliant, Chuck. Simply brilliant.— *Dan Wilburn, Pastor, Lakeland Community Church, Lee's Summit, MO*

Chuck Miller's teaching is a breath of fresh air! Never before have I ever heard or read anything like what Chuck lays out in this book. Absolutely no one else has ever clearly defined and explained how to both live and lead out of the Soul Room, to live and lead out of a relationship with God just as Jesus himself did. This book needs to be read and studied by all who take seriously the ministry of the kingdom of God in our world. —Jon Ciccarelli, *Lead Pastor, Escondido Seventh-Day Adventist Church, Escondido, CA*

For thirty-five years my ministry has been guided by the insights Chuck Miller spells out in his book *The Spiritual Formation of Leaders*. Chuck's insights have worked for campus ministry in Boston, a new church start in suburbia, and a refugee ministry in an urban Episcopal Church. Read, mark, learn, and inwardly digest this book! —*The Rev. David Montzingo, Associate Rector, St. Dunstan's Episcopal church, San Diego, CA*

Chuck Miller combines the organizational realities of leadership with the spiritual and inward realities of grace, and he does so with clarity, humor, and insight. Chuck leads us straight to Jesus himself as the model and the propellant for all leadership. This fresh, biblical teaching will strengthen your relationship with God the Father, Son, and Holy Spirit, and will give your leadership a more biblical shape—it has for me! Thank you, Chuck, for the precious gift of this book. I plan to use it and recommend it liberally. —*Jonathan Ball, Associate Divisional Director of InterVarsity Christian Fellowship, Greater Los Angeles*

Dr. Chuck Miller has recognized, along with many others, that the church in America is facing a crisis in leadership. However, unlike many others, *The Spiritual Formation of Leaders* moves beyond mere critique of the problems and advances realistic solutions. As one who has benefited greatly from his teaching, mentoring, and counsel for nearly thirty years, I appreciate the fresh insight Chuck has developed that weaves together the threads of spiritual formation and leadership into a tapestry that portrays the necessity of character development in the life of a leader. —*Jerry Root, Ph.D., Assistant Professor of Evangelism, Wheaton College, Wheaton, IL*

This is the book we've been waiting for! Chuck Miller speaks right to the heart of what Christian ministry and leadership are supposed to be all about: spiritual formation in Christ. It's a message that Chuck has lived out both personally and in his fifty years of pastoral ministry. Chuck's biblical insights, real-life examples, and compassionate prayers will draw you in to join him in abiding in Christ, loving others, and bearing witness. This is the way to a life and ministry in which we can exclaim with thanks to God: "My cup overflows!" —*William Gaultiere, Ph.D. and Kristi Gaultiere, Psy.D., Christian Soul Care, Psychotherapy and Spiritual Direction*

The sequence offered in this book—Pitcher/Cup… Saucer/Plate—continually helps me to prioritize the relationships, responsibilities, and opportunities God has given me. Interactive time spent with God in the morning or evening helps me to experience a fullness of joy in Christ, no matter how hectic the schedule. I know these insights can do the same for you. —*Erik Johnson, VP of Corporate Finance, QuikSilver, Huntington Beach, CA*

What could be more crucial for God's people in this and every age than the spiritual formation of our leaders? Chuck Miller has written a profoundly transformational yet extremely accessible book addressing this question. He skillfully helps us root ourselves and our leadership more deeply in the patterns Jesus gave all His followers in John 15: intimacy with God, expressing His sacrificial love for one another and reflecting God's love in the world. So, as you read, let God speak to you about how you view life and leadership and about the way you do both. —*L. Paul Jensen, Ph.D., Executive Director, The Leadership Institute*

Reading this guidebook for Christians in leadership is like a refreshing and challenging visit with a wise and experienced mentor. He knows the promises of following Jesus and shares his wisdom with those seeking guidance as leaders. — *The Rev. Dr. Roberta Hestenes, educator, pastor, and author*

This is a dangerous book! Read it at your own risk, but practice it only if you want to permanently change the way you—and 99 percent of other church leaders—have always done things in the church. Chuck Miller goes right to the heart of what I am called to do as a pastor and leader: the spiritual formation of the next generation of leaders. He talks about a ministry that really and truly flows out of the rich, joyful life of the Trinity. Chuck is a great teacher, and his concepts are as profound as they are simple. Just like his Lord's. —*Jim Pocock, Senior Pastor, Trinitarian Congregational Church, Wayland, MA*

We all think our leadership is to be an extension of our personal faith, but the daily application of this idea is challenged in our busy culture today. But God does an amazing transformation in our life when we—as Chuck Miller invites us to do—daily sit at His feet, spend time interacting with Him, pray, enjoy solitude with Him, and cherish our relationship with Him. If you allow God to use the truths in this book to impact your soul, it will transform your view of life and leadership. It's a journey I hope you will take! —*Kimberly Johnson, wife and mother*

Chuck Miller's idea that the Bible not only gives us God's message to convey, but also God's method of imparting it has shaped my ministry for the last 35 years. Whether I was teaching college students at Harvard, grad students in Africa, physicians in Mexico, or pastors in India, the ministry skills I imparted came from Chuck's insight into the Bible. Reading this book will draw you closer to the Lord and equip you to equip others. —*Charles White, Professor of Christian Thought and History, Spring Arbor University, Spring Arbor, MI*

During my formative days in seminary, I found a mentor in Chuck Miller. The life insights he taught were—and are—the basics of leadership that serve me still today. They are timeless biblical precepts that I've passed on to students and others for nearly three decades. In *The Spiritual Formation of Leaders*, a new generation can discover how they can make an impact for the kingdom. Every person who wants to make a difference for Christ should read it. —*Doug Clark, Director of Field Ministries. National Network of Youth Ministries, San Diego, CA*

Chuck Miller has it right. His analysis of the tensions we all sense between biblical leadership and modern corporate models is the clearest I've ever seen. His solution is even better. Don't be fooled by its simplicity. It is biblical. It works. Harried Christian leaders, don't dismiss this like the leper who derided bathing in the Jordan. Let God pour this book over your soul and your schedule. —*Clyde Cowan, North American Indian Ministries, Delta, British Columbia, Canada*

The church's greatest need today is for leaders, formed in the image of Christ, to teach others to do all that He commanded. And this book is one of the very best on how godly leaders are formed and what godly leadership looks like. *The Spiritual Formation of Leaders* is not a book of techniques and models to try. It is about lifestyle, about learning to live and lead as Jesus did: in intimate relationship with our heavenly Father. —*Karl Bruce, Director, The Spiritual Formation Alliance*

In these pages Chuck Miller guides the reader into what it means to become a leader fashioned after Jesus and fulfilled by God. Chuck calls leaders to recognize that godly leadership comes from the inside out. His concepts are completely biblical; his process, encouragingly practical; and his pages, purposefully targeted to leaders as well as laypeople who struggle and hope to bear lasting fruit for God's kingdom. —*Dr. Julie Gorman, Professor of Christian Formation and Discipleship, Fuller Theological Seminary, Pasadena, CA*

Chuck Miller's new book is a must-read for current and future leaders in ministry. It will enrich your relationship with God, challenge your commitment to the Word and prayer, transform your leadership style, and impact your ministry. —*Major Rudy Hedgren, Retired Salvation Army Officer who served as the Army's Territorial Youth Leader and Assistant Program Secretary*

This is the book so many of us have been asking Chuck Miller to write for years! I am thrilled that many more can now benefit from his godly wisdom, phenomenal insight, and gifted teaching. His focus will transform a person's relationship with Christ, the community of believers, and thus their perspective on priorities, prayer, the relevance of the Word, and, significantly, relational leadership." — *Carolyn B. Anderson, wife, mother, and attorney*

Too often, leadership development in Presbyterian (PCUSA) churches has meant information on how the denomination or congregation is organized and how church programs are developed and managed. How refreshing to have Chuck Miller set priorities straight in *The Spiritual Formation of Leaders* by beginning with the development of the leader's inner life in the Soul Room. —*Rev. Ted Schuldt, interim Presbyterian pastor, Seattle, WA*

In this volume, Chuck Miller offers not another ministry model to make us tired, but spiritual truths that revive our souls and bring our ministries back to life. What Chuck shares can lead to the fruitfulness that many of us stopped pursuing, thinking that it was a dream born of youthful idealism. Think again. —*Dr. Doug Burford, Pastor, Ward Parkway Presbyterian Church, Kansas City, MO*

Table of Contents

DEDICATION

God uses numerous people to impact our lives for our good and, more importantly, for His glory and mission, and some of these people shape and influence us throughout our life. This book is my thank you to three such people for their transforming and long-lasting impact on my leadership and life. I am in their debt.

To Dr. Lois LeBar
Professor of Christian Education at Wheaton College and Graduate School

Her pressing me to discover how Jesus did ministry and how He formed disciples and leaders laid the foundation for— and gave shape to—my lifestyle and ministry.

To Dr. Richard C. Halverson
Pastor of Fourth Presbyterian Church, Washington, D.C. and Chaplain of the United States Senate

His pastoral support, godly mentoring, and keen understanding of what the church is
enriched my theology as well as my lifelong commitment to the local church.

To Cathy Miller
She has been my best friend for over 50 years and my wife for almost 50 years.

Her love for Jesus and the Scriptures continues to challenge me.

Her desire to please God in life and ministry has refreshed scores of people, but especially me.

Her "merry heart that does good like a medicine" has carried us through times of ease and times of challenge.
We have written this book together for the last 50 years.
I love you, my Memphis lady.

ACKNOWLEDGMENTS

This book is the result of God's placing certain people along my path to shape the clay of my life—and it is my offering of thanks to Him for each one of you. So much of what I have become is because of your presence in my life and your love for the Lord and for me, and I'm grateful.

This book is also tangible evidence that God answers prayers. Many people have prayed for this project, encouraged me, and financially supported me. The book is a reality because they have been faithful.

This book is in your hands because of a team of special people.

The founders of *The Leadership Institute*—Paul Jensen, Wayne Anderson, and Jon Byron—and Alan Fadling did the storyboarding of the book with me. Thank you for helping me take the first step in turning this ministry dream into a reality.

Alan Fadling has continually interacted with the outline, with the manuscript, and with me. Your friendship, endurance, computer skills, and suggestions have been invaluable. Thank you.

Lisa Guest became a good friend as she did a remarkable job editing this book. You have improved immensely what I gave you, and your staunch faith and pleasant spirit have been greatly enjoyed and valued. Thank you.

Becky Roe, a professor of art and design at Azusa Pacific University and formerly in the college ministry at Lake Avenue Church in Pasadena, has done a first-class job on the cover and interior design of the book. Thanks, Becky, for your gentle spirit and excellent work.

Steve Bjorkman has cleverly captured the dominant idea of the book with his creative and fresh illustrations. Thanks, friend.

Finally, this book is in your hands because my dear brothers in the Lord who serve as the *Board of Directors of Barnabas* have supported this project and, since the midseventies, my ministry. Thank you.

Humbled by this list of people our good and gracious Lord has blessed me with, I close with a heartfelt "Thanks be to God!"

Chuck Miller

[The church today]
is one mile long, but
only one inch deep.
— Tokunboh Adeyemo

An Answer for the Leadership Crisis in the American Church:

Integrating Spiritual Formation and Leadership Development

Introduction

- Where are the healthy leaders?
- Why do we not see more leaders in the church today?
- And why are so many onetime leaders sitting in the bleachers?

   And the questions continue.

- Where are leaders of commitment, not convenience;
- Leaders of character and moral courage, not compromise;
- Leaders who serve for the long haul, not merely for a season?

   And where are leaders who have...

- A biblical foundation and a good understanding of contemporary culture;
- A Spirit-led inner transformation that expresses concern for the hurting among us;
- A God-given endurance for the hard times of life and of ministry?

   I praise God for the leaders in our church today, but how can we more effectively support and encourage them as they serve on the front lines? I also wonder what the church today can do to attract new leaders, especially from and for the younger generations. Finally—and of paramount concern to me—I want the church to develop leaders who, by God's grace, fully integrate spiritual formation and leadership development. Such leaders are able to effectively serve the Lord and His people as well as those people who have not yet named Jesus as their Savior.

THE CHURCH TODAY

It's hard to argue with theologian and writer John Stott who observed that evangelicals have "experienced enormous statistical growth … without corresponding growth in discipleship."[1] Echoing the same theme, African theologian Tokunboh Adeyemo lamented that the church "is one mile long, but only one inch deep."[2] Even more pointed is the observation of Oswald Sanders: "The supernatural nature of the church demands a leadership which rises above the human. And yet, has there ever been a greater dearth of God-anointed and God-mastered [people] to meet this crucial need?"[3]

Growing statistics, but stagnant discipleship…Shallowness versus depth… Leaders leading in their own power…No wonder the church today is struggling. The first step in solving this multifaceted problem is for Christians to become God-formed leaders who are living in vital and surrendered communion with the Lord and who will, in turn, guide others to become godly leaders living in vital and surrendered communion with Jesus Christ. In other words, the church needs you and me to become leaders who, like the apostle Paul with Timothy, can and will teach others how to be leaders. The church needs disciple-makers. Such efforts honor God as they fulfill His will for His church and His people. And such efforts must be rooted in a leader's life-giving relationship with God.

- Collin has been a pastor for over fifteen years. He has enjoyed God's blessing, but at times has felt run over, burned out, disillusioned, and not very appreciated. He is confused about whether he is called to preach or to manage. He's learned how to produce certain results, but he doesn't feel the presence of God in most of what he does.

- Jill and her husband have been volunteers in their church's high-school ministry for six years. They love the kids, but they feel detached from their own friends. They're also finding a big difference between being busy with ministry and being blessed by God. Jill feels as if she's starving spiritually. Her relationship with God occurs more through the high-school students than through personal intimacy with Him.

- Mike is a youth pastor. He loves the fun, goofiness, and tremendous potential of junior-high and high-school students. But he finds himself stressed and worn down. He runs more programs and leads more meetings than anyone else on the church staff. He also wants to cultivate his marriage and shepherd his own children well. All these demands at home and at church mean that Mike is rarely alone with God. When he does have time with the Lord, he's either rushed or emotionally and spiritually spent. He urges teenagers to have a love affair of intimacy and passion with God, but he feels that he's losing his own soul.

- Dan is on the governing board in a large church. He works long hours at the office, has a family, loves the Lord, and faithfully serves with others to do the work of the church. Yet too often he feels that the church is more a business than a movement of God. During his term he has been asked to do more and more—and his soul has gotten hungrier and hungrier. At this point, tired and spiritually empty, he can hardly wait until he's off the board.

Can you add your experience to this list—or could one of these stories be your own? In each of these situations, the demands of leadership and the leader's spiritual health are in tension. What's a person to do when loving God and trying to serve Him to the best of one's ability seems exhausting and draining, "more like a business than a movement of God," a matter of "being busy with ministry [rather than] being blessed by God"?

This book is a call for Christians to become God-formed leaders, to minister from a place of spiritual health and an intimate relationship with their Creator and King. This book is not another leadership model to try. Instead, it is about a way of living that God can use to form in us the heart—and develop in us the lifestyle—of a healthy leader. This journey integrates spirituality and leadership.

WHO IS A LEADER?

Before we go any further, who do you think I'm referring to when I talk about leaders? Let me be clear that I'm not using the word *leader*

to refer only to pastors, ordained elders, missionaries, or denomina-
tional executives. After all, kingdom ministry is carried out primarily
by laity (Ephesians 4:12). What I will share in this book about the formation of a leader applies not only to official, paid leaders, but
also—and just as effectively and fruitfully—to laity as they lead in the
marketplace, in the home, and as volunteers in the church. Stories in
this book tell of men and women living as influential people (leaders)
in their roles as moms and dads, salespeople and managers, attorneys
and teachers, and, yes, pastors and missionaries.

So realize that you are a leader. Wherever you live and wherever you work, you have the potential of being a leader of great
influence. In fact, I define leadership as "having influence." Every
single one of us has influence in the places we spend time and among
the people we encounter in our daily life—and sometimes we aren't
even aware of our influence. A word of caution is important. A careless leader influences others to carelessness. A money-oriented leader
influences others toward materialistic ends. But a godly leader influences others for God. God desires—and has designed—that each of
His people make a godly difference in the church and in the world.

IN SEARCH OF LEADERS

Think back to Collin, Jill, Mike, and Dan. The spiritual health of our
church leaders impacts not only them personally, but also those of us
who follow their lead as well as the ministry of the church in general.
We cannot afford to ignore the cries of the Collins, Jills, Mikes, and
Dans among us. And there are many among us.

Several years ago, for example, I asked our church staff to
document whenever one of our first-time visitors was a leader who
had left another local church. As we spoke with these people, we
heard them using words like "burned out," "tired," and "spiritually
empty." They often said, "I never want to be in leadership again." We
found that these tired and disillusioned leaders went to the bleachers
of non-leadership for a minimum of eighteen months before feeling
restored, nourished, and emotionally ready to take on any kind of
official church leadership again.

We as a society are becoming more and more aware of the importance of preserving our natural resources. We in the church must become more committed to preserving and developing the priceless resource we have in the leaders God gives us.

WHAT MAKES THIS BOOK DISTINCTIVE?

I'm going to answer that question with a word picture for you: I believe that we in America live in a two-room church. Let me explain.

In one room—which I call the Soul Room—are people excited about spiritual formation. They read certain books, develop a distinctive vocabulary, attend certain conferences, and focus on spirituality.

In the other room—the Leadership Room—are people excited about leadership. They read other books, develop a different vocabulary, attend different conferences, and focus on leading.

The church has tended to move type A people into leadership and the more reflective people toward prayer and spirituality. We end up forcing people to make an unnecessary choice between spirituality and leadership.

This book, however, is about both spirituality and leadership development. It integrates the Soul Room and the Leadership Room rather than keeping them separate or disconnected. In these pages, I will address both God's spiritual growth of the inner person and His development of that person's leadership knowledge and skills.

This focus on the inner person of the leader—the Soul Room—is rather countercultural. We are living at a time when leadership is based more on personality than character. When author and leadership consultant Stephen Covey studied the success-literature published in the United States since 1776, he saw that character was regarded as the key to success during our nation's first 150 years. What mattered in leaders were traits like integrity, fidelity, industriousness, and living by the Golden Rule. He noticed, however, that shortly after World War I the key to success began shifting toward personality. Success was increasingly seen as growing out of personality, public image, attitudes, behaviors, skills, and techniques. Some recent writings did mention character, but character was regarded as one of many elements of leadership and not the criterion by which success is defined or the foundation on which leadership is built. Covey concluded that America has moved from the character ethic to the personality ethic in its choice of leaders.[4] I believe that the church's view of leadership has been significantly influenced by this cultural shift. Sadly, less regard for the character of our Christian leaders has too often resulted in tragic moral failure. The church needs leaders of godly character, the kind of character described in Scripture and nurtured by the Holy Spirit.

Focusing on the personality rather than the character of our leaders is risky business, and this business has been supported by another development in our society. Over the last thirty years, the discussion of leadership—including leadership in the church—has come to emphasize effectiveness. With this emphasis comes the assumption that most important to leadership are the right personality type, an engaging charisma, a particular leadership style, appropriate spiritual gifts, an attractive personal appearance, and a carefully defined mission statement. I believe that basing our concept of leadership on such things is a fatal move. We in the church have already paid a high price: our leaders are wrung-out, struggling with moral failure, living lives that are out of balance, and feeling bitter toward, or disappointed in, the church and God.

But, sadly, we hadn't prepared these leaders to do otherwise. A consequence of thinking about leadership in terms of personality, style, and certain gifts has been our effort to shape leaders from the outside, in. Christian leaders are usually trained in theology, doctrine, speaking techniques, organizational methods, and church growth strategies. But if we are to reach our full potential as leaders—ordained or volunteer; in our homes, our workplace, our community—and if we are to see our work impact others for the Lord, we need to learn how to be God-followers in a way that transforms us and gives us life and strength from the inside, out.

Again, this approach is countercultural even within the church today. After all, we have many models of how to be Christian leaders. Take your pick—but know that such leadership models seldom address the intentional spiritual formation and transformation of the leader. Also realize that you will not find in the pages that follow any new techniques or surefire model for ministry. Instead, you will learn how leaders are empowered from the inside as they connect with God, the only Source of truly effective leadership.

THREE BOOKS IN ONE

We live in a culture of specialization. As reflected in the fields of medicine, law, engineering, and sales, we as a society are quite willing to pay a high price for specialists and the expertise they offer. The church has become a place that also values and is shaped by specialization: "What are your gifts? What are your passions? Join us and we will help you release these." Gifts for kingdom work are definitely from God, and the Holy Spirit certainly ignites passions in the human heart. But what does God say about the lifestyle of the person gifted for ministry? What does God expect in the lifestyle and values of the person who has passion for ministry?

It's significant to note that Jesus never talked about gifts while He was training the Twelve. Instead, He simply invited them to come and follow Him. He called His disciples then—and I believe He calls us today—to a life of integration, not a life of specialization; to a lifestyle that, day by day and moment by moment, integrates spiritual growth and leadership development.

If, however, we view the development of leaders with the eyes of a specialist, we will see that this book is actually three books. In fact, an author-friend of mine read one of the early versions and said, "Chuck, your book ends at the end of chapter 9." That is the viewpoint of a specialist: "Let's focus on growing spiritually, on becoming more intimate with the Lord." However, when Jesus was shaping the leaders of the early church, He wanted the tapestry of their lives and ministries to reflect the solid integration of *communion* with God, *community* with one another, and *commissioning* to live in the world. These are the topics of the three books you are about to read, and these three threads form the God-designed, God-ordained tapestry for leadership. For too long, though, we have isolated the threads and made them areas of specialization: "If you love quiet and solitude, you'll love developing intimacy with God. Come and join this ministry. However, if you're energized by being with people, small groups are where it's happening for you, and we'll introduce you to the leader of our small groups. Or if you have a heart for people not yet following Jesus Christ, join us in some of our outreach ventures. We need you."

Underlying this approach is the assumption that people in the church are fully integrating their personal spiritual growth and their leadership development efforts and therefore we are free to release them to specialize in an area of ministry—and this is a fatal assumption. Through the years I have seen too many believers become hardened and stuck in their place of specialization. A lifestyle that integrates spiritual growth and leadership development softens that hardness and enables healthy servanthood in a specific area of ministry. May this book, with its call to integration, therefore speak to the whole of your life and to the life of the church leaders you hope to develop. Only with a foundation of integration can we step out and specialize in an area of ministry and leadership. May the truths in this book cultivate a healthy lifelong integration that will in time empower healthy specialization.

WHY SHOULD YOU READ THIS BOOK?

- Are you enjoying your leadership role, but would like to gain more insights about how to lead?
- Are you exhausted from trying to be all things to all people and ready to quit?
- Do you love being involved in church leadership but realize that your life is out of control?
- Are you hurting, aware of having given a lot yet feeling used or, worse, betrayed?
- Are you holding your own or perhaps feeling lost, wanting to find answers to your questions and clearer direction for your ministry?

If you answered yes to any one of those questions, I'm glad you picked up this book, and let me tell you some reasons why you should keep reading.

This book will help leaders—and that's all of us—gain further insight into godly leadership as well as establish a foundation for a lifetime of healthy ministry and vibrant disciple-making. This book will give a renewed sense of purpose to leaders who are going through the motions and hungering for a renewed passion for ministry and for life. This book will help guide folks who are considering church leadership and who desire direction and training that will keep them strong in spirit. This book will also speak to leaders who are disengaged, disillusioned, or burned out, leaders who have gone to the bleachers. These pages will offer these tired servants hope and point the way to refreshment in God.

Basically, this book will encourage you in the lifelong adventure of:

- Meeting with God in the innermost room of your being, in your soul. *How long has it been since you felt comfortable sharing your frustrations, dreams, ambitions, fears, hopes, and disillusionment with your heavenly Father? When was the last time you felt deeply cleansed within and wonderfully refreshed by His living water?*
- Working alongside God in your home, church, workplace, and neighborhood, among the many people and in the various places to which He guides you along the way. *Are you feeling unfocused? Are you lacking energy, purpose, and any real sense of excitement or mission?*

I know from personal experience that leadership can be fun, enriching, fulfilling, and life-changing. It can also be exhausting, draining, frustrating, and overwhelming. Whatever leadership roles you find yourself in today and however you're feeling about those responsibilities, this book will speak to you. When you finish reading this book, you'll understand how to lead from a place of God-given strength and internal rest in the Lord as well as with a clear external focus and directedness. As it integrates spirituality and leadership, this book will shape and inspire the new, the casual, or the committed leader, any leader who is willing and ready to adventure with God.

Blessings on your journey!

Chuck Miller

Lake Forest, CA 2007

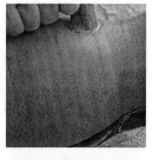

*Although potential
leaders are born,
effective leaders
are made.*
— *Bennie Goodwin*

I'm Not a Type A Person.
Can I Be An Effective Leader?

Becoming a Healthy Leader on Your Journey with God

A LIFELONG JOURNEY WITH GOD

Whether you are a pastor, a small-group leader, a youth worker, or a board member at your church, you may have asked many questions about Christian leadership:

- What can I do to become a more godly and effective leader?
- How can I protect myself and others from burning out and bailing out?
- How can we enlist and train more leaders, especially people from younger generations?

In this book, I describe a lifelong journey with God, a journey that offers answers to these and other questions about spiritual growth and about leadership. I am convinced a key to effective leadership is our personal, intimate, ongoing, and ever deepening relationship with God. I have found that when I meet with Him in what I call the Soul Room, He prepares me to serve Him and His people in the Leadership Room. By way of invitation to you, let me share a little about my own journey with God.

In both the Soul Room and the Leadership Room, I develop a growing awareness of my dependence on God, of my wayward nature, of my need for Him, and of the mystery of His person and presence.

In these rooms I keep learning about surrendering to God and allowing Him to form both the inner patterns of my life and the outer patterns of my lifestyle and leadership. As this happens, I also discover God working through me to radically transform people's lives for His glory. This two-room process continually increases my dependence on God, and it reminds me that He alone can change my heart and character *and* the heart and character of the people I lead. In this two-room process, I also learn to enjoy the mystery of God's work in my own life and in the lives of others.

This leadership process also offers me—just as it offers you—a growing experience of God's grace and the adventure of living with faith in Him. Imagine the privilege of cooperating with the God of the universe in His plan for His creation! In light of this very real privilege, the Soul Room and the Leadership Room can be places of daring adventure in our own spiritual formation and in the spiritual growth of others. When I spend time with God in the Soul Room, He extends His saving and strengthening grace to me. Then, when I go with God into the Leadership Room, He leads me and enables me to extend His grace and kindness to others.

In the Soul Room—the room too often ignored in our efforts to lead—the focus shifts from me to God. I find myself caught up in His majesty and embraced by His compassionate presence. In the Soul Room, God speaks to me as His friend. He joins in my excitement about leadership and ministry. He provides understanding for my struggles, my stumbles, my failures, and my sin. He speaks words of forgiveness, healing, and acceptance to my broken and burdened heart. He speaks words of hope to my discouragement and disillusionment. He refines my character, and He fires my imagination. In the Soul Room, I continually rediscover His love, His grace, and His refreshment. In the Soul Room, I become a worshiper of God. And in the Soul Room, the Father, Son, and Spirit form me into an effective leader for Their kingdom.

The Leadership Room then becomes an extension of the Soul Room. I'm led by the Spirit of God into the Leadership Room, and there I cooperate with Him as He develops my eyes, heart, and patterns of leadership. He fuels within me His passion for people, He helps me desire what He desires for them, and He allows me to see kingdom fruit.

No wonder I see both the Soul Room and the Leadership Room as critical in the formation of healthy Christian leaders, lay or otherwise. I also believe that God wants my lingering in the Soul Room to continually energize my impact in the Leadership Room.

So in this chapter I will compare leaders who are formed according to ministry models and those formed according to the biblical process reflected in Soul Room/Leadership Room. You will see the integration of spiritual and leadership development in diagram and biblical story. Read, reflect, and enjoy this journey. But first, let us pray.

Holy God, personal God, I thank You that You are alive and that You live with us and within us. Please meet and empower the person who is reading this chapter. Increase his/her excitement about You. Grow in him/her a greater understanding and stronger conviction to be a committed follower of the living Christ—in whose name I pray. Amen.

Today, since we are surrounded by many different cultural models of church, there is a great need for the church and its leaders to discover a biblical process for church leadership. By *biblical process* I mean the process by which God births and develops people, leaders, and ministries for His glory. And this biblical process—as opposed to a ministry model—must be central in the training of Christian leaders. As God-followers, we must discover and live within the biblical process rather than being borne along by the current "this-is-what-works" model.

Yet too often we may find ourselves wondering, "Are my struggles in leadership due to my failure to find the right discipleship program or church-growth model? I wonder if another model would fit me better. Or am I having trouble fitting in because I am not a type A person? Maybe I am not really a leader after all." I believe the simple answer to this concern is no. In fact, I believe this kind of questioning misses the larger issue: *I believe we leaders need to live according to a biblical process, not according to a ministry model.* This book is not about leadership technique or about a particular model for leadership. Instead, this book is about learning how leaders in the church, in the home, and in the world can be empowered from the inside as they connect with the hidden Source of energy and imagination, strength and wisdom, grace and love.

UNDERSTANDING MINISTRY MODELS

At one time or another, every one of us involved in Christian leadership has gained insight and benefited from various models of ministry, each one based on a focused need that has often been unaddressed in our own congregational life. The goal of resolving this particular unmet need was established somewhere, and a program was designed to reach that goal. The model's specific suggestions and approaches provide solutions that have worked in a particular place or ministry.

During my forty-plus years in Christian leadership, for instance, I have personally benefited from many models that may or may not be familiar to you. *Body Life*, a book written by Ray Stedman, pastor of Peninsula Bible Church in Palo Alto, California, provided insights into the importance of living in authentic community rather than living as separate islands. *Evangelism Explosion*—from the ministry of Dr. James Kennedy, pastor of Coral Ridge Presbyterian Church in Coral Ridge, Florida, before he went home to be with the Lord— helped me learn to strike up conversations with people not yet following Jesus. The seeker-sensitive model brought to us by Bill Hybels of Willow Creek Community Church reminded me that I must understand well the words, pictures, and values of the culture into which God has sent me to communicate the gospel. The spiritual-gifts model popularized by C. Peter Wagner and others caused me to realize that God's people are not only servants, but also gifted individuals empowered by God to share His grace. Most recently, God has used *The Purpose Driven Church* by Saddleback Church pastor Rick Warren to richly bless His people and, in my case, to prompt me to ask myself—and others—"Why am I here? What is God's intention for my life?"

Such models have strengthened the church where it has been weak. Furthermore, these models are packaged and easily shared, they often raise leaders' confidence in their work, they bring new ideas and new ways to a church body, they help church communities break new ground, and they can simplify a leader's life and clarify that person's approach to ministry. I have studied all of these models, read the books, and often received specific training. In recent years, I have also served on church staffs that follow one or more of these models.

The problem with models, however, is that we often use them as templates for developing leadership and ministry. These models become the blueprint that completely defines the ministry playing field—and they often take us many steps away from the Bible's pattern of developing leaders.

A LEADERSHIP/MINISTRY MODEL VS. AN ONGOING GOD-PROCESS

Consider with me the differences between a particular ministry model and what I call an ongoing God-process. We'll look at the strengths and contributions of ministry models and, as we do so, realize that the distinction between model and process is not merely a matter of semantics. Case in point.

A friend of mine candidated for a position on a pastoral staff. During the interview he was asked, "If given this position, what would you do, how would you do it, and what outcomes would you expect?" The committee liked my friend's answers and eventually called him to the position. He went to the church and did what he said he would do, but the outcomes that he had forecast and that the committee had dreamed of did not occur. My friend felt discouraged, disillusioned, out of place, and significantly judged by the congregation's lay leadership. He desired to leave. His sad story brings into focus six key differences between model leadership and process leadership.

Observation #1

A model presents a product.

Biblical process presents a path.

In a model, the outcome is established. It is defined and often able to be measured. In the biblical process of leadership, the specific outcome is often unknown. It is prayed for, dreamed about, and often unquantifiable. In his interview, my friend presented a model. He and the committee dreamed about the product and imagined the outcomes. But a year later the model hadn't produced.

And I know this experience personally. Once I was talking with a man who helped church plants by sending out zip-code mailings. He told me that if we mailed out so many thousand pieces to our city, he could guarantee that two hundred new people would attend our church the following Sunday. We sent the pieces. Eleven new people came.

Beware lest the seeming security of a model's promised outcomes distracts you from focusing on God, God-process, and the path He provides. The following experience echoes that warning.

Recently, I was on the phone with a friend whose pastor had attended a popular leadership seminar. When he returned to his church, he took the staff and lay leaders on retreat to focus on this new way of doing church and impacting the world. His excitement level was high, but my friend shared with me, "Our church today is severely divided and diminished over this new model that has been introduced." They are discovering that what works in Phoenix doesn't necessarily work in Pittsburgh. In other words, the model that worked well where it was developed wasn't transferring well to this new setting. A model became a blueprint rather than a resource to be drawn upon as needed.

Observation #2

A model arises from a situation and provides a sense of closure.

Biblical process recognizes that God is continually at work in a situation.

A model develops in the context of a unique situation and embodies insights and skills gained over time in that situation. The model may very well have taken shape as a result of an encounter with God, but the model tends to only pass along the "how to do it" elements. A model shares a product rather than a process. Models present the template and the tool kit. They send the message "Come and learn from us." A model provides a sense of measurability and closure. It defines completed goals and steps to take to reach those goals.

With process, however, there is a sense of something unfolding, a sense of mystery and the unknown. Rather than being a closed container, process is open ended. And instead of beginning by offering defined steps toward measurable goals, biblical process celebrates who God is, what He has done, and what He continues to do. This process acknowledges that God will lead us to take specific steps, and some of those steps will involve something measurable (e.g., more people attending worship). Leaders, however, must always be aware that God is present and doing many things that are both unseen and unmeasurable.

Observation #3

A model draws attention to itself saying, "Look at *it*."

Biblical process draws attention to God and says, "Look to *Him*."

Almost always leaders are measured against the model they adopt. Few "God questions" are asked by anyone. With process, however, leaders are mindful of the constant presence of God and His ongoing work in circumstances and in individual hearts. Process asks the question "What is God doing in the people, in us?" rather than "What does the model tell us to do next?" Asking the God question protects us from focusing on—and being enslaved to—a model.

And a model can be a cruel master—as Barry learned. He was an energetic youth pastor whom God was using in a wonderful way to reach teenagers with His truth and love. Eventually, God called Barry to a new church in another city. He arrived with excitement and confidence that he'd see God work. Barry envisioned the kinds of blessings he experienced in his previous church being reproduced in his new church. So he dreamed, labored, designed, and tried hard, but it seemed that the more energy he gave, the more the ministry unraveled. He became discouraged, and this caused tremendous stress on his marriage. Furthermore, he and the church became disillusioned with each other. Finally, a defeated and discouraged Barry left the church and the ministry. The model that worked in the first church didn't work at the second one. Could one reason be that, while models do indeed provide focus for ministry, success in reaching the set goals according to the model's way can lead to rigidity?

In contrast to this kind of rigid adherence to a plan that worked for someone somewhere, biblical process relies on the leader's growing relationship with Christ from whom comes focus, ministry ideas, and Spirit-led flexibility. That's why leadership according to biblical process keeps one open to flexibility and change. As former Chaplain to the U.S. Senate Richard Halverson noted, "The church has its own alpha and omega. The alpha: 'We've always done it that way.' The omega: 'We've never done it this way.'" Too often the church becomes frozen in its blueprint.

I have, however, had the pleasure of knowing many church leaders who are open to biblical process and God's mysterious but faithful guidance. One such leader was Dr. Donald McGavran, a missionary in India for many years who, year after year, saw God do amazing things. New believers came to faith in Christ, and the community of saints was built up to God's glory. In Dr. McGavran's later years, he brought to the worldwide church the church-growth model. He and I were speaking and consulting with a well-known international missions agency. Its field directors from around the globe were gathering in Northern California for a think-tank experience. They were there to plan, dream, and identify their mission goals for the next three years.

Dr. McGavran and I were sharing a cabin. One of our days together began at about 5:30 in the morning and went until late evening. As I walked up a steep hill at about 10:30 after our long day, I noticed a light on in our cabin. When I opened our door, I saw Dr. McGavran seated in the far corner of the room. This man—in his midseventies and thirty-plus years my senior—was reading his Bible. I moved quietly in the room until he finished reading. When he was finished, I asked him, "May I make a comment?"

Dr. McGavran invited me to speak, and I said, "Please don't assume that my generation does what you were just doing. Lingering in God's presence and reflecting on a biblical text is not a prominent part of our life. When we come to the end of a day, we turn on the television or read the paper. We don't typically sit and read our Bible like you were just doing."

Now, we may have varied opinions of Dr. McGavran's church-growth model, but I'm more concerned about the many leaders who have taken his model for ministry, but not his life process. They did not understand that behind the model was a man who lived in a deep, intimate relationship with God. Dr. McGavran looked to the Lord to direct his ministry and guide his steps. What resulted was a model for others to see, but I think such models go wrong when they become detached from their living source—from the God-process of the particular person or group that developed the model. We need to look to the God whom we want to serve!

Observation #4

Models run their course.

Biblical process is ongoing.

If you were leading a college ministry in the late sixties and early seventies, you needed a coffeehouse. So our college ministry fixed up a wonderful coffeehouse. It was to be a comfortable, nonthreatening place for us to connect with one another and to welcome new students. Coffee, music, and conversation in a casual atmosphere were cool, and we wanted to do our coffeehouse ministry with excellence. By the time we got our coffeehouse refurbished, though, that coffeehouse model for ministry had run its course. The season had passed, and coffeehouses were definitely a thing of the past. We'd missed the prime season for that model.

In biblical process, however, God continually connects with me and refreshes me in Christ. He keeps me alert to present and changing situations. Of course we can draw valuable insights and even how-tos from models, but those models must never become a blueprint for developing healthy leaders and ministries. Let me also mention that I have seen many leaders seem strong and effective when the model is going well, but when the model begins to run its course, these leaders floundered and didn't know what to do. Models have their season, but biblical process—and the nurture and power it offers leaders—will never be out of season.

Observation #5

Models say, "Follow it."

In the biblical process, Jesus says, "Come, follow Me."

"It" may be a model of a ministry for children or couples. "It" may be a model for a singles ministry or leadership development. Whatever the need being met by the model, advocates say, "Follow it." By nature of its established design, a model may not be able to address unique circum-

> *Beware lest the it of a model diverts you from the Who of the biblical process.*

stances or changing needs. By nature of its design, however, biblical process can constantly respond to unique circumstances and changing needs.

Consider that, when Jesus instituted His leadership training process, He put the focus on Himself, not on the trainee or the model. So listen carefully for Him say to you, "Come, follow Me." Also ask the God-process questions like "What are the needs right now?," "What is God saying?," "What is on God's heart?," "Where is God working now?," "What is God doing?," and "What can we do to follow Him and join Him in this work?" Beware lest the *it* of a model diverts you from the *Who* of the biblical process.

That warning was often voiced to me by a man of God I greatly respected. In the sixties I had the privilege of working for six years on a pastoral staff with a man I quoted earlier in this chapter: Dr. Richard C. Halverson. He was senior pastor at Fourth Presbyterian Church in Washington, DC and later became chaplain of the United States Senate. Even after I moved away to serve at another church, our intimate relationship continued until God took him home in November 1995. During those years, we often had meaningful discussions prompted by how disturbed Dr. Halverson was by models and by how quickly Christian leaders gave their allegiance to them. Early in his Christian life, Dr. Halverson felt that models manipulated people and shoved God aside. He also saw that too often people's confidence shifted from trusting in God to trusting in models. And I agree.

OBSERVATION #6

Models tend to focus on management.

Biblical process acknowledges mystery.

When I follow a model for ministry, I see the whole, the end from the beginning, and every step in between. The tool kit—the implementation kit—is complete, and my primary task is to manage the tools effectively. This job assignment can give me a nice sense of security and control.

In a biblical process of ministry, though, I see God alone. He enables me to see the road, but often not very far down it. And in contrast to a model's complete, no-surprise package, biblical process promises only God's companionship and many holy surprises along the way. Understandably, biblical process may inspire feelings of both trust and insecurity. Beware that the pressures of model management can distract us from the mystery of God's presence with us in ministry.

MOVING FROM MODELS TO PROCESS

I remember lecturing in a doctor of ministry course being taught by Dr. Robert Munger at Fuller Theological Seminary. At the time, he was president of the board of my ministry Barnabas Inc. and occasionally he asked me to speak to these pastors on the next-to-last day of his intensive two-week course. Every time I had that privilege, I said to the pastors, "Your elders and leaders aren't exactly excited about your coming home from this course." They would wonder what this crazy lecturer meant, so I continued.

"The leaders in your church remember when you went to a weekend conference awhile back," I said. "You gathered many new ideas and then went home to try them. They also remember how, after about three to six months, the whole thing ran out of gas. Later, you went to another conference and got a new model and another set of ideas. After you tried this one back home for a few months, it too ran out of gas. Imagine what your church leaders are thinking now that you've been gone a whole two weeks! They're expecting you to come home with a new model and a truckload of thoughts and ideas—and they are scared stiff!"

After the laughter subsided, I talked to the pastors about an alternative to new models and plans and ideas. I taught them about the biblical process for forming healthy leaders. As I've mentioned, I think of that process as happening in the Soul Room and the Leadership Room—and, as the diagram illustrates, the two are completely integrated. (The diagram below shows the two rooms in which this godly leadership process develops.)

We are soul creatures. We have feelings, desires, thoughts, longings, fears, and loves. We also need relationship, and we were created for communion with God. As Blaise Pascal put it, "There is a God-shaped vacuum in every person." We are people with an inner life that is not to be ignored; we are people of the Soul Room.

We also have an outer life, and we're on a journey that is quite observable. We develop friendships. We live in people groups. We have the opportunity to influence others; we are people of the Leadership Room.

What happens in the Soul Room spills into the Leadership Room. What happens in the Leadership Room is brought into the Soul Room. This biblical leadership process is a two-room process.

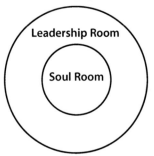

Where can you learn more about this Soul Room/Leadership Room process of God? Will you ask the successful church leader? read a book? go to the season's hottest new leadership seminar? I maintain that none of those resources will be as helpful as what God Himself has already said on the subject of leadership. So let's open His Word and see how God develops one of the Bible's greatest leaders.

GOD CALLS A LEADER

Few people would disagree with the statement that Moses was one of the most significant leaders in all of human history. Jews, Christians, and Muslims alike all look to Moses as a respected and influential leader.[1]

Moses was raised in the home of the Egyptian pharoah, the world leader of his day. A privileged child, Moses had opportunities that few others had. He also lived at the Egyptian crossroads of dominant trade routes of the time, so he interacted with many influential people.

As a young man, Moses witnessed the attack of a Hebrew slave by an Egyptian. He responded by taking matters into his own hands and killing the Egyptian. The next day he noticed two Hebrews fighting. When Moses stepped in to resolve their conflict, one of them essentially said, "I saw you murder that Egyptian yesterday." Moses was terrified. The news spread, and Pharaoh himself heard what Moses had done. Moses was a marked man, and he fled for his life. Talk about a huge black mark on his record! Why would the God of process pursue this man with such a bloody stain on his resume? Had Moses forfeited his opportunity to lead?

Many years later, we meet Moses again. He is married, has a family, and works for his father-in-law tending sheep. He doesn't look much like a potential leader and hardly an influential one. But one day at work, Moses notices a bush that is on fire but is not turning to ashes. As he approaches it, a voice from inside the bush calls him by name. The Voice tells Moses to stop and remove his sandals because he's standing in a holy place. The Voice then identifies Himself: "I am the God of your father, the God of Abraham, the God of Isaac and the God of Jacob" (Exodus 3:6). Moses covers his eyes and is afraid to look. We see here the process of God revealing Himself as the God of history and a God of relationships. We see here a lesson for each of us: Before God calls us to mission, He calls us to a personal and ongoing relationship with Himself. **This call to relationship is the starting point of the process by which God forms leaders for His church**.

During this encounter, God expresses His concern for the suffering of His people in Egypt. God also declares His intention to rescue the Hebrews and take them to a better place. This divine plan calls for human leadership, and God asks Moses to become that leader who will confront Pharaoh and lead the Israelites out of Egypt. In response, Moses asks God a question that you may have asked yourself: "Who am I to do that job?" Moses doesn't feel qualified for the task. In fact, murderer that he is, he might even feel completely disqualified. He knows he can lead his father-in-law's sheep, but he's not sure about people.

But God refocuses Moses and says, "Moses, I am at the center of this, not you".

After Moses asks, "Who am I?" God says, "I will be with you" (Exodus 3:11-12). God's reply doesn't sound like an answer to Moses' question. That's because it really isn't. Moses is looking for a little personal affirmation about his ability to lead such an endeavor, but God doesn't address that issue at all. Moses is asking, "God, do I have the right temperament, the right gifts, the right passion, enough charisma?" But God refocuses Moses and says, "Moses, *I* am at the center of this, not you. I am the Speaker, and you are the listener. I am the Initiator, and you are the responder. I am the Inviter, and you are the invited."

Do you see what is happening here? Moses' leadership of God's people is to be based on his relationship with his God and on God's ongoing presence with Moses during the journey ahead. Moses will not lead as a solitary "I." Moses will be a leader who is "we" with God. Moses will not go to Pharaoh alone; God will be with him. Moses alone will not lead the Israelites out of Egypt; God will be with him. Moses alone will not lead the Hebrew nation into the Promised Land; God will be with him. God's process for integrating spirituality and leadership development is birthed in Moses (and all of us) in the place of relationship with God—and that is where our leadership skills continue to grow. (Notice that God even has Moses spend forty days alone with Him on a mountain. Talk about developing a solid relationship!) In the life of Moses, God demonstrates how He continually forms leaders: this biblical process begins with—and continues to be based on—the truth of who God is, not who the leader is.

GOD'S PROCESS FOR MOSES—AND FOR YOU

I confess that, as a leader who works diligently in the Leadership Room, I find myself occasionally assuming that I am in charge. After all, that is what the organizational chart says, and I feel I need to solve the problems in the Leadership Room. But when the going gets rough, I know I have God available as a consultant in the Soul Room if I need Him. Whenever I enter the Soul Room, though, God gently shifts this agenda of mine. He invites me to take a seat, and He calms my leader's anxious heart. I may have come with some urgent problem that needs to be addressed right away, but He makes it clear that what I need first is simply… Him. He reminds me and reassures me of both His bigger picture and His loving support. He wants me to understand anew that the Leadership Room is *His* room, not mine.

> *He wants me to understand anew that the Leadership Room is His room, not mine.*

Then, in His time, He takes me to the windows of the Soul Room to look into the Leadership Room of my life. He speaks passionately to me about His deep concern for the people and situations that I am dealing with there. God gives me insight into my leadership roles as well as into the people I'm leading. He looks with me at some of the frustrating and puzzling situations I'm facing. He reminds me that, because He is Lord, the problems out there are His and that He's not expecting me to carry them as my own. When I meet with God in the Soul Room, He expresses His love for me, He enlarges my perspective on the kingdom work He wants to do through my ministry, He clarifies my thinking about the problem I face, and He renews my passion to do His work and to love His people. There in the Soul Room, I worship Him and renew my commitment to go with Him out into the Leadership Room.

Then, as we enter the Leadership Room together, God begins to show me around. I start to realize once again that He's been there a lot longer than I have and that He's far more aware of who is there and what is happening than I had realized.

And I am definitely not the only person who has discovered the value of recognizing God's presence with us as we try to lead. In *Under the Unpredictable Plant*, Eugene Peterson offers this encouraging truth about our interaction with God in the Leadership Room, a truth based on Mark 16:6-7—"He has risen… he is going before you to Galilee; there you will see him, as he told you." Hear these encouraging words:

> In every visit, every meeting I attend, every appointment I keep, I have been anticipated. The risen Christ got there ahead of me. The risen Christ

is in that room already. What is he doing? What is he saying? What is going on? In order to fix the implications of that text in my vocation, I have taken to quoting it before every visit or meeting: "He is risen ...he is going before you to 1020 Emmorton Road; there you will see him, as he told you".... When I arrive and enter the room, I am not so much wondering what I am going to do or say that will be pastoral as I am alert and observant for what the risen Christ has been doing or saying that is making a gospel story out of this life.... We are always coming in on something that is already going on.... Always we are dealing with what the risen Christ has already set in motion, already brought into being.[2]

Aren't we leaders supposed to enter a situation, exert our influence, and make something happen? No. Instead, before entering the Leadership Room, we should first connect with God in the Soul Room. There His presence and grace become increasingly central in our life. Then God will invite and enable us to join Him in what He is already doing in the Leadership Room. Being with and listening to God in the Soul Room positions us to receive His direction for cooperating with Him in His work. He may invite us to come alongside specific people, to take charge in certain circumstances, or to just sit and listen in another setting. He may have us hold our tongues, express our concern, or pray with someone. Our work in the Leadership Room becomes more and more an expression of the work He is doing in us when we meet with Him in the Soul Room.

In the God-process,

relying on Him is always primary.

God of both the Soul Room and the Leadership Room, *please refresh me and transform me as I encounter You in both rooms and as I open myself to learning what kind of leader You want me to be. May Your Spirit teach me how to move back and forth between these two unique and crucial rooms. In a world where leaders often focus on the Leadership Room and struggle to find time for the Soul Room, help me to root myself in the Soul Room, and when I'm there, enable me to welcome whatever You desire to do in my life, whatever You need to do to continue to form me into Your image, so that I will be effective in the Leadership Room for Your glory. In the name of the God—the Father, Son, and Holy Spirit—who develops character in leaders. Amen.*

Before You Take the Next Step

What insight in this chapter did you find especially helpful? Why?

What models have helped you in ministry and leadership? Be specific about how they helped.

In what ways have you been tempted to rely on models more than on God Himself? Talk to Him about this.

May God nourish your life in the Soul Room and in the Leadership Room.

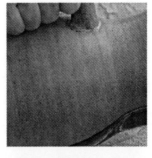

Which resume is more accurate for your life up to this point: one that shows you are in control or one that shows you are an apprentice of the Master?

Who Me? A Leader?

Learning to Lead by Following the Master

Jesus has a mission for His followers, and He is very clear about it: "Go and make disciples of all nations, baptizing them in the name of the Father and of the Son and of the Holy Spirit" (Matthew 28:19). The implementation of this plan for spreading His kingdom on earth depends on effective leaders. The people Jesus trained personally did—by God's grace—carry out this mission, and in doing so they started a chain reaction that continues even after twenty centuries. And you and I, enabled by God's grace, can participate in that chain reaction because Jesus left His training manual for us, and in it Jesus shows us how to cooperate with the Holy Spirit in developing leaders for His kingdom work. Our understanding of His approach to leadership development is vital to our own growth as leaders as well as to our efforts to develop both the present and the next generation of godly and effective leaders for His church.

In this chapter we will examine a passage of Scripture and see how Jesus—who longs for us to know the Father—went about building leaders. Jesus is well aware of our circumstances, and He responds by extending to us a remarkable invitation. As we look at this invitation, we will see what Jesus means by "learn," and we will identify the dominant characteristics of the Master Teacher's classroom. Finally, we will gain insight into how God uses yokes to develop us into leaders.

Lord God, the world offers many ideas about leaders and how to train them. I want to be Your kind of leader, so please use these pages to capture my heart with a new and powerful sense of Your presence. Help me hear Your voice and study well Your leadership training process. Please grant me deep and life-changing insights into myself as a leader and into Christ's leadership process. And, Holy Spirit, please also refresh my soul and mind. I pray this in the name of the Triune God, the ultimate Developer of leaders. Amen.

JESUS RESPONDS TO WHO I AM

In Matthew 11 Jesus is teaching some people who are very resistant to His message. Upset by the hardheartedness of humanity, Jesus has denounced the cities where He performed miracles but the people remained unbelieving. Our Lord's heart is heavy as He sees such resistance to the gospel. Yet He chooses not to act according to His sadness and frustration with these resistant people. Instead He extends praise to the Father and a remarkable invitation to us. Let's listen to what Jesus has to say to the Father and to us as He stands between heaven and humanity:

> At that time Jesus said, "I praise you, Father, Lord of heaven and earth, because you have hidden these things from the wise and learned, and revealed them to little children. Yes, Father, for this was your good pleasure.
>
> "All things have been committed to me by my Father. No one knows the Son except the Father, and no one knows the Father except the Son and those to whom the Son chooses to reveal him.
>
> "Come to me, all you who are weary and burdened, and I will give you rest. Take my yoke upon you and learn from me, for I am gentle and humble in heart, and you will find rest for your souls. For my yoke is easy and my burden is light." (Matthew 11:25-30)

Whenever I read this passage, I'm tempted to rush through the first three verses and focus my attention on the last three. I want Jesus to provide a quick solution for whatever problem I'm struggling with or challenge I'm facing. I want to hear His sympathetic, comforting words—and I want to hear them right now! But those wonderful words of verses 28-30 become even richer when we see what Jesus says in the three verses preceding them. So take a moment to read this passage again before I share my observations. And remember that spiritual leadership formation is a process that happens in God's presence. Enjoy His presence as you walk through His process.

JESUS REVEALS HIS FATHER TO US

It is a remarkable privilege to be able to listen in on Jesus' words to the Father. Jesus wants us to know His Father better, and He wants us to share in the kind of intimate relationship They share with each other. So, while Jesus could have prayed these words off by Himself somewhere, He instead prays them where the people could hear Him and where we can hear Him. Let's listen, learn, and enjoy.

Jesus first speaks praise to His Father, exalting Him as Lord of heaven and earth. Jesus brings us with Him into His Soul Room and opens our eyes to His Father's vast kingdom of heaven and earth. Talk about enlarging our perspective! Jesus also talks about God's way of revealing His truth—not to the wise of the world, but to those who trust Him in the same way that children trust their parents. This plan was, according to the Son, a source of pleasure for the Father. Jesus focuses us on a Father who takes pleasure in what He does.

Now think for a moment about your own image of God, the one you carry deep in your emotional being. Is He a God who enjoys pleasure? Does He wear a scowl or a stern expression? Or is the Lord of heaven and earth smiling and saying, "I feel good about that" and "I feel good about you"?

So, as this passage from Matthew opens, Jesus praises His Father as Lord of heaven and earth. He affirms His Father's decision to hide some things and reveal other things. He acknowledges His intimate relationship with His Father. And He shares His desire to reveal His Father to us. In our world of broken relationships, Jesus models for us—and invites us to experience—an eternal relationship built on admiration, love, and trustworthiness.

Try for just a moment to imagine what life would have been like if Jesus had not chosen to reveal His Father to us. What if He had decided, "I don't want anybody else to know Him"? In that case, we wouldn't have the invitation and promise of verses 28-30; we would receive nothing from the Father. But, by His grace, the Son wants people—He wants you and me—to know His Father and to know Him. Jesus wants to be in relationship with us. Therefore we receive from Him a remarkable invitation: "Come to me."

THE MOTIVE BEHIND JESUS' INVITATION

Let's not miss who is extending this invitation! It is from the Son who has an eternal and, as I said earlier, a uniquely intimate relationship with the Lord of heaven and earth. Now this holy, loving Jesus has been observing you and me. He sees that we are weighed down and wearied by burdens beyond our human ability to manage. Christ knows that we have been giving it our best shot and that we are running out of gas. He has noticed our struggles to keep up and our longings to live life more fully. Jesus loves us, He wants good things for us, and He has significant dreams for us. Most important of all, Jesus wants us to enjoy meaningful relationships not only with people but especially with Him and with His Father. He wants to see us live life from a different center, a different source—as His invitation indicates.

Jesus' desires for us are evident in the three imperatives of His invitation: "Come to Me"; "Take My yoke"; and "Learn from Me." These are not unrelated invitations. Instead, they are three essential components of a framework for a fulfilling life lived with the Father, the Son, and the Spirit. And, again, it is not insignificant that this gracious three-part invitation comes from the One who loves us enough to have died on the cross for us. At this very moment, how do Christ's desires for you make you feel?

JESUS INVITES US TO COME: "COME TO ME."

Jesus longs to be in relationship with us. He does not invite us to go to a place, embrace a vision, do a job, or fulfill a mission, but to enter into a personal relationship with Him: "Come to Me." Our motives for coming to Him and His reasons for inviting us, however, are often quite different. We go to Him for fulfillment; He invites us to enjoy friendship. We go to Jesus for insight; He invites us to experience intimacy with Him. We go to Him for direction; He invites us to reunion with our Creator. In a world where our mission in the vocational world often suggests a measure of our life's value, Jesus instead wants the value of our life to be measured by the intimacy of our friendship with Him. This relationship with Jesus is what matters most in life.

So let's review some of what we know about the One who invites us to come to Him. Jesus is the Son of God who knows and reveals the Father to us (John 1:1-18). He is the Risen Christ who reconciles us to our holy and almighty God (1 Corinthians 15). Jesus is the Grand Designer and Overseer of the heavens and the earth, and He has called us to reign with Him over the world (Revelation 5). What a backdrop for His call to us to lead! What a classroom in which to learn from the Master! And once we've entered into a relationship with Jesus as our Savior and Lord, our relationship with Him is like a living textbook, written on our heart by the Holy Spirit.

And this wonderful Jesus is saying that as we come to Him, He will give us rest, relief, and refreshment. The rest Jesus gives us rejuvenates and satisfies us like nothing the world offers. But are you and I truly receiving and fully embracing this gift of refreshment? Are we wholeheartedly coming to Jesus and allowing our weariness and wornness to be replaced as we enjoy communion with Him? And are we continuing to come to Him day-by-day, even minute-by-minute, so that we live life based on our relationship with Him and not on task and performance?

Jesus Invites Us to Take:
"Come to Me and take My yoke upon you."

Jesus continues to respond to our condition by inviting us to "take My yoke upon you." Most of us have had little and probably no experience with yokes. When we think yolk, we think eggs. But a yoke was as familiar and common to Jesus' audience as an automobile is to us. The people in Jesus' day used yokes to join oxen together to work their fields. A yoke was part of their everyday lives.

In their own history, the Jews used this very familiar image of a yoke to describe a burdensome expectation from someone in authority (see 1 Kings 12:10). They also used the imagery of a yoke as a metaphor for apprenticeship and discipleship.[1] "Take my yoke" is a way of saying to the hearer "Join me in this work" and "Make my work your work." Spoken by Jesus, "Take My yoke" therefore calls you and me to journey with Him.

Consider what Dietrich Bonhoeffer wrote:

> "Take my yoke" is a way of saying to the hearer "Join me in this work" and "Make my work your work."

> If they follow Jesus, men escape from the hard yoke of their own laws, and submit to the kindly yoke of Jesus Christ.... Only the man who follows the command of Jesus single-mindedly, and unresistingly lets his yoke rest upon him, finds his burden easy, and under its gentle pressure receives the power to persevere in the right way. The command of Jesus is hard, unutterably hard, for those who try to resist it. But for those who willingly submit, the yoke is easy, and the burden is light.... The commandment of Jesus is not a sort of spiritual shock treatment. Jesus asks nothing of us without giving the strength to perform it. His commandment never seeks to destroy life, but to foster, strengthen and heal it.[2]

Yet we often resist this life-giving yoke and instead keep our own yokes. In fact, while few of us have ever seen an actual yoke, we have all experienced being yoked to someone or something—being bound to a person, a dream, a possession, or a personal trauma—and finding that yoke to be anything but life-giving and easy.

Some of these heavy yokes are placed on us by other people. I call them "outer yokes." If you work for someone else, for instance, you are in a sense wearing that person's yoke of shared goals, purpose, and commitment. A marriage relationship is another kind of outer yoke, again one characterized by shared goals, purpose, and commitment. We may also have a sense of being yoked in our experience of church life. In Jesus' day many Jews had come to know the yoke of God's law. And in our day we may also find ourselves laboring under ideological yokes like the culture's beliefs that identity is found in achievement, power is found in position, and possessions bring fulfillment. These cultural ideas tend to become heavy emotional, social, or spiritual yokes that can burden and overwhelm us. Outer yokes like these can profoundly impact every aspect of our lives, draining our energy, dragging us down, and weakening our relationship with Jesus.

As you can see from even this short list, some outer yokes are healthy and beneficial, but many others are unhealthy and limiting, if not stifling. When outer yokes become heavy and cumbersome, they cease to be good for us. They can diminish who we are and who Christ longs for us to become. They begin to hinder God's transforming work in us, His process of making us His leaders, disciplers of His people, and His influence in the world.

The yokes I call "inner yokes" can do the same kind of damage. These yokes that we place on ourselves can bind and enslave us just as much as any outer yoke can. They grow heavier and heavier over time, and they can come to control us. Let's look at two inner yokes.

First, some of us have perhaps grown up feeling that we were never the honored child. We may have responded by taking on the yoke of perfectionism and working hard to prove that we are good enough. This lifestyle becomes heavy and stressful.

Another example—and a yoke that is very difficult for leaders especially to cast off—is what I call the "take control" yoke. It says, "I'm in control. I'm in charge here." After all, aren't leaders meant to exercise control in the places where God puts them? Of course! But the "take control" yoke is dangerous when Soul Room habits are thin or nonexistent and responsibilities in the Leadership Room dominate one's life. The Holy Spirit is too easily ignored when the "take control" yoke drives leadership style and activities. This yoke quickly grows heavier and more constrictive whenever life and ministry circumstances seem out of control. At such times the leader is tempted to take even more control to try to solve the problem. Jesus' leadership design, however, does not distinguish between things that we feel we can control and those things that are clearly beyond our control. Instead, He calls us to relinquish every aspect of our life and leadership to His control. He invites us to discover what it means to come to Him, to take on His yoke, and to submit to His control. To the leader trapped by the "taking control" yoke, Jesus says, "Trust Me. My yoke is specially fitted for you."

In fact, Jesus sees how badly all of our outer and inner yokes fit us. That's why He extends to us wearied and burdened people the remarkable invitation to take on the only yoke that truly fits us—His yoke.

Perhaps before you can put Jesus' yoke on, though, you need to identify the yokes you need to take off. What yokes have you experienced in your life? What yokes are you wearing now? Where have they come from? What impact are these yokes having on your life? on your relationship with Jesus? on your leadership?

And that last question may prompt in you a question for me: "What do yokes have to do with leadership?" You might be thinking, "I'm all for helping people who are discouraged and wounded find rest in Christ, but I also want to see better leadership in our church. We need our burned-out leaders to be restored. We need to get on with ministry and leadership development." And these indeed are legitimate, if not pressing, concerns. But let me reassure you that we are in an intentional process, and we will get to those questions. As you read on, you'll see that Jesus is not only helping the weary, but He is also enlisting leaders from among the weary.

JESUS INVITES US TO LEARN:
"COME TO ME. TAKE MY YOKE UPON YOU. LEARN FROM ME."

First Jesus invites us to come to Him—to establish a growing, dynamic, ongoing relationship with Him. Then He invites us to take on His yoke—to commit ourselves to our relationship with Him and consequently to relinquish our life and our concerns to His control. Third, Jesus invites us to learn from Him—to be continually transformed by our relationship with Him who is our good and gracious, our loving and powerful Lord.

"Learn from Me." What images come to your mind when you think about learning? Do you see yourself in Mrs. Simmons's first-grade class reciting the alphabet? Do you remember dissecting a frog in high-school biology? Perhaps you think about cramming for an American history exam in college. Or maybe you thought about a training seminar you recently attended. In all of these settings for learning, there was a body of information for you to master and be tested on.

Today we find ourselves buried under an avalanche of information, and the flow of new information continues. Until the explosion of this Information Age, people basically went to school for twelve years, received some vocational training or attended college, went out and worked in the same place for forty years, and finally retired. Today, however, we may not only change jobs eight or more times, but we may even change careers two or three times. Some of the jobs that will be most vital in 2025 may not even exist yet! In this rapidly changing environment, it is essential for us to be lifelong learners.

In our information-overloaded context, do we have what we need—brain power, emotional power—to be able to listen to Jesus' invitation to learn from Him? And even if we do, does Jesus think of learning the same way we do? Put differently, what exactly does Jesus mean when He invites us to learn from Him? Perhaps we'll be better able to answer these questions if we first ask ourselves, "What kind of a teacher is Jesus?"

First think about flesh-and-blood teachers you've had. Have you ever taken a course from a teacher with a large ego? Or have you ever sat in a classroom with a teacher who has a great understanding of the material, but not much ability to connect with the learner? How did teachers like either of these make you, the learner, feel?

Do you realize that Teacher Jesus is very different from these two types? In His own words, He is "gentle and humble in heart" (Matthew 11:29). One writer described Jesus the teacher in this way:

> To be a pupil of Jesus is to have a very gentle and humble minded teacher, who is never impatient with those who are slow to learn and never intolerant with those who stumble. It would of course be boastful for any merely human teacher to claim gentleness and humility as his primary qualifications. But Jesus the Christ does not hesitate to do so. "Learn from me," He says, "for I am gentle and lowly in heart" (RSV). It is precisely this feature of the divine invitation which renders the description of it in the Book of Common Prayer, a "comfortable" word; for we all know from experience that it has been the teachers who have possessed something of these lovely qualities who have most influenced us for the better.[3]

Being in the classroom with Jesus, the Master Teacher, elevates your self-worth, whets your curiosity, and increases your understanding of leadership. Being in the classroom with Jesus is better than being in the best class or with the most wonderful teacher you've ever experienced. Jesus, the Teacher who is gentle and humble in heart, establishes an atmosphere conducive to learning, connects with His students in very personal ways, and grows in us a hunger to learn from Him. So what exactly does Jesus want us to learn?

THE UNIQUENESS OF JESUS' CLASSROOM PARADIGM

The word Jesus uses for "learn" is directly related to the word He uses for "disciple." In fact, the words are basically interchangeable in the New Testament. *Disciple* appears some 250 times in the Gospels and the book of Acts, presenting us with a totally new paradigm for learning. As we visit Jesus' classroom, we'll focus on four distinctives of His learning paradigm. You'll also see that disciple-makers—that leaders—are at the same time learners.

One element of Jesus' learning paradigm is relationship. In many of our own classroom experiences, we received information, but no relationship developed between teacher and learner. In the classroom of Christ, however, a relational connection between Jesus and the learner always develops. As one Bible scholar explains, the New Testament word for disciple "always implies the existence of a personal attachment which shapes the whole life of the one described as disciple."[4]

What makes this trait of relationship in Jesus' classroom so significant for our culture? Talk to an elementary-school teacher and ask her to describe the students in her classroom who have attachment disorder. These children have experienced the breakdown of so many primary relationships in their lives that they find it impossible to trust or attach to anyone. A marvel of Christ's invitation to you, then, is that when you personally attach your life to Him—once you enter into relationship with Him—He will never leave you. He has not merely invited you to a weekly meeting. Instead, He looks forward to this ongoing relationship. He will always be there for you. These truths breathe intimacy and security as well as fresh anticipation into the learning situation.

A second element of Jesus' learning paradigm is transformation. In other learning situations, the learner's goal is usually to gain information or to develop a new life skill. Our learning from Jesus is different. Learning from Him involves far more than merely acquiring head knowledge. It brings transformation to our inner life and character. Through Him we experience soul nourishment from which comes a radically different lifestyle.[5] Let me explain.

The first-century language Jesus uses makes plain that He has the power to form and transform the thinking and the life of the learner. He is the One who brings new shape and resolve to our inner life. In the classroom of Jesus, the information He imparts is infused with His transforming power to bring deep inner change to the learner. This inner change affects the learner's behavior. One believer describes the transformation like this: "God's whole purpose, conceived in a past eternity, being worked out for and in his people in history, to be completed in the glory to come, may be encapsulated in this single concept: God intends to make us like Christ."[6] That is a profound transformation.

> *the information He imparts is infused with His transforming power to bring deep inner change to the learner.*

A third element of Jesus' learning paradigm is the matter of control. In many modern educational settings, the student exercises a great deal of control over the learning process. Students, for instance, often design their own educational focus through the selection of particular courses or instructors. The classroom of Christ is set up differently, though. We have been invited to come and learn from Him, the Master Teacher who continually reminds us that He is in control.

And that's not as tyrannical as it sounds. Imagine, for instance, studying with a world-class artist. You consider the opportunity to learn from her a real honor. You are glad to come under her authority and direction and to be her apprentice. In light of her stature in the art world, you don't even question that she completely controls the learning process.

Likewise, in the classroom of Christ, you have the incredible opportunity to study with the One who created all the people you will see today. He is the One who has created every tree, every bush, every flower, and every animal that you will pass along the way. He is the

One who has placed the sun, the moon, and the stars in the heavens. This Master calls you by name when taking roll and honors you with His invitation to apprentice under Him.

"Learn from Me" is indeed Jesus' invitation to "Be My apprentice." Christian author and pastor Eugene Peterson writes, "*Disciple (mathetes)* says we are people who spend our lives apprenticed to our master, Jesus Christ. We are in a growing-learning relationship, always. A disciple is a learner, but not in the academic setting of a schoolroom, rather at the work site of a craftsman. We do not acquire information about God but skills in faith."[7]

When you and I struggle with the issue of control as we take a leadership role in Christ's church, which is wiser: for us to try to control what happens or for us to give control to Him? Which resume would be stronger: one that shows we are in control or one that shows us as an apprentice of the Master? As you answer those questions, remember that an earthly resume won't last like a heavenly one will. Furthermore, when Jesus takes the initiative and invites us to learn from Him, He makes it quite clear that He is in control, but He honors us with His invitation to apprentice under Him, to be His disciple. This apprenticeship is lifelong and comprehensive. There is no aspect of our soul, our lifestyle, or our character development over which the Lord Jesus is not Master. He is in charge of our learning to make disciples… be people of influence… and be leaders.

A fourth element of Jesus' learning paradigm is the matter of outcomes. What outcomes from time spent at the Craftsman's worksite can we anticipate? And how will we measure those outcomes? As valuable as goals are, they can be the wrong goals. We live in a pressure-driven, task-oriented world where the bottom line is the dollar. But to Jesus, people are the bottom line, not task or dollar. The salvation of people and their development into disciples and disciple-makers, into leaders in His church, are the outcomes that matter passionately to the Christ.

In the time of Jesus, most rabbis had disciples, and the rabbi was indispensable to his disciples whose goal was to learn the Torah and become like their rabbi. Furthermore, everyone knew that the day would come when the rabbi would be gone, and then one of his disciples would replace and perhaps even surpass him. In this sense, the rabbi was a stepping-stone along the student's life journey.

In the classroom of Jesus, however, the outcome of being a disciple is not merely a first step; it is not a stage of life we eventually leave behind; it is not merely a stepping-stone on our journey of faith. Instead, being a disciple of Jesus Christ is the lifelong process of being molded by Him into His image and taught by Him how to teach others to be like Him. This lifelong apprenticeship in making other disciples enables us to be servant-leaders in Christ's church: we are being discipled by the Master even as we disciple others. We learn this disciple-making process from Jesus in the context of a personal relationship with Him, and in that context we witness our ongoing transformation and apprenticeship. Our mission, then, in making disciples is to reproduce Jesus' classroom for people who are burdened and who need a different yoke.

In summary, Jesus' classroom for leadership development is one of relationship with Him and transformation by His power and His presence in our life through the Holy Spirit. This dynamic learning paradigm involves relationship, transformation, Christ being in control, and remarkable outcomes. By being with Jesus, we become more like Him, our gracious Master who extends understanding and grace to each of His students. We also continue to discover the wisdom of letting Him be in control as we lead in His church. Jesus' desired outcome for those of us in His craftsman's workshop is that, as lifelong apprentices, we—by the power of the Holy Spirit—will become leaders who are making disciples for the Lord and who are being people of influence in the world. We are not to be people merely going to events, but people impacting and discipling other people.

LEADERS AS FOLLOWERS

As we close this chapter, please read my paraphrase of Jesus' invitation to you:

> "I have seen the condition you are in; I know how weary and weighed down you are by yokes that hinder your life and leadership. So, as your compassionate and gracious God, I have sent you a special invitation, and accepting it will mean leaving behind those heavy and unmanageable yokes. I desire that you live life rooted in a different source, rooted in Me.

So come to Me. You see, I want us to live life together. I want to see you restored and refreshed as you spend significant time in the Soul Room with Me. When you have been renewed, we'll go together into the Leadership Room where you can simultaneously be discipled by Me and learn to disciple others. We will be team-building leaders. Then, together, we can go out and make disciples of all nations.

"On a more technical note, though, know that I am definitely passionate about forming leaders, but My development process attends to the soul condition of each leader. I seek to provide them with the right yoke for developing their character and preparing them for the specific work they will be doing for the kingdom. As they travel on a path of continuous nurturing, My leaders are ready to both learn from Me and be a leader with Me. On a more personal note, know that you must continually draw upon Me as your source of guidance and insight, power and wisdom, as you yourself follow Me and lead and make disciples."

Jesus wants us to make a difference in the life of person after person as we grow both as believers and as leaders in our lifelong relationship with Him. And this relationship with Jesus is not a distant "professional" one; rather it is an up-close-and-personal relationship of companionship and intimacy that reflects His relationship with the Father. Jesus wants us as leaders, then, to come alongside others and develop meaningful relationships with them. We befriend people in the Leadership Room and shortly thereafter lead them into the Soul Room where they might encounter our Lord.

Of course, we need to keep coming back to Jesus to be refreshed and restored. We must also stay on guard against the yokes that others try to slip on us, and we must continually ask the Holy Spirit to release the inner yokes we take upon ourselves that hinder our journey of life. Bottom line, Jesus desires that we live as influencers in the neighborhood, the office, the school, the community, and the church where He has placed us. So He invites us to come to Him, to take His yoke upon us, and to learn from Him, the Master Teacher and the Servant-King, how to lead.

CHRIST INVITES YOU TO BE A LEADER
AND TO MAKE DISCIPLES.

God, forgive me when leadership becomes something
*I strive to do in my own power or by the world's methods. May I
never lose my sense of awe and wonder at the invitation to come to
You, to take on Your yoke for me, and to learn from You how to lead.
May Your presence with me be a continuous source of awe and
excitement for Your kingdom work and for the transformation of my
soul. Lord, may I then enter every situation with You—and may I, by
Your power and grace, be an effective servant leader, an apprentice of
Jesus, the Master Leader. I pray this in the name of the unique
Builder of leaders, the Lord Jesus Christ. Amen.*

Before You Take the Next Step

What insight in this chapter did you find especially helpful? Why?

What outer yokes do you find yourself bearing? What inner yokes? What yokes
do you need to set aside in order to take on Jesus' yoke?

What aspect of Jesus' learning paradigm of relationship, transformation, control,
and outcomes is most meaningful to you? Why?

The Bible is a book
of stories about
pardon and process,
not about performance
and perfection.

Plenty of Ideas—But Where's the Wisdom?

Story, Message, and Way: The Bible as the Christian's Guidebook

You may easily identify with this pastor's frustration: "Our church is always in need of leaders. We never have enough. People move, burn out, or quit. What can we do to create a healthy community that attracts new people? And what can we do to continually enlist and develop new leaders? Where do I turn for insight and help?"

The answer to this pastor's last question holds the seeds for answers to his other questions. So allow me to ask you where you turn for insight as you lead. Specifically, for example, when you prepare a sermon for your church or plan a leadership training class, what is your primary source? As you design the curriculum for a new members class, what is the main text you open? As you develop the agenda for a leadership gathering, where do you turn first? I ask these questions because they raise some big-picture issues for us: Why do you do what you do in ministry? Why do you do it that way? What is your primary source of authority, counsel, or inspiration for how to select and train leaders?

In my conversations with Christian leaders, I hear them talk about the Christian books they've read, the conferences they've attended, or the other ministries they've visited more than I hear them talk about the ways that Scripture itself has given them confidence, guided their efforts, and fueled their passion for the leaders they build and the work they do. And I am convinced that when we regard Scripture as the authority for just the message but not also as the authority for the way we live out that message, we limit what God intends Scripture to be for us.

It seems to me, for instance, that we turn to the Bible for the process of how to lead someone to faith in Christ, but when we wrestle with the process of how to build leaders or develop a ministry to youth, we first look to other sources for insight, direction, and inspiration. It's almost as though we feel that we'll find more wisdom in the writings of other people than in God's Word. We act as if God has said, "Here's My message, but you'll have to figure out how to implement it and apply it to people's lives."

But I believe that God gave us the Scriptures not only to inform us about what to believe, but also to provide for us a written guide of *how* to live—how to build ministries, develop leaders, and grow healthy, godly, transformed people beginning with ourselves. When the Bible is not the authority for what we do as we lead, one tragic outcome is that the elegant, grace-filled, life-changing news of God is packaged in trite, manipulative, and faddish processes.

> Allow the Bible to be the authority not only for what you believe but also for how you live, how you lead, and how you train leaders.

So we will let the Bible be our primary text in our study of leadership development. We will look at both the message of God and the ways of God. We will allow the Bible to be the authority not only for what we believe but also for how we live, how we lead, and how we train leaders. We will also visit Christians in different places along their faith journey and learn from Scripture some ways God might develop them further into effective kingdom leaders.

Put differently, we will consider Scripture from the perspective of the Father, who wrote our sin and our redemption into His *story*. We will consider Scripture from the perspective of Christ, who came to earth with a *message* of hope for us. And we will consider Scripture from the perspective of the Holy Spirit, who dwells within us to enable us to live in a *way* that honors and glorifies God. Story, message, way.

Dear Father, Son, and Holy Spirit, thank *You for the Scriptures. Thank You that they are so much more than just another book. Thank You that they are Your written authority for my life. God, may I appreciate afresh the majesty and grandeur of Your book. In our Lord's name I pray. Amen.*

HEALTHY LEADERS READ THE BIBLE AS *Story*: YOUR BIOGRAPHY AND MINE

From beginning to end, the Bible is an unfolding story comprised of many particular "people stories"—stories of individuals who exhibited faith and of others who didn't. Stories of people who loved God and of others who strayed from Him. Stories of people who listened to God and of others who ignored Him. The Bible is a book of grace, containing people stories of pardon and process, not of performance and perfection.

The Bible's story begins with a people story about a couple who knew harmony with the Father and all of His creation. Adam and Eve knew no shame, no embarrassment, and no poor self-image. But then they listened to the serpent and disobeyed God's command. Brokenhearted yet overflowing with compassion, the Father longed to reconcile with Adam and Eve, to reestablish His relationship with them, and to continue His redemptive story, which graciously is the story of our redemption as well.

Why did God give us a book that is essentially a collection of stories like this one? Wouldn't it have been better if He had given us a book of rules or proverbs, of how-tos to try or principles to follow? Of course the Bible contains some rules, some how-to nuggets, and some insights into the way things work. But why the centrality of story?

Eugene Peterson offers an answer to this question in his reflections on the Gospels. Hear what he says about the importance of story in the larger context of the Bible:

Stories invite us into a world other than ourselves, and if they are good and true stories, a world larger than ourselves. Bible stories are good and true stories, and the world that they invite us into is the world of God's creation and salvation and blessing.

Within the large, capacious context of the biblical story, we learn to think accurately, behave morally, preach passionately, sing joyfully, pray honestly, obey faithfully. But we dare not abandon the story as we do any or all of these things, for the minute we abandon the story, we reduce reality to the dimensions of our minds and feelings and experience. The moment we formulate our doctrines, draw up our moral codes, and throw ourselves into a life of ministry apart from a continuous re-immersion in the story itself, we walk right out of the presence and activity of God and set up our own shop.[1]

> *The Bible is the story of God at work in people's lives.*

When the biblical story is only an occasional point of reflection rather than the all-encompassing story in which we live and breathe, we miss God, and we set aside the biblical process for life and leadership. In subtle or perhaps not-so-subtle ways, we take charge of our own journey even though we may still hold to what we understand to be a biblical belief system. We must be aware of this danger, and we can avoid it by allowing the Bible to be what it is: the Bible is the story of God at work in people's lives. And God works in our lives today just as He worked in the lives of those who lived centuries ago.

As we journey through the Christian life, God is rewriting our stories. He is transforming our hearts, growing our relationship with Him, and consequently changing the paradigm for how we lead. The kingdom of God is breaking in to our lives, bringing us new understandings, new ways of doing things, and a new perspective on our life.

I've seen leaders get very excited when they gain this new perspective and see their own story—their biography—being rewritten by the Spirit of God. They begin to sense that God's Spirit truly is alive within them and enabling them to become more than they ever dreamed they could be. Nothing engages leaders more than seeing transformation in their own lives as well as in the lives of others. So, when developing our people into leaders, we must connect with their stories, for their stories help us develop compassion for them and provide insight for encouraging their growth as leaders. We must also help leaders see how God is rewriting their story and encourage them to open themselves—their hearts—to His wondrous revision. When people see how God is rewriting their story, it is amazing how their view of themselves changes and their impact on others begins to increase.

HEALTHY LEADERS READ THE BIBLE AS *Message*: GOOD NEWS TO HEAR AND TO SHARE

In addition to being our story, the Bible is also a message of good news for you and me. The Bible clearly shows God giving hope to humanity. Its pages tell the ongoing story of His redemption and love—and invite us to participate in it. Therefore reading the Bible can help us see that our leadership is a way of being part of God's story. Now for some details.

> *In addition to being our story, the Bible is also a message of good news for you and me.*

The Father brought clarity to His story by sending Jesus Christ with a grand message that introduces us to God and His characteristics. Jesus' message also defines our humanity for us. We learn that we are made in the image of God and that this image has been marred by human rebellion against Creator God. But the message goes on to tell us what we men and women can become. It brings us hope that meaningful and significant life transformation can occur on this earth.

The message of the Bible that we both hear and are to declare also gives us God's vision for the outcome of the human story: Christ is coming again. We mortals will put on immortality. The perishable will put on the imperishable. Death will be swallowed up in victory through the resurrection of Jesus Christ. This grand and all-encompassing message of the Scripture adds hope and transformation to the biographies of those who respond to God's gracious invitation to reestablish relationship with Him.

Finally, the Bible as our message book stands as our authority for what we communicate to others on His behalf. As spokespeople for God, we confidently communicate this message of grace and forgiveness, of love and eternal life, with conviction and compassion.

And, as we continue to grow in our understanding that the Bible is our message book, the following passages can help answer some foundational questions about God's message:

- Who is God and what is He like? Exodus 34:6-7; Psalm 139; Isaiah 6; John 1:1-14; John 16:5-15; Colossians 1:15-20

- How does God see humanity? What is His purpose and design for us? Genesis 1:26-31; Psalm 8; Romans 1:18-32; Romans 3:21-24

- What are God's intentions in creating us? What potential for recovery does He offer us? Isaiah 6; Psalm 51; John 7:53-8:11; 2 Corinthians 5:14-21

- How will our story end? Job 19:25-27; John 14:1-6; 1 Corinthians 15; 1 Thessalonians 4:13-18; Revelation 21-22

Answers to questions like these are important to how we live out our faith. Not long ago, for instance, I talked with a woman who had known only a legalistic faith system that had both exhausted her emotionally and defeated her spiritually. After we spoke for a while and I had the opportunity to share the Bible's message about God, humanity, and redemption, she responded, "I've done my best to please God, but I fall far short. No matter how hard I try, I never seem to measure up. Now I hear you telling me that God's Son paid the penalty for the wrongs I have committed. You say my life needs to be about a relationship *with* God rather than a performance *for* God. You've told me that God, in His grace, forgives my sins and empowers me to live in a relationship with Him that is both healing and transforming. I'm tired of climbing the never-ending ladder of performance, and I want this relationship you've described. This is a new message for me."

And it's a message she had ears to hear that day—clear evidence that the Bible as message book speaks with conviction and compassion to people right where they are and that it invites them to begin a new chapter in their biography.

One more note. When the Bible is our authority for *message*—as it should be—we have a filter through which to evaluate what we and what others teach. When we do not have this filter, heresy is inevitable. Likewise, when the Bible is our authority for *way*—for method, for how to—we have a filter for discerning the process of how we as well as others do life and ministry. When we do not have this filter for *way*, man's ways tend to rule the day, and fads and manipulation seem inevitable.

HEALTHY LEADERS READ THE BIBLE AS *WAY*: GOD'S METHOD FOR LIFE AND LEADERSHIP

In the Bible the Father's story unfolds, Jesus brings the message, and the Holy Spirit, living within us, shows us the ways of God. And God's ways—what He does and how He does it—reveal His character. God's ways also give us His paradigm for life, leadership, and ministry development. And God's ways tend to be quite unusual compared to our ways. They often surprise and even contradict our human methods.

If, for example, you were going to send an important message to the ruler of a neighboring kingdom, whom would you send? Your most skilled ambassador, your highest-ranking general, or a seasoned politician? Or would you go out to a plantation and ask someone who is picking fruit to deliver your message? God's way was to send the fruit picker—the prophet Amos.

Or if, for instance, you were to choose a family for a person of significant influence to be born into, would you find a solid married couple longing and ready for a child? Would you select a young, engaged couple with lots of promise if not lots of life experience? Or would you decide on a young girl who is pledged but not yet married to an older man? Would she be the mother of this significant individual even though, in her day, becoming pregnant outside of marriage could mean death? From among the various ways God could have chosen, He selected a virgin named Mary to be the mother of His only Son.

Finally, suppose you have a life-changing message that you want the world to hear. Whom will you select as your primary messenger? What will that person's background or training be? What will his resume look like? You probably wouldn't select someone who had spent his life so far doing everything he could to discredit your message and destroy your followers. But God chose just such a man, and we know him as Paul the apostle.

As these three examples illustrate and as the prophet Isaiah clearly states, God's ways are different than our ways:

I don't think the way you think.
The way you work isn't the way I work.
For as the sky soars high above earth,
    so the way I work surpasses the way you work,
and the way I think is beyond the way you think. (Isaiah 55:8-9, MSG)

So, if we are going to develop godly leaders who will lead God-centered ministries among God's people and in God's world, we must identify and learn how to cooperate with God's ways and methods. We must learn how to allow God's Spirit to take us into the ways and methods of God. Basically, we must build our lifestyle and leadership on a paradigm that is radically different from the ways of conventional, worldly wisdom. Our efforts to develop spiritual and effective leaders for life must therefore involve learning and following the ways of God.

"Teach Me Your Ways"

When we read Genesis 1 and 2, we see that sin's entrance into the world means radical changes in how life is lived. God's ways are ignored and man's ways rule. "What would God want me to do here?" is set aside. "How do I want to live and do life?" rules the day. God's judgment follows because His directives for how to live life are ignored (Genesis 6:12-13).

Therefore, in every generation, the news of God and the ways of God must be taught and received, absorbed and lived. Desiring to know the ways and methods of God, Moses cried out, "If you are pleased with me, teach me your ways so that I may know you and continue to find favor with you" (Exodus 33:13). Centuries later David echoed that plea: "Show me your ways, O Lord, teach me your paths. ... Good and upright is the Lord; therefore he instructs sinners in his ways" (Psalm 25:4,8).

Yet God's ways often surprise His followers. First, Christ Himself baffled His disciples when He spoke about God's plan that "the Son of Man must suffer many things and be rejected by the elders, chief priests and teachers of the law, and that he must be killed and after three days rise again" (Mark 8:31). This idea was offensive and very disturbing to Peter. He had never imagined that suffering and death would be part of the program. In his thinking, being rejected and killed was no way to establish a kingdom. Convinced that the wrong methods were being used, Peter pulled Jesus aside to reprimand Him. Jesus responded by saying, "Get behind me, Satan! You do not have in mind the things of God, but the things of men" (verse 33). Peter's idea about how to usher in the kingdom of Jesus Christ did not match the Father's method at all. Cultural process and biblical process were completely at odds.

In the exciting early days of the church, God's ways continued to surprise His people. In the book of Acts, for instance, the Holy Spirit is developing leaders and enabling first-century believers to follow the ways of God. He overrides His long-standing distinction between Jew and Gentile because Jesus brought them together at the cross. Women were never honored in first-century culture, but God lifts women to a position of dignity and respect. The worship patterns of the people of God change, and the new pattern is to worship on Resurrection Day—the first day of the week.

The same Holy Spirit who transformed the life of leaders in the early church is continuing this work in the twenty-first century: He is still calling and enabling Christian leaders in the lifelong challenge of taking on the ways of God. God's ways are often radically different from the ways I would naturally choose, so I must continually be aware that, when I begin planning a program or solving a problem, my way may not be God's way. When I hang on to this awareness, Scripture and the Holy Spirit become God's vital transforming agents in my life.

In the early church, believers like you and me needed to learn to do things the way God would do them. In fact, the early church became known not only as people of Christ, but as "people of the Way" (Acts 9:1-2; 19:9,23; 24:14). I often wonder what it would be like in our church and in our world if our lives were so completely reshaped according to God's paradigm that the way we live—our attitudes, behaviors, values, and responses—was distinctly different from people who live without Christ. Christian leaders would not lead the same way a cultural leader does. As the Holy Spirit transforms us, we live and lead differently.

"Lord, teach me Your ways. How do *You* live? How do You

develop healthy, lifelong kingdom leaders? How can *Your* ways truly become my ways?"—this kind of prayer is a mark of God's leaders.

HEALTHY LEADERS RESPOND TO THE GUIDEBOOK: INTEGRATING STORY, MESSAGE, AND WAY

- The Bible tells the *story* of our rebellion against our heavenly Father and His desire to reconcile with us. Longing for the sin-filled chapters of humanity's story to be different, the loving Father sends His one and only Son to earth.

> *Our* story changes and will change under the Father's sovereign hand and according to the message of Christ as—in the power of the Holy Spirit—we follow the way He shows us.

- Jesus Christ proclaims with His words and His life a life-changing *message* for sinners estranged from the Father: "I have come that they may have life, and have it to the full.... I am the way, the truth and the life. No one comes to the Father but by me.... Now this is eternal life: that they may know you, the only true God, and Jesus Christ, whom you have sent" (John 10:10; 14:6; 17:3). And Jesus speaks of the Holy Spirit.

- The Holy Spirit is our Counselor, the One who comes alongside to help us live and lead the *way* God wants us to. This Counselor, the Spirit of Truth, will be with us forever, living with us and in us (John 14:16-17).

Do you hear that the Trinity is saying to us, "Here is the message of truth that clarifies who Jesus is, why He came, and where He is going. But the message alone doesn't transform life or develop leaders. The Holy Spirit's presence and His power are essential if the message is to move into your life and into your neighborhood. A teachable response to the Christian's guidebook and the presence of the Holy Spirit is vital to developing healthy leaders."

But, you may be wondering, *how does this message and the way of the Holy Spirit make sense of my past, my life today, and my life tomorrow?* First of all, the Father, who is still writing the story, has written His grace in our story past, and His grace continues to break in upon us and breathe new life into us. Our *story* changes and will change under the Father's sovereign hand and according to the *message* of Christ as—in the power of the Holy Spirit—we follow the *way* He shows us. And this happens as we give Scripture the place of primacy in our life, in our growth as leaders, and in our encouragement of other leaders that it deserves.

Now let's meet some Christians who are at different places in their faith, at points in their life where story, message, and way are not yet well integrated. Consider what might be some growth steps for them, because only when integration of story, message, and way happens can we lead as God wants us to.

Growing Beyond Where They Are

The New Christian — This man in his early forties recently came to Christ, and I asked him to tell the congregation what happened to him. His excitement that the Father is rewriting his story and that his life is changing is evident in his words to me—"I'm a different man. I'm doing things differently"—and his eyes light up when, using words from the Gospel of John, he says, "I have crossed from death to life" (see 5:24). This young Christian is occasionally finding time to study Scripture, but when I ask him to share what happened to him, he is hesitant.

"Chuck, I'm afraid that if I share this, I'll injure people if they hear me swear or do something wrong. I don't want to injure them." Notice that he views the Christian life as one of perfection rather than progression, and he knows he hasn't arrived. Clearly, this new believer needs to immerse himself in the biblical story so he can see that God's pattern for our lives is determined by His grace and acceptance, not by our perfect behavior. God's way is to extend forgiveness when He is asked. God's process involves new beginnings. These patterns of God are radically different from the cultural patterns around us.

Furthermore, the Spirit of God is present within us to conform our character and our leadership to the ways of God. May this young Christian come to understand that the Holy Spirit is present with him and within him to help write his story. No one in the Bible other than Christ has a spotless story. We must help new believers—these potential leaders—understand the difference between perfection and progression.

The Longtime Christian — Having known the Lord a long time, she has become a student of Scripture who has a solid knowledge of the Word. But its truth has become for her a set of principles or character patterns that she is trying to live up to. In fact, she often feels as if she's living according to a check-off list rather than as a pilgrim on an exciting journey with her God. She is living out what writer John Eldridge describes like this: "The problem with modern Christianity's obsession with principles is that it removes any conversation with God."[2]

Unfortunately, the principles of Scripture have so captured this longtime believer's thinking and imagination that she has lost touch with the Bible's presentation of God's ongoing ways and overarching story. Scripture's people stories have been overshadowed by her focus on biblical principles. The Bible has become for her a set of principles to live up to rather than a collection of stories about the exciting work of God in people's lives and, by extension, of His work in her life—and these would be stories she could, in obedience to Scripture, share with others (see Psalm 145:4). Enabled by the Holy Spirit, may she experience her life story being enfolded in the stories of Scripture.

Big-Event Christians — We don't often see this couple at church. When they do attend, it's because a large and exciting Christian event is soon going to occur in the area, and they are enthusiastic spokespeople enlisting support for this major happening.

The Bible as a grand story has indeed captured their imaginations. They love to be part of what God is doing in history, so at big-event times they generously give of their time, energy, and money. But they are missing the Bible as message, as God's statement defining the Christian life and the church. The biblical message, for instance, makes clear that the church is a body, a family, not a series of big events. Yet, to these big-event believers who live for emotional highs, the message has the feel of mundane routine. Their life and leadership would be richer if they were more open to the Bible's statement of life's purpose and its clear teaching about the daily role the church is to play in the lives of believers. The Scriptures not only communicate God's message, but also God's ways. Big-event Christians often fail to enjoy the richness of God's day-to-day guidance in their lives. May this big-event Christian couple become more enfolded in a healthy church and learn to appreciate the richness of God's presence and activity in their lives.

The Tired and Disillusioned Christian — She used to love God so much, and now her love for Him is pale in comparison. One reason is that she's overwhelmed with more unpleasant questions than she can list: *How could an elder in her church leave his wife for another woman? How could people who claim to love Jesus gossip so much about one another? Why is the church a place of so much conflict and hurt?* These human stories and others have disillusioned this believer and disconnected her from God's story. What aspect of the Bible does she need to draw upon at this time?

> The Bible is a book of grace about pardon and process, not about perfection and performance.

This disillusioned believer may need to be reminded that part of the message of the Bible is that there are none righteous, not even one (Romans 3:23), and that the human heart is deceitful and desperately wicked (Jeremiah 17:9). In God's story, she'll find honesty about the human condition. She'll read about Sarah, Abraham, and Hagar taking matters into their own hands (Genesis 16); about the sinful adultery of David, the man after God's own heart (Psalm 51); and about the apostle Paul's murderous past (Acts 8–9). God includes all these sordid details—and others—in His ongoing story. The Bible is a book of grace about pardon and process, not about perfection and performance. And its power is released when leaders who discover this truth in their own journey share it with others.

God's power is also at work when a disillusioned believer realizes that He values fallen people and that He forgives us and offers us new beginnings. After all, every kingdom leader knows sin and failure. The Father's way is to redeem those chapters of our lives that we'd prefer to tear out of our story, and He makes those scenes of pain and loss a critical part of our testimony of His power and love. May the Scripture therefore be the book of the Way... the *how* of redemption. May this tired and disillusioned Christian allow the Scripture to bring her hope and take her to new places in her journey with God.

The Professional Christian — He is a pastor who feels extreme pressure to produce. Leaders in the church have brought the culture's paradigm for leadership and management to him. They want clear goals established, the mission clarified, and the outcomes well defined and measurable. In addition to his board's input, this pastor feels pressure from the books on church management he's read and the recent seminar on church leadership he attended. As an evangelical, of course he goes to the Bible when he needs to prepare a sermon or talk. But, unfortunately, when it comes to his managing and leading the church, the Bible doesn't have much influence on him. Instead, he tries to copy the ways of the successful church across town.

Now, goals in and of themselves aren't bad, but a problem arises when professional Christians establish clear, realistic goals with only passing reference to God or even independently from Him. This happens because of our very human desire to be in control: we tend to define and manage away any sense of mystery. When we do so, our own ego expands, and we find ourselves on the precipice of "Look what I did!"

We don't like living with the tension of mystery; we prefer the specifics of management. Besides, aren't Christian leaders supposed to—and aren't they even often paid to—manage? God wants to enlarge our vision of leadership development to include the real-life stories of real places, real people, and real times, real-life stories of events that aren't easily contained or quantified. God's story and God's ways always preserve the sense of mystery. May God's Spirit help this professional Christian leader learn to live with the holy tension of mystery and management.

The Achiever Christian — I have worked with church leaders whom the culture considers successful. Often these people have brought their leadership and management skills to the church, pressed them upon their congregation, and "succeeded." Sadly, though, as I've gotten to know these people, I have discovered that their own communion with God in Scripture and prayer is almost nonexistent. God's Spirit is an afterthought in their leadership process rather than the ever-present, energizing Person who leads the process. For many Christian leaders, "Christ as Lord over my paradigms of thought, over my attitudes toward myself and others, and over the manner in which I live" is a rather foreign concept. Too often the Bible is the authority over the message these leaders believe, but it is not also the authority for the process by which they live and lead.

Effective and godly leaders, however, see that the Bible tells us about the lives of real people—about their moments of great faith and their moments of great lack of faith. This aspect of the Bible challenges growing leaders to allow God a greater presence in the development of their own story. Also, realizing as they read God's Word that His ways are not our ways, healthy leaders keep discovering and responding to God's ways.

Still, I know that it is easier to check off items on the culture's or even the church's list of essential leadership qualities than it is to experience a growing intimacy with God that continually transforms our behaviors, attitudes, and thoughts. The dominant question in our growth as leaders must therefore be "What is happening on a daily and continuing basis between the Father and me... the Son and me... and the Holy Spirit and me?" Such a perspective makes our leadership an ever-enriching and ever-expanding story.

So may God help this "achiever" Christian frequently ask the questions "How would God do this?" and "What method would God's Spirit use in doing what we are considering?"

As these examples illustrate, we do well to embrace the wholeness of the Bible so that our spiritual formation and leadership skills can be enriched by its profound and life-giving truth. The *story* of the Bible—God's record of His ongoing transformation of people's lives—must capture us and give us hope for what He can do in our own lives and ministry. The *message* of the Bible—God's news for all generations—communicates who God is, who I am, what God's dreams are, what I can become, why am I here, etc. In addition to answering these questions, the Bible invites me to become a vital part of the Bible's story, of His story. Finally, however countercultural it is, the *way* of the Bible—God's instructions for how to establish a relationship with Him, how to live on this earth, how to make disciples, how to build leaders, etc.—must be breathed into our thoughts, our manners, and our behaviors by the Spirit so that God can express Himself in us and through us in the world.

May each one of us allow Scripture to be all that God intends it to be. May the Bible as *story* become the place where our leadership story is born and grows. May the Bible as *message* continually be good news that we bring to the world ... and remember ourselves. May the Bible as *way* direct our life and our leadership. May we allow the Father, the Son, and the Holy Spirit to be, respectively, the Writer of our own story, the Focus of our message as we live and lead, and our empowering Companion along the way. Such a response to God's message not only makes a difference in us, but the Holy Spirit living in us uses us to make a difference in the lives of others as we become salt in the world and light in their eyes. As Eugene Peterson says, "The Jesus way and the Jesus truth must be congruent. Only when the Jesus way is organically joined with the Jesus truth do we get the Jesus life."[3]

Let me close this chapter about God's Word with a passage from it. Paul, in training Timothy, offers this young leader—and you and me—an important insight about the value of God's Word: "All scripture is inspired by God and is useful for teaching the faith and correcting error, for re-setting the direction of a man's life and training him in good living. The scriptures are the comprehensive equipment of the man of God and fit him fully for all branches of his work" (2 Timothy 3:16-17, PHILLIPS). This insight still holds true for twenty-first-century leaders like us.

**THE BIBLE IS
TELLING US GOD'S STORY,
MAKING CLEAR GOD'S MESSAGE, AND
SHOWING US GOD'S WAYS
OF DEVELOPING LEADERS.**

God, in a world overflowing with both ideas about life and books about leadership, we sometimes feel overwhelmed by the challenge of leading in Your church. We wonder how we will become the leaders You want us to be—and how we will develop the kind of leaders You desire to see do Your kingdom work. Thank You that You have given us the Bible to tell us Your story, to make Your message clear, and to show us the way to become and to build people of influence. May Your book be our one and only, our primary guidebook for developing people of character and leaders of impact. In our Lord's name I ask this. Amen.

Before You Take the Next Step

What in this chapter most refreshed or affirmed you? Give God thanks.

Which aspect of the Bible—story, message, or way—is most familiar to you? Why? Which aspect is most unfamiliar? Why is that?

Which of the six kinds of Christians mentioned in this chapter have you been at some point of your faith journey? What did God do—or allow to happen in your life—to grow you beyond these places?

What is the Lord saying to you about the soil of your life right now? Prayerfully interact with the Lord about this topic.

The Way that is Jesus
cannot be reduced
to information
and instruction.
The Way is a person
whom we believe and
follow as God-with-us.
— Eugene Peterson

What Keeps Leaders Energized and Healthy?

"Come Unto Me" & "Come, Follow Me":
The Propellant for the Christian Life

He had been born into the right family, one well ensconced in the upper crust of society. He had been trained at the Harvard of his day and tutored by the best professor around. He had followed all the rules to the nth degree. He had climbed the corporate ladder of his religion. His resume outdid all resumes. From a human perspective, he had everything going for him. His name was ... Saul.

But one day, on a journey to a town called Damascus, this Jew's Jew encountered the risen Jesus and made a remarkable discovery (Acts 9). Saul—soon to be called Paul—realized that he had been persecuting the very God he thought he'd been serving. The resulting transformation of Paul's heart also transformed his paradigm for life. The things he once valued and treasured, his achievements and his position—he came to consider all this loss for the sake of Christ. In fact, he came to consider everything a liability compared to "the surpassing greatness of knowing Christ Jesus my Lord" (Philippians 3:8). Suddenly what mattered most to him was intimacy with God. Paul's passion was to know everything of Christ he could—both Christ's power and His sufferings.

Looking back on his life, Paul recognized this leadership secret:

> But by the grace of God I am what I am, and His grace to me was not without effect. No, I worked harder than all of them—yet not I, *but the grace of God that was with me.* (1 Corinthians 15:10, emphasis added)

Godly leadership is an extension of the leader's relationship with God.

The only way Paul could explain his influence and leadership in the Christian church he had once persecuted was by highlighting the grace of God as the key to both his identity and his enabling. Paul didn't point to a man-made model. Instead he regarded whatever he had contributed in his ministry as an expression of the grace of God and the God of grace. And when I speak of the grace of God, I'm speaking of the presence of God. When God's grace is with us, God Himself is with us. Simply put, then, godly leadership is an extension of the leader's relationship with God.

In fact, the secret of godly and effective leadership is indeed God Himself. You're probably thinking that this doesn't sound like much of a secret or too striking an insight. But the Triune God—the Father, the Son, the Holy Spirit; the God who knows all, who can do anything, who is present everywhere, who has always been and always will be; the all-sufficient, ever-faithful God who never changes—is the secret of godly leadership.

Lord God, I am grateful that You call me Your child, and I'm honored that You've called me into leadership. But, Lord, I'm afraid I'll blow it. I know people who started the race strong but grew tired and, in their tiredness, turned away from Jesus. God, I don't want to be like them; I want to finish strong. I want to lead in a godly and effective way for Your kingdom. So I need to know more about what will enable me to serve You faithfully all my life long. Please teach me. In the name of my Lord, I pray. Amen.

LETTING THE BIBLE DEFINE THE CHRISTIAN LIFE

In our quest to determine—based on the Bible's teachings—what enables Christian leaders to lead effectively and, let me add, to avoid burnout whatever the demands of ministry, let's look to Jesus. We'll open the fast-paced book of Mark, "the gospel about Jesus Christ, the Son of God" (1:1).

As Mark's story quickly unfolds, he tells about Jesus walking beside the Sea of Galilee and talking to Simon and Andrew, two brothers who are fishing there.

> "Come, follow me," Jesus said, "and I will make you fishers of men." At once they left their nets and followed him.
>
> When he had gone a little farther, he saw James son of Zebedee and his brother John in a boat, preparing their nets. Without delay he called them, and they left their father Zebedee in the boat with the hired men and followed him. (1:17-20)

These fishermen have done nothing to try to be noticed by Jesus, but He has chosen them to know Him. These fishermen are not nameless men to Jesus: He calls them by name. And these fishermen receive a clear invitation from Jesus—"Come, follow me." You—and Jesus knows where you are and who you are—receive that same invitation.

JESUS' INVITATION: "COME"

"Come." The word speaks warmly of being recognized and chosen for something specific, something special. When Jesus speaks that word of invitation, His "Come" is a call to join Him wherever He is. Our response involves leaving wherever we are and whatever we're doing, and coming to where He is. This word dislodges us as it invites us to go to a new place. Sometimes I resist coming to Jesus because His call interrupts where I'm already going and what I'm already doing. Furthermore, it presses me to release control of my life to Him and to make a commitment to Him. Besides, it seems more exciting—and less threatening—to go do ministry than to come be with Jesus. And it's much easier to stay where we are, on the path we're on. But what an honor to have Christ invite us to come to Him, to join Him where He is. This invitation clearly implies that He has a place for us—for you and for me—and that He wants us to join Him there. So He says, "Come. Come here."

Notice in Matthew 11:28 what Jesus is inviting us to receive when we come: "Come unto me all you who are weary and heavy laden and I will give you rest." Among boats and fish or with a group on a hillside, Jesus invited people to come to Him. Clearly Jesus recognized that His first-century hillside hearers were worn out and in need of rest from carrying their heavy burdens. I am therefore certain that Jesus sees that His twenty-first-century hearers—living as we do in our busy, performance-oriented culture that is plagued by the hurry-up disease—need rest as well. His invitation challenges us to admit our exhaustion, the weight of our sins and failures, our need for forgiveness and rest. Until we admit our condition, we will seldom make intentional time in our hectic schedules to come to Him. Burnout, midlife crisis, high blood pressure, emotional weariness, sleepless nights, guilt, anger management seminars, drug addiction—these and many other things reveal our profound need for rest.

The rest that those who come to Christ receive from Him connects us with Him and brings us renewal, refreshment, and rejuvenation. This rest calls for far more than my merely making space for Him in my day or taking a time-out from my schedule to read the Bible and pray. Receiving this rest comes when we make space in our schedules and our hearts to develop an intimate personal connection with the living Christ. In this relationship with Jesus, I am restored, rejuvenated, and transformed more and more into His image.

Hear again Jesus' invitation to you: "Come unto me all you who are weary and heavy laden and I will give you rest." My ongoing response to this invitation gives Jesus the opportunity to restore my soul and grow my character. In responding to this invitation, I am a leader tending to my inner journey so that my healthy leadership is formed from the inside out. "Come unto me" is the first ingredient in the propellant that keeps leaders energized and healthy.

Jesus' Invitation: "Come, Follow…"

We don't come to Jesus in order to just sit with Him, though. "Follow" is a call to go with Christ wherever He goes. It requires a willingness to let Another lead, to let Someone else make the decisions and be in charge. Simply put—and to coin a term—biblical leadership is followership.

Unfortunately, many Christian leaders feel that they've grown beyond the place of following, that following is a step down. They've been trained, they've earned their credentials, and they've paid their "following dues." They have outgrown following; they are now leaders. Following has become a foreign, if not unwelcome, concept.

But look again at the gospel scene. In time, the fishermen Jesus calls to follow Him become significant leaders in the early church. Because they are willing not only to come to Jesus but also to follow Him, these fishermen go places they never would have gone, they see things they never would have seen, and, most important, they become men they never could have imagined becoming. And their obedient lives of followership impact the course of history beyond their wildest dreams and imagination. Outside of Jesus' circle, is anyone else from the first century still influencing people around the world in the twenty-first century?

JESUS' INVITATION: "COME, FOLLOW ME"

When we come and follow Jesus in response to His invitation, we are not following after a goal, an enterprise, a vision, a mission, or a job description. We are following a Person, the Person Jesus, and our following is all about a developing, ongoing, lifelong relationship with Him. Passion and vision are of value, but their value is secondary to our focus on Christ.

When we follow Jesus, as we live with Him and in awe of Him, community and camaraderie develop. We live lives of worship, our friendships deepen, a sense of mission develops, and our inner transformation continues. All of this happens as we focus more and more on Christ Himself, on coming to Him and following Him. Godly leadership is rooted in our response—day-to-day, moment-by-moment—to Jesus' invitation "Come, follow Me." His invitation is a continual expression of God's grace to us.

WHO OR WHAT MATTERS?

The Christian life is to be an ongoing relationship of intimacy with Jesus. In his gospel, John expressed it this way: "Yet to all who received him, to those who believed in his name, he gave the right to become *children of God*" (1:12, emphasis added). Clearly, at its heart, the Christian life is a matter of Who, not what. The Christian life is about friendship, relationship, intimacy, and connection with Jesus Christ; it's about coming and following Him.

But in our leadership efforts, not to mention in today's approach to leadership development, does the Who remain prominent? Does vital relationship with Jesus remain the top priority? Or do we allow the planning of events and the development of ministries to become a long list of whats that interfere with or distract us from an intimate relationship with Christ?

> Our relation-
> ship with our
> Savior is the
> only source of a
> truly godly life;
> it is the propel-
> lant of our
> journey with
> Jesus as well as
> the reason we
> serve Him.

We live in a culture that places many demands on us. We are very good at accomplishing tasks; the whats of life drive us. It is too easy for us to focus on doing all that we feel needs to be done and let our close relationships with others suffer.

Consider married couples struggling with tensions or even hostility in their relationship. In most of these cases, marriage has become little more than a collection of whats—the long "to do" list of paying bills, cleaning the house, doing the laundry, tending the kids, and so on. When relationship is reduced to "honey do" lists, the joy of marriage fades, and a couple's desire to work on their marriage can significantly diminish.

For many believers, the Christian life and Christian leadership can also become a collection of whats—the long "to do" list that includes going to church, reading the Bible, saying prayers, memorizing Scripture, teaching Sunday school, attending meetings, planning for the next churchwide event, and on and on. When activities like these begin to feel like requirements, our excitement about Christ fades. This is why God calls us in His Word to focus on our relationship with Jesus (see John 15:4-10; Philippians 3:7-9; 1 Peter 2:9-12; 1 John 3:1). Our relationship with our Savior is the only source of a truly godly life; it is the propellant of our journey with Jesus as well as the reason we serve Him. Our motivation to serve God must be rooted in our relationship with Jesus, in the Who rather than in any what.

YOUR CURRENT RESPONSE TO THE INVITATION

Think about the current state of your Christian life. Which of the following presentations of Jesus' invitation best reflects how you're doing in your relationship with Him?

"***Come***, Follow Me."

"Come, ***Follow*** Me."

"Come, Follow ***Me***."

The first option suggests that you most need to respond to the word *come*. Are you unwilling to move from where you are to a place of relinquishing to Jesus full control of your life?

Or perhaps, according to the second option, you need to work on *following* Jesus. Where do you need to allow God to break your attitude, get certain items off your "to do" list, release you from your perfectionism, or reorganize your schedule?

Maybe, though, you have readily run to Jesus and willingly said, "I'll follow," but things that have come into your life have changed your focus. Have you been captured by a dream, propelled off course by a desire, or distracted by responsibilities and, in the process, lost your *focus on Jesus Christ*? You may need to discover afresh—or maybe for the first time—that the Christian life is a life focused on a robust relationship with Jesus Christ.

THE PROMISED OUTCOME

Having considered the Lord's invitation to us to "Come unto Me" and "Come, follow Me," now think about the promised outcome of our following Him: "Come, follow me, and I will make you fishers of men" (Mark 1:17). The original language makes clear that "it would be a slow and long process, but Jesus could and would do it. He would undertake to make fishers of men out of fishermen."[1] When we follow Jesus, we become something we weren't before, and that becoming grows out of our relationship with Him. That transformation results from our intimacy with the Triune God and our willingness to allow God to completely transform our character and our life.

Too often, however, the development of leadership skills takes precedence over our focus on followership and relationship. We try to get the outcomes of following Jesus without following Him. We reduce leadership to certain skill sets and assume that the results of followership will happen. But Jesus makes it very plain: fishing for men—working effectively in His kingdom for His kingdom purposes—comes with following Jesus. Today, however, in presentations at seminars and conferences as well as in conversations with fellow believers, I often hear more about outcomes than about following; more about programs than about Jesus; and more about gifted leaders than about committed followers of Christ.

> *Leaders in Christ's church ... must learn followership because biblical leadership is followership.*

We too often talk about leadership by answering questions like "Who am I—and who am I becoming?" and "Do I have the right stuff—the right personality, the right resume, the right appearance, and the necessary leadership skills?" We tend to reduce Christian leadership to me and my abilities. Oh, I may invite God to hone my skills, but even then my focus is on me rather than God. We have bought into our culture's do-it-yourself mind-set even when it comes to being effective Christian leaders. We hope that God will somehow be there in the middle of all we're trying to do for Him, but are we really acknowledging Him as Lord and truly living under His leadership?

I believe that the church today is in desperate need of true followers of Christ. In case you're not yet convinced, let me explain. The Bible clearly teaches that the Christian life begins when I receive Jesus Christ, the One who knocks on the door of my life, forgives my sin, and issues the amazing invitation to come unto Him and follow Him. From that point on, the intimacy of my relationship with Him is the God-provided propellant of the Christian life. Leaders in Christ's church—and that's all of us, both leaders who are official and paid and leaders who are not—must learn followership because biblical leadership is followership. Recognition of this truth changes attitudes and softens hearts, ideal conditions for the Holy Spirit to continue transforming the character of God's people.

KEEPING OUR FOCUS ON JESUS SHARP

I have been honored to know Christ for more than half a century. I still get goose bumps to think that the Father really loves me. He doesn't only love you or the person next door, but He also loves me. What amazing love! And how amazing and humbling to realize that, prompted by love, the Son suffered His Father's rejection that I might know forgiveness and love. And then, perhaps the most amazing of all aspects of the gospel truth, Jesus invites me to follow Him and be in intimate relationship with Him. He invites me—just as He invites you—to open those two remarkable invitations every morning.

Sometimes, however, I lose my focus on following Jesus. Sometimes I have focused more on the blessing of what is happening than on the One who authored those blessings. At other times I've found myself in the valley of discouragement and gone to the want ads ("There must be something else I could do") rather than going to Him. In those moments, God has kindly called to me in His still, small voice, "Chuck, come to Me and follow Me."

When Jesus calls us to follow Him, He never says the road will be easy. Consider again the experience of Paul:

> I have worked much harder, been in prison more frequently, been flogged more severely, and been exposed to death again and again. Five times I received from the Jews the forty lashes minus one. Three times I was beaten with rods, once I was stoned, three times I was shipwrecked, I spent a night and a day on the open sea. I have been constantly on the move. I have been in danger from rivers, in danger from bandits, in danger from my own countrymen, in danger from Gentiles; in danger in the city, in danger in the country, in danger at sea; and in danger from false brothers. I have labored and toiled and have often gone without sleep; I have known hunger and thirst and have often gone without food; I have been cold and naked. (2 Corinthians 11:23-27)

That kept Paul going on his missionary journeys as he confronted death and hardship and suffering? He answers that question for us with these wonderful words from his letter to the Romans: "I'm absolutely convinced that nothing—nothing living or dead, angelic or demonic, today or tomorrow, high or low, thinkable or unthinkable— absolutely nothing can get between us and God's love because of the way that Jesus our Master has embraced us" (8:38-39, MSG). Intimately knowing God and His love kept Paul going despite the dangers and the pain.

A man I know is one of the most respected patent attorneys in the country, has loved Jesus for years. And for the last forty years, he has taught the eleventh-grade Sunday-school class at his church. Yes, forty years. Why does he keep doing this? What keeps him going despite the time required and the challenges faced in a high-school classroom? He would tell you, "Loving these teenagers keeps reminding me just how much God has loved me. God has made me feel so special that I want these high-school juniors to know how special they are."

> *The propellant of lifelong godly motivation is God's incredible love and the relationship with Him that we have through Christ.*

And no less remarkable will be your testimony, the reason you will give for responding to Jesus' invitations, following Him, and persevering in your area of leadership, whether it is the office or home, the neighborhood or the board room, the local church or an international ministry. The words will be your own, but the God those words will point to is "the Lord, the Lord, the compassionate and gracious God, slow to anger, abounding in love and faithfulness, maintaining love to thousands, and forgiving wickedness, rebellion and sin" (Exodus 34:6-7).

THE ONLY SURE PROPELLANT OF A GODLY LIFE

The secret to—and the propellant of—faithful and lifelong leadership is God. The propellant of godly living and effective leadership is not a vision, a "to do" list, a new ministry, a revised mission statement, or anything else. The propellant of lifelong godly motivation is God's incredible love and the relationship with Him that we have through Christ. Only when we are truly acknowledging Jesus as Lord and living under His leadership will we have the propellant that will enable us to be His faithful servants for life.

You'll find support for this fact when you hear others speak of their conviction that God Himself and His great love for them motivated them to faithfully live for Him. Consider these four examples:

> From this time many of his disciples turned back and no longer followed him.
>
> "You do not want to leave too, do you?," Jesus asked the Twelve.
>
> Simon Peter answered him, "Lord, to whom shall we go? You have the words of eternal life. We believe and know that you are the Holy One of God." (John 6:66-69)
>
> But because God was so gracious, so very generous, here I am. And I'm not about to let his grace go to waste. Haven't I worked hard trying to do more than any of the others? Even then, my work didn't amount to all that much. It was God giving me the work to do, God giving me the energy to do it.—The apostle Paul in 1 Corinthians 15:9-10 (MSG)
>
> Eighty and six years I have served this Christ, and he has done me no wrong. How can I deny him now?—Polycarp, Bishop of Smyrna, about 100 A.D.
>
> He is no fool who gives up that which he cannot keep, to gain that which he cannot lose.—Jim Elliot, martyred missionary to the Auca Indians in Ecuador in the 1950s

Clearly, the apostle Peter saw Christ as the source and answer to his life, now and forever. Paul the evangelist also knew well that a life fruitful for the kingdom comes because of the grace of God released in us. Polycarp kept his eyes on Christ even as he was burned at the stake. And, in a world that worships material possessions and resume building, Jim Elliot knew that only what we do for God will last.

What brings me this kind of clarity when I'm confused by the details and demands of life? God's presence with me. Where do I find the motivation and propellant for continuing my journey of faith when I'm tired or discouraged? In God's presence. What prompts you and me to keep going through the hard times of life? God's presence. Nothing more and nothing less. Nothing else.

So, as you reflect on your own life, is something or someone other than the Living God serving—or trying to serve—as the propellant of your life and leadership? Do you keep on keeping on because of a vision, the hope of a job promotion, a goal not yet realized, a new ministry opportunity, or the expectations of others? As fine as some of those reasons might be, history has shown again and again that the greatest life unfolds when the Master's love and grace serve as the continual, singular propellant. So open the invitation the Lord Jesus extends to you. Hear His words "Come unto Me" and "Come, follow Me"—and respond now.

HEALTHY LEADERS
ARE ABLE TO CONTINUE LEADING
BECAUSE THEY ARE ENERGIZED BY THE PROPELLANT
OF "COME UNTO ME" AND "COME, FOLLOW ME."

Dear God, *You who are the Living God, the Creator, the Sustainer, and the Lord of the universe, I am humbled to think that, in the vastness of space and in the vastness of humanity, You personally invite me to come and follow You. You take up residence within me. You bring forgiveness and love and purpose to my life. May I so linger with You and get to know You that nothing of this world will motivate me, only the Christ who lives in me and loves me. And in whose gracious name I pray. Amen.*

Before You Take the Next Step

How did this chapter encourage you in your understanding of leading as a Christian?

When you think about Jesus' invitation "Come, follow Me," which of these words is most significant to you right now—*come, follow*, or *me*? Why?

What motivates you most in your Christian life and leadership? In what ways are you sensing God's invitation to allow companionship with Jesus to increasingly be your sole propellant?

What is something in this chapter that you might share with a friend in the next week?

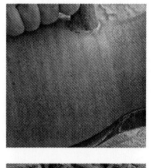

In a world of busyness
and distractions,
the Gardener and
the Vine are life-giving,
life-centering, and
life-sustaining for
those of us who
are the branches.

Too Many Things to Do!
What Really Matters?

Abiding, Loving, and Bearing Witness:

A Christian's Priorities

When we accept Christ's gracious invitation to come follow Him, what does our following Jesus look like in daily life? Does the propellant of His love and grace merely give thrust to my life, or does it give me direction? Does following Jesus help me decide whether to teach Sunday school, help in worship, join a small group, or go to Kenya when I'm already busy and don't know what I can add to my schedule? What influence do God's love and grace have on my daily life and regular schedule? Bottom line, as Christians who are either in paid, formal leadership or in lay leadership, we want to understand what is essential in the life of a leader—and then be sure we're living it!

In this chapter, we will join Jesus in the Upper Room as He spends His last evening with His disciples before His arrest and crucifixion. As He anticipates going to be with the Father, He desires to communicate to His closest followers what matters most because they are the ones who will carry on His ministry. So, based on Christ's teaching, we will examine the priorities of a godly lifestyle that He wanted these first-century church leaders—and you and me twenty centuries later—to understand and develop. God's gracious love—the propellant for our life as His people—leads us to live according to three specific priorities. Many Christian leaders become driven in ministry when they lose sight of these priorities.

God, the invitation to come follow Your Son is gracious and wonderful. But what does that following look like in the twenty-first century? Lord, please give me insight, soul refreshment, and a willingness to obey. Give me clarity about the priorities that will bring shape to my acceptance of Your invitation to follow Jesus. Then help me to yield myself to You so that, by Your Spirit's power, I can live according to these priorities in the way You desire Your people to live. I pray this in Jesus' name. Amen.

JOINING JESUS IN THE UPPER ROOM

So how does my relationship with Jesus shape my life? In what specific ways does this relationship define the passions, priorities, and playing field of my daily experience? In other words, what does following Jesus look like as I live and lead?

I believe Christ answers these questions. In fact, He speaks with great clarity to His disciples about how their relationship with Him is to be nourished, protected, and strengthened; how it is to affect the way they live and lead. Jesus needs the disciples to whom He entrusts His ministry (and that includes you and me) to thoroughly understand the normative Christian lifestyle. Jesus wants His followers to know that the Christian life is not merely information to believe, but a Person to trust in and live with every moment of every day.

So take a moment right now and imagine that you and I have joined Jesus Christ and His disciples in the Upper Room. It's Christ's last night before the Cross, and I encourage you to really hear His words, watch His movements, pay attention to His responses, notice His facial expressions, and feel His passion. That kind of attention is key to intimacy, and God longs for an intimate relationship with us. That's one reason Jesus has invited His disciples (He calls them "friends") to celebrate the Passover meal with Him. And remember that this is His last meal before He will be arrested and led away to die.

John 13–17 is the account of Jesus' time with His disciples in the Upper Room, and the first verse in those five chapters says, "Having loved his own that were in the world, he now showed them the full extent of his love." Jesus takes off his outer clothing, puts a towel around His waist, pours water into a basin, and starts to wash the disciples' feet. You are in that circle. What are you noticing? What are you feeling? When Jesus comes to you, kneels down, washes your feet, and then dries them, what are you sensing? What are you thinking? Why do you think you'll never forget this moment?

Suddenly, you hear Peter saying, "Jesus, You can't wash my feet." This remark catches your attention. But, after exchanging a few words with him, Jesus does wash Peter's feet along with the rest of the disciples' and then He sits down. While the group is reflecting on what has just happened, Jesus asks a question: "Do you understand what I've done for you?" (3:12). Do they see the significance of His actions?

Jesus answers His own question: "You call me 'Teacher' and 'Lord,' and rightly so, for that is what I am. Now that I, your Lord and Teacher, have washed your feet, you also should wash one another's feet. I have set you an example that you should do as I have done for you" (13:13-15). While they are still together, Jesus longs for His disciples and friends to catch His passion for serving one another, for washing the feet and meeting even the very practical and unglamorous needs of one another. Jesus adds that, in doing so, they will enjoy God's blessing: "Now that you know these things, you will be blessed if you do them" (13: 17).

TEACHING US WITH WORDS AS WELL AS ACTIONS

As we linger at the table with Jesus and the others, we hear Him say, "I'm telling you ahead of time so when it happens you will understand and know that I am sent by God.... One of you is going to betray me" (see John 13:19, 21). Judas leaves the room, and the Son of Man says, "Now I'll be glorified, and so will my Father" (see 13: 31). He continues: "Now I need to tell you about something that is very important to Me. I want the community that we have begun to continue, and this is the key to its survival: You must love one another—and I'm not talking about the way the world and others say you should love. I don't want you to love one another whenever and however you feel like loving someone, but rather love one another the way I have loved you—sacrificially and unconditionally. This kind of love will enable the world to know that you are My disciples" (see 13:34).

Do you hear the passion in Christ's voice? As we live in His presence, we not only gain insights from Him, but we also feel the driving power behind His ministry. We also begin to sense that the Christian lifestyle is about living in His presence.

As we linger right now in His life-giving presence at this Upper Room table, the conversation shifts. Jesus tells His friends that He is leaving to prepare a special place for them and that they can't join Him where He is going. But He is quick to add, "Don't worry. Don't be stressed. I'm concerned about you. Trust in God and trust in Me. Rely on Me" (see 13:36 and 14:1).

What a remarkable announcement! Christ is leaving us to get a place ready for us. After He goes, He wants us to continue to rely on Him. He longs for a community on earth that will one day be with Him and His Father in heaven. Until then, He says, "If you love me, you will obey what I command" (14:15). He explains the importance of this command: "Your obedience is an expression of your love for Me. And, as you're obeying and following Me, realize that you are part of the community of the Father, Son, and Spirit and that We long to see you become more than you ever dreamed you could become. For the Father sent Me to you, and I'm going to ask Him to send You a Comforter, the Holy Spirit. When He comes, He will teach you all things. As My follower-leaders, you are to be learners and obeyers."

And exactly how are we sinful, weak human beings going to be able to be obedient lovers and leaders within the community of the Father, Son, and Holy Spirit? Jesus addresses that issue.

An Image for Life

By painting a vivid word picture, Jesus teaches about the key to our ability to be learners and obeyers. In John 15 our Lord describes a vineyard and says that He Himself is the Vine. In fact, He is our Vine of nourishment, and His Father is the Gardener who tends the branches that receive sustenance from the Vine. In other words, God tends you and me and our lives, and Jesus makes clear that the Father is a good Gardener. He will prune the branches so that they might draw more deeply from the life of the Vine and bear more fruit. By bearing fruit, we glorify the Father and show ourselves to be disciples of Jesus Christ (15:8).

Using this imagery of the vine and branches, Jesus then identifies three passions that He desires to have become our passions. These key priorities of a disciple of Jesus Christ will guide the lifestyle as well as the leadership of every Christian. And, when the propellant of God's love and grace is present in our lives and as the Holy Spirit works in us and enables us to obey Jesus' commands, we will be able to live out these three priorities.

Let's listen in again on the Upper Room conversation. "Peter," says Jesus, "I really like you. You're a decision maker, you have high energy, and you make things happen. The downside of this God-given nature of yours is that you can easily run ahead of My leading. That's why I want you—and all My followers—to be captured heart, mind, and soul by what I'm about to say." What follows are vital directives for the first leaders in the early church, and these instructions are just as essential for the leaders of the twenty-first-century church.

LIFESTYLE AND LEADERSHIP PRIORITY #1

> "If you abide in Me, and My words abide in you, ask whatever you wish, and it will be done for you." — John 15:7 (NASB)

"If you abide in Me..."

Christ says to us, "I want you to abide in your relationship with Me. Remain connected to the Vine. Stay rooted in our relationship and protect our relationship." Christ is speaking of the primary life and leadership priority—abiding.

At the center of God's passion for us is intimacy, connection, and dwelling. You and I may not use the word *abide* in everyday conversations, but it is vital in the writings of the apostle John. He uses it forty times in his gospel and twenty-six times in his epistles. What exactly does that word mean? As one commentator explained, "[*Abide*] is used to communicate the enduring character of Christ, and more importantly, when used with the preposition 'in' and a personal object, it points to the relationship of mutual indwelling of the

Father, the Son and the believer."[1] The key to both effective Christian living and Christian leadership is to abide *in* Christ.

Notice the role of abiding in Christ's own life. (Yes, He practices what He preaches!) Jesus says, "Do you not believe that I am in the Father, and the Father is in Me? The words that I say to you I do not speak on My own initiative, but the Father abiding in Me does His works" (John 14:10, NASB). Commenting on this verse, Richard Foster says, "When Jesus told His disciples to abide in Him, they could understand what He meant for He was abiding in the Father."[2] The disciples knew what to do in response to Jesus' command to abide because they saw Jesus abiding in the Father.

> *The effectiveness of our leadership hinges on the degree to which we are abiding in Christ.*

And I believe that the Son's abiding in His Father—that His dynamic and constant relationship with His Father—was key to the effectiveness of Christ's ministry. The energy source of His leadership was His relationship, His abiding, with His Father. Too often, though, we have drawn on other sources, such as resume, theology, vision, spiritual gifts, or friends, for energy and leadership. More than anything else, though, the effectiveness of our leadership hinges on the degree to which we are abiding in Christ. The fruitfulness of our life and ministry is evidence of our abiding.

"[If] My words abide in you"

Abiding in Christ involves the Bible, the written revelation of who God is and what Jesus wants us to be. So, in a sense, Christ issues this invitation to us: "Abide in My book. Stay in the book that describes who I am and who you are. Investigate My book and discover all that I desire you to be and become. Linger in My book and learn how I indwell leaders and carry out My mission through them. Dwell in My book and see the story of which you are a part."

Jesus' words abiding in us give foundation, substance, and framework to our lives and our leadership. Jesus wants His words, the Scripture, to lodge in our heart, settle in our mind, abide in our being, and transform us. He wants the Word of God to influence our thinking, our feelings, our choices, and our behaviors.

Jesus is saying to the emerging leaders of the first-century church and to His twenty-first-century followers as well, "If you will abide in Me—if you will really tend our relationship—and if My words abide in you—if you continue to meditate on and cling to My thoughts, My attitudes, and My life choices—ask whatever you wish and it shall be done for you." Let's consider this amazing promise.

"Ask whatever you wish and it shall be done for you"

I have to confess that I'm much better at asking the Lord for things than abiding in His presence. I know how to ask God for help and healing and guidance and blessings. I find it a bit more challenging, though, to remain in Christ and in His Word—and I'm guessing that you can identify with me. But the sequence of Priority #1 is abiding and then asking. I often find, however, that my sequence is reversed—that I ask and maybe sometimes I abide.

Why do we find it so hard to abide in Jesus and in the Scriptures? One reason is that we live in a busy, driven world. As a result, it is often difficult to slow down, stop, settle in, and simply abide in God's presence and His story. That's why it's very good news that you and I don't have to wait for the perfect time or circumstances to abide. I can abide in Christ's presence while driving a car, going to work, or caring for the children. That kind of abiding is very important, but so is stopping and letting God's Word abide in us. As someone has asked me on occasion—and now I'm asking you—"Do you marinate in the Scripture? Are there times in your day when you intentionally stop, open your Bible, and reflect on what God is saying to you?"

When I spend time in a text of Scripture, I grow in my under-standing of the character of God, and I experience rich communion with Him. When I allow God's Word to abide in me, He forms and restores His passions and priorities in me; His character reshapes my character; His Spirit enlightens my spirit. Abiding in Him, abiding in the Vine, becomes the center of my life and impacts all I think and do, my internal as well as my external activities.

I believe that one weakness of the American church is that we often take on the mission of God without taking on the priorities of God—without living the lifestyle of the Upper Room. Just as He did with the Eleven, Christ looks to you and me with a heartfelt longing that we would enjoy deeper intimacy with Him. Too often, though, our mission *for* Him is not an extension of our communion *with* Him. This Vine/branch relationship, this communion with God, involves an open Bible. When mission stems from this place of connection with God through Scripture, we will be blessed with a growing sense of God as the Source of our strength and direction in ministry and as our Companion as we serve.

Let me share some further insights into this dynamic from J. I. Packer's study of the Puritans.

> We are so busy doing things *for* Him that we don't often take time to be alone *with* Him.

First, we cannot but conclude that whereas to the Puritans communion with God was a great thing, to evangelicals today it is a comparatively small thing. The Puritans were concerned about communion with God in a way that we are not. The measure of our unconcern is the little that we say about it. When Christians meet, they talk to each other about their Christian work and Christian interests, their Christian acquaintances, the state of the churches, and the problems of theology—but rarely of their daily experience of God. Modern Christian books and magazines contain much about Christian doctrine, Christian standards, problems of Christian conduct, techniques of Christian service—but little about the inner realities of fellowship with God. Our sermons contain much about doctrine—but little relating to the converse between the soul and the Savior. We do not spend much time, alone or together, in dwelling on the wonder of the fact that God and sinners have communion at all; no, we just take that for granted, and give our minds to other matters. But how different were the Puritans! The whole aim of their "practical and experimental" preaching and writing was to explore the reaches of the doctrine and practice of man's communion with God. In private they talked freely of their experiences of God, for they had deep experiences to talk about.[3]

Do you agree with this evaluation of the twenty-first-century church? I certainly do. When we Christians meet, we do tend to talk about our Christian work and Christian interests, but all too rarely do we talk about our day-to-day interaction with God. We are so busy doing things *for* Him that we don't often take time to be alone *with* Him. No wonder we don't have much to say about that kind of intimate interaction with our Lord!

Granted, some of us really do thrive on being with others. Those of us who find people a source of energy may find it difficult to sit quietly and be alone with God. Silence and solitude can be very threatening. We must remember, however, that Jesus Himself went off early in the morning to be alone with His Father. Following Christ therefore requires our diligence and ongoing intentionality to sit alone, to abide in His presence and in the Scriptures. Read this observation by Andrew Murray:

> 'Tis only the abiding that can really satisfy the thirsty soul and give to drink of the rivers of pleasure that are at [God's] right hand.... You did well to come; you do better to abide. Who would, after seeking the King's palace, be content to stand at the door when he is invited in to dwell in the King's presence and share with Him in all the glory of His life?[4]

It is indeed in the King's presence that our love affair with Christ is enriched.

And it is important for us to remember that, at its heart, the Christian life is a love affair. It is not a straightedge to try to measure up to or a long "to do" list for us to accomplish, but a love affair with God: He pours His love into us, He focuses His affections upon us, and we come to love Him with more and more of our being. And the more I am with Him—the more time I am abiding in the Scriptures and abiding with Him—the more I take on His character as well as His passions for my life and ministry. And our own relationships teach us this principle.

Recently, for instance, I had lunch with a friend. We were talking about marriage, and he said he wanted to develop greater intimacy with his wife. I told him that the way we husbands can do that—the way we can discover the interests, concerns, excitements, and passions of our wife—is simply to be with her. The more I am with my wife, the more I begin to share her concerns and her passions—and intimacy with God develops in a similar way. When I pause to sit with the living God and His Book, what matters to Him comes to matter more and more to me. The beauty of the Christian life really does lie in abiding in Christ's presence.

That's why I see Priority #1 of the Christian life and of leadership in the church as abiding in Christ. This ongoing and growing commitment to Jesus Christ involves spending time alone with God in Bible study, prayer, and personal worship. This time alone lays the foundation and is at the heart of Christian leadership, of the entire Christian life. That's why, in chapters 6, 7, and 8, we will discuss how you can develop and enrich your life of abiding. Chapter 9 will focus on abiding for others. Abiding in God and in His Word is the key to living a fruitful Christian life.

Now let's return to Jesus' conversation in the Upper Room. Hear Him as He addresses two other disciples: "James and John, you are brothers, and I know that, as brothers, you have experienced conflict with each other. That's just part of life as brothers, and it will be part of the life you'll experience with your brothers and sisters in the church. Remember that, in the midst of that conflict, the community of faith must be protected and formed.

"And how can you do that? How can your communion with God and your community with one another be restored and preserved especially as all of you are tempted to go off on your own and do something alone in My name or even in your own name? I have a word for you that will help you preserve the unity of your fellowship, a word that is crucial for your ongoing joy and effectiveness in the mission I've given you. This passion and priority is essential for you who are growing as leaders and disciple-makers." Let's move on to this word, Priority #2.

LIFESTYLE AND LEADERSHIP PRIORITY #2

> **"This is My commandment, that you love one another, just as I have loved you." — John 15:12 (NASB)**

As Christ continues to speak to the leaders of the early church and of the church today, He voices what really matters to Him, and it is the key to making and leading disciples, to carrying on His ministry. The key is love.

But notice a word in this verse that is not politically correct. It is the word *command*. Wouldn't people today be much more comfortable if Jesus had said, "This is My suggestion," "Let Me propose an idea, and you might form a committee to evaluate it," or "Here is a recommendation you might consider"? But in the Upper Room, as Jesus passes the torch of leadership to the first generation of leaders who will soon be without His physical presence, the Lord straightforwardly issues a commandment, *His* commandment. It isn't just a suggestion, an idea, or a recommendation. Jesus commands His people—then and now—to love one another.

To be honest, I wish the verse stopped at that point. I wish the Lord had left His command at "love one another." If He had, I could define for myself just how I'm to care for the people of God with whom I come in contact. But the Lord didn't stop with that phrase. Instead He said, "This is My commandment, that you love one another, *just as I have loved you.*" Whoa! Jesus expects us to love with the same selfless attitude and in the same sacrificial manner in which He has loved us. Jesus loved us not just in words but also through His actions. And that's why the gospels help us learn to love. In fact, you might enjoy reading through one of the gospels with this simple question in mind: "How did Jesus show love to those around Him?" You would gain many insights from that experience, but allow me to share one thought about how Jesus showed love.

Before we consider a scene from our Lord's life, answer two questions. First, do you like to be interrupted? And, second, do you enjoy having something unexpected come up in the middle of your well-planned day? Let's see how Jesus responds to just such a situation in John 1.

The Lord is walking along when He suddenly notices two men following Him. He stops and asks them, "What do you want?" They respond with the deep and profound theological question "Where are you staying?" He simply says, "Come and see." Jesus invites these two men into His schedule, and the three of them spend the day together. (You can read about it in John 1:35-39.) The point I want you to consider, though, is this: Am I open, as Jesus clearly was, to those holy interruptions that God might bring into my life? Am I open to extending love in the same selfless, sacrificial way Jesus did?

Now we return to the Upper Room and more teachings from our Lord: "This is My commandment, that you love one another, just as I have loved you.... I have called you friends, for all things that I have heard from My Father I have made known to you" (John 15:12,15).

To appreciate the significance of what Jesus is saying here, take a piece of paper and write down the names of people who, when they talk about their friends, would write your name on their list. For example, I'm pretty sure my wife would put my name on her list. Take a few minutes to complete your list.

A List of Friends

Now look over the list of those who would call you their friend. Did you write the name Jesus? I've been doing this exercise with people for over thirty years. I read John 15:12-15 aloud, slowly and with emphasis, two or three times. I then instruct the people to make a list of people who would call them a friend. When they have finished, I ask them, "How many of you put Jesus on your list?" Despite what these verses state very clearly, seldom do more than one or two people in a group of fifty write Jesus' name.

I'll admit that this is sort of a sneaky way to make a point, but it is effective. I still remember when I had been abiding in this passage and God first led me to write my own list. I took a blank sheet of paper and began listing people who I felt would likely include me on their list of friends. When I got down to the eighteenth or nineteenth name, I wrote the name Jesus Christ. I was absolutely blown away. I could hardly imagine that, when Jesus talks about His friends, He talks about me. What amazing, life-changing news! Do you want empowerment in your Christian life and leadership? Here it is!

I think the reason that we don't automatically list Jesus among our friends is because we haven't connected with Jesus at the emotional level the way we do with our flesh-and-blood friends. We don't find it easy to emotionally connect with the possibility that if Jesus were chatting about His friends, He would talk about you and me. Too often we see God's friendship as being dependent on our performance. We would do much better to "quit keeping score altogether and surrender [ourselves] with all [our] sinfulness to God who sees neither the score nor the scorekeeper but only his child redeemed by Christ."5 Yet not only His child. Also *His* friend.

Now I don't know about you, but I have always enjoyed the old hymn "What a Friend We Have in Jesus." The lyrics express our gratitude about having Christ as our Friend. But in John 15:15, Jesus reverses and personalizes the sentiment: "What a friend I have in Sue,

Cathy, Paul, Wayne, and _____." Place your name in that blank. Know that Jesus sees you and describes you as His friend. Pretty amazing, isn't it?

And that's not all. As we live in God's presence and allow Him to—by the power of His grace—form His life in us, we begin to hear more clearly our Friend's voice. We also begin to understand things we've never understood before. For example, I've often felt that God is late to respond to a situation, but as He keeps growing me and helping me see from His perspective, I realize that God is exactly on time, on His time.

As we spend time reading God's love letter to us, we hear what is on His heart and we see, among other truths, that He is the God of community—the Father, Son, and Spirit. We also see that the Father, Son, and Holy Spirit want our shattered relationship with Them to be restored and enriched. They desire to deepen and broaden our relationship with Them. This growth happens as we abide in Christ. That's why, during His last moments with His leadership team before His arrest and crucifixion, Christ emphasizes, "Protect your time alone with Me and your time reading My love letter to you."

This first priority—an ongoing and growing commitment to Christ—is the nurturing soil for the second priority. Our Lord's second concern for healthy leaders is obvious in His command that we love one another. Jesus says, "Don't disperse; don't go off and do your own thing. Instead, love one another the way I've loved you. This kind of devotion to one another, your sacrificial love for one another, is how people will know that I'm real and that you're Mine" (see John 13:34-35).

Challenges to Loving One Another

Have you ever made the effort to care for someone in the church and gotten hurt in the process? Do you know how it feels, whether in a leadership or nonleadership role, to be ignored, slighted, or injured by a fellow believer? Or perhaps you meant to say or do something good, but your brother or sister in Christ took it the wrong way. We learn that we are able to genuinely love others only when we are centered and firmly abiding in Christ. In that abiding, in being called a friend of Christ, our identity is formed and grounded. There in God's presence we know the security of His acceptance and care, and that is a solid place from which to reach out and love someone in the body of Christ. Then, if I'm injured in the process, I'm not destroyed because, as I sit alone with Jesus and an open Bible, I hear my Lord reminding me that I am His friend.

Let me make this point another way. Many people make the mistake of going into Christian leadership in order to *establish* their identity. They feel—consciously or unconsciously—that becoming a leader will make them someone important, give their days meaning, and cause them to feel good about themselves. That backward approach to leadership is a surefire way to open oneself to further injury. Instead of looking to a leadership role to establish my identity, my identity must be rooted in Christ and in my relationship, my holy friendship, with Him. My identity is formed as I abide in Christ and in the Scriptures. My identity is strengthened and expressed when I share the love of Christ with His people.

Next, having called us to love one another, Jesus continues to share His heart with us in the Upper Room: "Each of you is a special friend. Each of you is unique. Each of you is different from the others. But I have told all of you to love Me and abide in Me (Priority #1); I have commanded all of you to love one another (Priority #2). And there's one more thing." Jesus clarified the first disciples' mission—and ours—with Priority #3.

LIFESTYLE AND LEADERSHIP PRIORITY #3

"When the Helper comes, whom I will send to you from the Father, that is the Spirit of truth who proceeds from the Father, He will testify about Me, and you will testify also, because you have been with Me from the beginning." — John 15:26-27 (NASB)

During our time in the Upper Room, we've heard Jesus' thoughts and passions, and we've seen many remarkable sides of our Savior and Lord. We've seen Him as a Foot Washer, a betrayed Friend, a Son longing for His Father, and our Friend challenging us to love one another. No wonder the Upper Room is a place of many conflicting emotions. Jesus knows that Judas will betray Him and that He is headed to the cross. He loves us: He looks into our eyes and calls us His friends. As the disciples process the news that their Teacher and Friend is leaving them, their body language and facial expressions show shock, hurt, and love. Into this mix of emotions, Jesus speaks about the mission He wants us to carry out: "When the Counselor comes, whom I will send to you from the Father, the Spirit of truth who goes out from the Father, he will testify about me. And you also must testify, for you have been with me from the beginning" (John 15:26-27).

Let's put this mission in context. Here in the Upper Room Jesus has been sharing His heart: "I am concerned about your inner world and your character development. I long for you to recognize your sin and your need for Me so that you can fully experience forgiveness, cleansing, acceptance, and healing. I want you to know My great love for you. As you spend time with Me and become more aware of the extent of My love for you, you will have a greater sense of value and worth [Priority #1: Abiding].

"My plan for your life includes more than that, though. I want you to become an intimate, supportive community with and for one another [Priority #2: Loving one another]. And I'm equally concerned that the life you receive from Me and that you are living out in community be given to the world [Priority #3: Bearing witness]. The world desperately needs the light, life, and healing that only I can offer. So, just as I sent the Holy Spirit to you to bear witness to Me, I am also sending you to the world to bear witness of Me.

"You see, I am passionate about reconciling the world to Myself. My Father is a brokenhearted Lover who desires and seeks reconciliation with rebellious humanity. Therefore I am sending you to live out My presence in the world. I came into the world as a servant, and now I am sending you out as servants. I, the Son of Man, did not come to be served, but to serve and to give my life as a ransom for many [see Mark 10:45]. Therefore, I am sending you into the world as My servants, people of influence, leaders. Know that, wherever you go, I will be there with you. Through you, My presence will be in schools, in offices, in gyms, and in neighborhoods because I am already there and you will be bearing witness to Me."

This third passion of Jesus Christ—this third priority for us, His followers and friends—is a commitment to the work of Christ in the world. Scripture sets forth two aspects of this kind of bearing witness. One is the *evangelistic* mandate. We are sent out to share good news with lost people (Isaiah 61:1-4). We are to bring light to those in darkness, hope to those who are hopeless, and new beginnings to those who are defeated. We are to follow the example of Christ: "For the Son of Man has come to seek and to save that which was lost" (Luke 19:10, NASB). In addition to this evangelistic mandate, God also sends us a *cultural* mandate: We are in the culture in order to give a cup of water to people in Jesus' name. We are in the culture to speak words of grace and kindness in Jesus' name. And we are in the culture to minister God's love and mercy regardless of people's color or race, income or status. We will further explore the evangelistic mandate and the cultural mandate in chapters 15-18.

The Heartbeat of God

As we return to the Upper Room, we continue to hear the heartbeat of God, this time as Christ prays in John 17. We hear again about the importance of intimacy with the Father, the Son, and the Spirit. And we hear Jesus say, "Now this is eternal life: that they may know you, the only true God, and Jesus Christ, whom you have sent" (17:3). As Jesus says these words, we realize that eternal life is not merely a dynamic of time, but a dynamic of relationship. And we will see that, because of this relationship of eternal life, we are able to live out in God's presence and in the world the passions and the priorities of Christ, expressed in His words in John 15 and in His prayer in John 17. We live as godly leaders.

In light of the Upper Room conversation, then, what is the Christian life? *It is an ongoing relationship of deepening intimacy with Jesus Christ.* The Christian life is more of a *who* than a *what*. And followers of Christ live the healthy Christian lifestyle when they take on the passions and priorities of Jesus Christ: an ongoing commitment to Jesus Christ (Priority #1), ongoing commitment to the body of Christ (Priority #2), and ongoing commitment to the work of Christ in the world (Priority #3).

Now it's one thing to say that these priorities matter to us; it's quite another to let them shape our schedule and define each of us as a person. Living out Priority #1—communion with God—establishes our identity as children of God and servants of Christ who are being shaped into His image. In our times of abiding, we need to revisit the truths that, by God's grace, we are His precious creations, His ambassadors in this world, and His beloved sons and daughters. In Priority #2—loving fellow members of the body of Christ—we express our identity and reveal who we are in Christ even as the Holy Spirit continues to make us more like Him. Finally, in living out Priority #3 and bearing witness to God by our loving service and words of testimony, we further express our identity as His children even as He continues to shape that identity and often affirms it.

It is a great honor to be organizationally positioned as a leader, whether as a pastor or as laity. (We need to realize, though, that it is an equal honor to live as a person of Christian influence in every and any setting we find ourselves!) We must, however, always guard against allowing a leadership role to become our identity. In my work in the world and in the church, my identity as a follower of Jesus is to be expressed, not formed. Our answers to the following questions can help warn us if the opposite is happening:

Do I feel my identity is in jeopardy?

Do I fear someone is going to beat me out or replace me?

Am I being tempted to establish my identity through ministry or leadership?

Pay attention to what your answers tell you about why you are leading and serving. Take note of what your answers tell you about the source of your identity.

Do you see the genius of God's plan? He has established the Christian life on a relationship between Him and me, a relationship that keeps growing in intimacy and closeness. This relationship manifests itself as I live and lead. The remaining chapters will offer some important insights and suggest some specific patterns for living out this lifestyle of the Upper Room.

Before we take those steps, let's take just a moment to review where we've been. In the previous chapter, we examined the propellant of a godly lifestyle and godly leadership: Christ's gracious and loving invitation to "Come, follow Me." In this chapter, we have seen that God's grace and love are to shape the priorities of our lives.

Picture those three priorities of the Christian life as three concentric circles. The innermost circle is abiding—Priority #1, ongoing commitment to Jesus Christ. This is lived out in our alone time of abiding with the Father, Son, and Holy Spirit and with God's Word. The next circle is loving one another—Priority #2, ongoing commitment to the body of Christ. This commitment is lived out in our loving one another in our immediate family as well as in the larger body of Christ. The third circle is bearing witness—Priority #3, ongoing commitment to the work of Christ in the world. This is lived out in the homes, neighborhoods, schools, and marketplaces of our lives.

At this point it's very natural to wonder how these three priorities actually become the heartbeat and core of our life. What can we do to enter in to the process by which God forms leaders? by which He makes these priorities fundamental to who we are and what we do? by which He transforms our inner thoughts, attitudes, behaviors, and responses to be more the person He wants each of us to be, to be more like His Son? If you desire to be salt and light in the world, if you want to be a godly influence and an effective leader in the church as well as in the community, keep reading. Part II of this book walks you through the transformational process.

MOTIVATED BY GOD'S GRACE,
WE DEVELOP A LIFESTYLE AND A LEADERSHIP STYLE BASED ON
ABIDING, LOVING ONE ANOTHER, AND BEARING WITNESS.

To the One who calls me His friend,
I ask Your help. There are so many voices, so many responsibilities, and such limited time and energy in my life. Lord God, enable me to look at my schedule with Your eyes. Help me yield it to You so that You can reshape it as You wish. As You know, I sometimes feel so driven. I long instead to be directed, led, and empowered by Your Spirit. Help me—by Your grace—to learn to live and lead according to Your priorities, plans, and timing. In our Lord's name. Amen.

Before You Take the Next Step

In your own growth in Christ, which of the three priorities has received the most emphasis? the least emphasis?

As you reflect on the three priorities of abiding in Christ, loving one another, and bearing witness of Jesus to the world, which do you find more natural for you? less natural? Talk to the Lord a bit about this.

We've looked closely at the words Jesus spoke in the Upper Room. What impact will these words have on your praying and planning in the coming week?

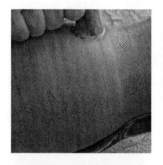

Simple table items provide a picture of the lifelong God process for spiritual growth as well as leadership and ministry development.

Developing the Lifestyle
of a Healthy Leader

The Process That Integrates

Spiritual Formation and Leadership Development

We all know that a picture is worth a thousand words. So let me give you an image that will help you better grasp an essential concept in this book. As we've seen, God forms us into His leaders in the Soul Room and the Leadership Room. I like to describe this process using the image of Pitcher/Cup...Saucer/Plate. Let me explain.

- The *pitcher* represents all that God is and all that He longs to pour into the cup of my life: His very being, His existence as Father, Son, and Holy Spirit, His character, and His desires for my life.

- The *cup* represents my life. It is the unique and distinctive cup of who I am—of who God created me to be and of all that God longs for me to become. God desires to continually pour Himself into the cup of my life until it overflows with His character and grace.

- This divine overflow spills onto the *saucer*. The saucer represents relationships, the network of people my life touches, however frequently or infrequently.

- Finally, the *plate* represents events, the places, and the organizations where God's gracious presence in my life can further overflow through me and, at times, through my leadership responsibilities.

This Pitcher/Cup … Saucer/Plate process involves the whole of my being, the whole of my life.

NOURISHING OUR SOUL

This Pitcher/Cup … Saucer/Plate reality was vividly illustrated by an experience I had at a gathering of the regional field staff of a very large and well-known ministry. I had never met any of these people, yet my assignment was to teach about nourishing our souls. Here is the afternoon agenda; I am item #3.

1. What is our vision?
2. What is our budget?
3. How do you nourish your soul?
4. What are the tensions and stresses between the home office and field staff?

After we had spent two-and-a-half hours on vision and budget, I was given forty-five minutes to offer some insight about the nourishment of our souls. I began by reminding the group of the richness of God's love for us and His amazing availability to us. Then I gave them the opportunity to meet alone with this great and gracious God. They received a sheet that included a Bible passage and two reflection questions for their time alone with God. Before that time began, I played the Graham Kendrick worship song "For This We Have Jesus." After the song, I prayed. Then I encouraged these leaders to continue praying, to prepare their heart to be a sanctuary where God could meet with them, speak to them, touch them.

I had planned to give them—and myself along with them— fifteen minutes for solitude and reflection. My Scripture page was as blank as theirs. As much as anyone sitting around that table, I needed God's Spirit to touch my life. I needed a Holy Spirit encounter with God, not just some unique technique for acting like a Christian.

After about eight minutes, I noticed a woman who was crying. Clearly, her heart was heavy; something was weighing her down. A few minutes later, another person at the far end of the table began to weep. As we came to the end of the fifteen minutes, I encouraged these remarkable people to turn and share what God had given them with the person on either their right or left. Then, after giving them some time to talk, I encouraged them to pray with that same person.

As the prayer time ended, I asked, "What did God do as you were quiet in His presence with this passage?" The responses were stunning. One woman said, "We share the same office, and there has been something going on between the two of us for weeks. We've just never stopped to deal with it. When we turned to share with each other what God had given us from the passage, our hearts were broken and reunited. We asked for each other's forgiveness."

Next, another staff member shared that she had come to this day tired, stressed, and wondering if anyone cared about her. She said, "In this quiet place I discovered that God is here, and He reminded me that He cares for me. Then, as we shared and prayed with one another, I discovered that others here care about me as well."

At this point, my forty-five minutes were up, and the staff team began listing the tensions and stresses that existed between the home office and the field staff—agenda item #4. Such tension is inevitable in large ministries, and these special people desired to have an honest and beneficial problem-solving time. Freely sharing about the stresses, they came up with a list of fifteen items that were written on flip-chart pages and hung on the wall. Emotions were strong, convictions were high, frustrations were deep, and the problems seemed insurmountable.

As this time drew to a close, though, one man spoke up: "As I look at our long list of tensions between my field office and the home office, I'm realizing that if I were tending my soul better, all but one of these stresses would be removed from the list." Other heads immediately nodded in agreement.

Do you see what happened here? Before addressing tensions and stresses, each individual had gone to the Soul Room and reestablished their essential bond with the Lord. This deep connection not only restored the leadership community (forgiveness was asked for and received; one leader realized that people genuinely cared about her), but this connection also enabled clarity about leadership and administrative issues. When spiritual formation is an intentional part of the leadership agenda, there is the God-given potential for repentance, confession, reconnection, new perspective, creative ideas, and restored and restorative community. I wonder what would have happened in this gathering if we had begun with spiritual formation—or, on the other hand, if this time set aside for spiritual formation had been completely omitted from the agenda on the assumption that it was happening in each individual's personal schedule.

A LESSON FOR LIFE

In light of this real-life illustration about the importance of Pitcher/Cup ... Saucer/Plate, allow me to ask you a few questions:

1. How important is your personal spiritual formation and development to your leadership responsibilities and decisions? Look, for instance, at how much time in a typical week you devote to your personal spiritual growth.

2. Is your spirituality foundational to your effectiveness as a godly leader and disciple-maker, or is your spiritual health a peripheral enhancement to your leadership? And does your calendar or Day-Timer support your answer?

3. Do you consider spiritual formation a good thing to attend to—when you have the time?

4. Or is your solitude with God and your silence before Him the primary source of energy and guidance for your leadership as well as a dynamic part of your daily life and therefore a key item on your leadership schedule?

Reflect for a few minutes on the questions above. Give thoughtful responses to them. Then consider what your answers reveal.

The process of godly leadership must begin with our spending quiet and focused time with God Himself—Father, Son, and Holy Spirit. In our fast-paced world, creating space for God by establishing a regular time of solitude and silence with God in the Scriptures is a constant and difficult challenge. In hopes of helping you meet this challenge, I will answer in chapters 6-8 some questions about the Soul Room you may have—questions about what happens in the Soul Room and how you enter it. Rest assured that I'm talking about far more than just reading and studying the Bible. Then, in chapter 9, we will talk about entering the Soul Room not just for our soul and life, but now also for the souls and lives of others.

Chapters 6-9 address the *Pitcher/Cup* aspects of the process of integrating spiritual formation and leadership development. Whenever you spend time with God in the Soul Room, He pours His presence into the cup of your life. May these four chapters therefore help you develop an awareness of a place and some patterns that foster a spiritual passion for enjoying the Lord and for going with Him into the Leadership Room.

Chapters 10-14 address relationships and events (*Saucer/Plate*) in the context of the local church. We become Soul Room/Leadership Room people living out Lifestyle and Leadership Priority #2 ("loving one another").

Chapters 15-18 offer a deeper understanding of the world in which we live and insights about how to build relationships in this world. We become Soul Room/Leadership Room leaders living out Lifestyle and Leadership Priority #3 ("bearing witness").

"May the God of hope fill you with all joy and peace
as you trust in him, so that you may overflow with hope by the
power of the Holy Spirit." — Romans 15:13

*The Triune God
desires your presence
in the Soul Room,
and upon your arrival
the Father, the Son,
and the Spirit welcome
you with genuine love
and wholehearted
acceptance.*

Does God Really Care
about Spending Time with Me?

Being Blessed by the Community of Father, Son, and Holy Spirit

Often when I am talking with Christian leaders, I ask them two questions: "What matters most to you?" and "What are some of the key ingredients of your leadership?" These remarkable folks usually give me the right answers—being a person of prayer, being committed to a team, caring for people, etc. Then I ask them if they have their calendar with them. If they do, I ask them to walk me through the past two weeks. After they've done so, I share my genuine excitement about their life and my appreciation for the overview of their ministry. But too often I then have to comment, "Your schedule over the past two weeks doesn't show that you have set aside significant time for nourishing your soul, for spending meaningful time alone with God." Their response is usually "I know I need to be more consistent in my time alone with God, but I've been so busy" or a more discouraged "I just can't find the time."

What would the calendar of the past two weeks of your life reveal? Would you be able to point to specific and substantial blocks of time you spent with the Lord, blocks of time when He was able to nourish your soul? Or would the way you have lived these past two weeks reveal a gap between what you would identify as some of the key ingredients of your ministry (prayer, meditation, quiet time) and the reality of your actual schedule?

This one-on-one time with the Lord, this abiding alone with our God, is crucial to our spiritual health, our spiritual growth, and, yes, the effectiveness of our leadership.

Sadly, the vast majority of these people I've talked to were, at that moment, in leadership roles in the church, and I believe that this careless neglect of soul nourishment is a major weakness of the American church. Too infrequently do we who are leaders make our ongoing spiritual formation *primary* and not *secondary* in our life, much less in our ministry. Consequently, more often than not we are ministry-driven rather than Spirit-led. We enter leadership and ministry settings more frequently and freely than we enter into God's presence to abide in Him and commune with Him. Yet this one-on-one time with the Lord, this abiding alone with our God, is crucial to our spiritual health, our spiritual growth, and, yes, the effectiveness of our leadership.

Do God the Father, God the Son, and God the Holy Spirit know you as an occasional visitor to the Soul Room or as an abiding friend? Scripture reveals that alone-with-God times formed the pattern of Christ's life as well as the pattern of Abraham's life. God's Word also teaches that Christ Himself longs for us to come away and be with Him.

Very early in the morning, while it was still dark, Jesus got up, left the house and went off to a solitary place, where he prayed. — Mark 1:35

Early the next morning Abraham got up and returned to the place where he had stood before the Lord. — Genesis 19:27

If you remain [or abide] in me and my words remain in you, ask whatever you wish, and it will be given you. — John 15:7

Spending time abiding in Jesus is an act of intentionality on our part; it won't happen automatically. But when it does happen, you will be glad you made the effort. After all, your time of worship and fellowship in the Soul Room is the time when the cup of your life is filled, the time when your soul is nourished.

It is all too easy for us leaders to run through life—from

meeting to meeting, from sermon to sermon, from crisis to crisis, from event to event—without tending to our constant need for the cup of our lives to be filled and refilled by the Pitcher. God Himself desires to pour into the cup of our lives all that He is and all that He longs for us to become. This is what happens in the Soul Room—you are filled and nourished by your sweet communion with God the Father—and this is the focus of chapters 6, 7, and 8.

God—Father, Son, and Holy Spirit,

You know my heart; You know what I'm feeling. You are well aware of the level of excitement and exhaustion, the intensity of the joy and/or pain I'm feeling, and my struggle for direction and insight. Lord, I pray that You would meet me and minister to me in a very real way as I read this chapter. Please grant me the ability to focus my thoughts…to experience refreshment in my soul…and to freely venture into new waters of relating intimately with You, my God and Father. I pray this in the grand name of the living Christ. Amen.

THE SOUL ROOM: A PLACE OF COMMUNITY

As I enter the Soul Room to abide and be spiritually fed, I come as one known by God. And He knows whether I am excited or exhausted, focused or floundering, delighted or disillusioned. He knows if I am running or crawling, healthy or hurting, forgiven or feeling guilty. Whatever my condition, God is pleased and excited that I am coming—that I am entering His presence to be with Him. And I am pleased and excited too.

Some of you, though, may feel unsure about entering the Soul Room. Perhaps you felt closer to God in the past than you do now and you're afraid to come back. After all, when there was distance in other relationships, you may have been replaced when you finally dared to return. You may be concerned that this will also happen in the Soul Room.

For others of you, the Soul Room may be a very new experience. You wonder who is there, what God is like one-on-one, and how He will make you feel. Will He treat you like an intruder, a freshman to be initiated, or a newcomer needing to pay your dues?

Let me try to put you at ease by letting you know what awaits. Whenever you and I enter the Soul Room, we can be sure that Someone is always there to greet us, understand us, listen to us, care for us, and respond to our situation. That Someone is there for us to interact with, and with that Someone we can develop a strong and intimate relationship. This Someone is God, and He is present as the community of the Father, the Son, and the Holy Spirit. They are the Soul Room community into which we are received.

And it's a community we read about in the Bible.

> At that time Jesus came from Nazareth in Galilee and was baptized by John in the Jordan. As Jesus was coming up out of the water, he saw heaven being torn open and the Spirit descending on him like a dove. And a voice came from heaven: "You are my Son, whom I love; with you I am well pleased." (Mark 1:9-11)

> May the grace of the Lord Jesus Christ, and the love of God, and the fellowship of the Holy Spirit be with you all. (2 Corinthians 13:14)

As you consider this Triune God and getting to know Father, Son, and Holy Spirit more intimately, think too about this observation: "The fact that our view of God shapes our lives to a great extent may be one of the reasons Scripture ascribes such importance to seeking to know him."[1]

May this chapter facilitate your seeking. Learn now more about who will greet you in the Soul Room, what They are like, and what They desire for you.

IN THE SOUL ROOM COMMUNITY: GOD THE FATHER

The longings of God the Father—and the metaphors with which those are described—reveal much about the Almighty and about us. God, for instance, is **a brokenhearted Lover** who desires and seeks reconciliation with those who have forsaken Him. God is also **a brokenhearted Father** who longs for His loved ones to come home. If God is Lover, then we are beloved. If God is Father, then we are sons and daughters.

The following verses from Jeremiah incorporate these powerful metaphors:

> I myself said, "How gladly would I treat you like sons and give you a desirable land, the most beautiful inheritance of any nation." I thought you

would call me "Father" and not turn away from following me. But like
a woman unfaithful to her husband, so you have been unfaithful to me,
O house of Israel. (3:19-20)

Do you feel the Father's heartbreak? It's hard to miss His longing to
be called "Father" and His passionate desire to share and celebrate His
life with His children. You may very well be surprised by the Father's
warmth as He welcomes you into the Soul Room. Just remember that
"His heart is the most sensitive and tender of all. No act goes unno-
ticed, no matter how insignificant or small. A cup of cold water is
enough to put tears in the eyes of God. Like the proud mother who is
thrilled to receive a bouquet of wilted dandelions from her child, so
God celebrates our feeble expressions of gratitude."[2]

The longings of the Father reveal key truths about Him, but
consider other facts we also know about Him, facts that prompt us to
worship Him. God, for example, is the **Creator of all things** in
heaven and on earth. The tree I'm climbing, the flower I'm holding,
or the sunset that is mesmerizing me all reveal His craftsmanship and
skill (Genesis 1–2). Listen to the words of Psalm 19:1-3 (NLT):

The heavens tell of the glory of God.
The skies display his marvelous craftsmanship.
Day after day they continue to speak;
 night after night they make him known.
They speak without a sound or a word;
 their voice is silent in the skies.

Often growth in my relationship with God—and this may be true for
you—occurs as I observe more closely His physical world that sur-
rounds me. When God's nature book captures my attention, it reveals
Him to me. Kallistos Ware, a bishop of the Greek Orthodox Church,
makes this comment:

It is to see God in all things and all things in God—to discern, in and
through each created reality, the divine presence that is within it and at the
same time beyond it. It is to treat each thing as a sacrament, to view the
whole of nature as God's book.[3]

God the Father as loving Creator impacts my leadership lifestyle by
affecting how I value, care for, and live in God's creation—including
the people He has lovingly crafted in His image and then entrusted
to my care.

Yes, we can see—if we look—the image of God in the people we live with as well as in the people outside our neighborhood, beyond our country's borders, and across the ocean. In the Soul Room, we sharpen this ability to see humanity through God's eyes, and this ability influences and convicts me about how I treat others. Do I show respect for people of other social backgrounds, races, and ethnic origins? As a leader do I see both women and men as graced and gifted by God the Father?

We see more about our Creator God when we consider that He also **designed the plan for our salvation**. Again, this broken-hearted Lover has desired and sought reconciliation since the Fall (that's a one-sentence summary of the biblical story from Genesis through Revelation), and He developed a plan to bring about this reconciliation. His plan involved the coming of a Redeemer. And Jesus, our Redeemer, is also present in the Soul Room.

IN THE SOUL ROOM COMMUNITY: JESUS CHRIST, GOD THE SON

Abiding in the Soul Room allows me the opportunity to develop my relationship with God the Son, Jesus Christ. In the Soul Room, I get to know more about what He is like and what He desires for me.

We know from His earthly itinerary that when Jesus sees crowds of lost people, He is moved with compassion. He describes the people He sees as "harassed and helpless, like sheep without a shepherd" (Matthew 9:36). Jesus also sees everything that would rob people of life and declares, "I came so they can have real and eternal life, more and better life than they ever dreamed of. I am the Good Shepherd. The Good Shepherd puts the sheep before himself, sacrifices himself if necessary" (John 10:10b-11, MSG). Jesus is our **compassionate Shepherd** who desires to both give and protect life.

As He carries out the longings of His shepherd's heart, Jesus will act as **Liberator**.

> The Spirit of the Lord is on me,
> > because he has anointed me to preach good news to the poor.
> He has sent me to proclaim freedom for the prisoners
> > and recovery of sight for the blind, to release the oppressed,
> to proclaim the year of the Lord's favor. (Luke 4:18-19)

He is the **Champion** for the poor, the imprisoned, the blind, and the oppressed. He is the Father's love in a human body, and He presses me to ask myself leadership questions like "Do I see—*really* see—the people around me? Am I willing to go to them regardless of their condition? Am I willing to work as a liberator with Christ, my **Liberator**, to help others become all that He desires them to be?"

As we observe the Son, we also see Him as a **Model of endurance** for us leaders. After all, how do you handle the rough seasons of Christian ministry? How do you cope with rejection? How do you handle discouragement and lack of motivation in yourself as well as in others? Jesus handled all this and much more (see Isaiah 53:2-12; Mark 14:32-36). Will the life of the Lord Jesus be your model for lifelong endurance in leadership, in your efforts to make disciples?

Finally, the Son is **Savior** of my soul, the Lamb of God who died on the cross for my sin. In His presence, I am overwhelmed by His amazing love and immeasurable grace, and I am compelled to worship Him. As I stand in His presence, I am also reenergized with passion for the meaning and direction He has given me for life. A busy leader who is involved in the lives of many people, I am once again brought to the bottom line of my faith: the thrilling honor of knowing Christ Jesus as Savior, Lord, and Friend and of sharing the good news about Him—news that brings us human beings from death to life—with everyone and anyone He puts in my path.

By the way, notice that what Christ can do as Liberator and as Savior, He does in order to fulfill His longing that the lost sheep of this world will come to know Him as their Good Shepherd. As the Son of God reminds me of this truth, He ignites in me the very longing to serve Him by living and sharing with others that He is my Liberator and my Savior. Don't miss the truth that energy and power for the Leadership Room comes from the Soul Room.

IN THE SOUL ROOM COMMUNITY: GOD THE HOLY SPIRIT

The Soul Room welcoming community is not only God the Father and God the Son, but also God the Holy Spirit. This third Person of the Triune God was given to me and you by the Father at Christ's request: "I will ask the Father, and he will give you another Counselor to be with you forever—the Spirit of truth…. You know him, for he lives with you and will be in you" (John 14:16-17). Father, Son, and Spirit share a special concern for my life and leadership—and for yours as well. Let's consider the role of the Spirit.

Jesus teaches that the Holy Spirit will live with us and will be in us (John 14:17). This language offers a picture of communion—of God the Holy Spirit being in an intimate relationship with us and partnering with us in ministry and life. In fact, when Paul wrote to the Romans, he described the Holy Spirit as One interceding before the Father on our behalf "with groans that words cannot express" (Romans 8:27). Clearly, the Holy Spirit longs to be an active presence at the deepest levels of our life and leadership.

And He is able to do that by virtue of His nature. The Holy Spirit, for instance, is the **Paraclete** who comes alongside to help me, and He will be my **Companion** forever. Klaus Issler refers to the Holy Spirit as "my roommate and copilot." He explains:

> Imagine your relationship with the Spirit to be like that of a pilot and copilot flying a multimillion-dollar passenger airplane through the friendly skies. Similar to an airplane, human life, a priceless and miraculous creation of God, is expressly designed to be a two-pilot arrangement. God has so fashioned human nature that both a human person and a divine person can occupy the pilot's quarters together. Yet the Holy Spirit does not become the senior pilot in this arrangement, although He is the superior expert. The Spirit is our divine mentor, our flight instructor as it were, to help us live our lives to the glory of God.[4]

Too often the Christian life is seen as an "I" proposition. Similarly, leadership often focuses on "I"—what I am going to do and why I am going to do it. When I abide in the Soul Room, though, I realize more and more the truth that the Christian life is not the journey of an "I" but an adventure of a "we." The Spirit with me and in me means that I am never alone. I am part of a "we," living with Another.

As my constant companion, the Holy Spirit also serves as my **Guide**. In our world of vast and not always correct information, He guides me into all truth, He reminds me of everything Jesus has taught me, He helps me understand those teachings, and He thereby establishes my leadership on reliable ground. As the Spirit does these things for me, He guides me along the journey of life.

Jesus teaches that another one of the Spirit's roles in my life is that of **Convictor**. Present in the world, the Spirit exposes and convicts the world of its sin and rebellion against God. Present in me, He does the same thing on a personal level. As Convictor, He reveals my sin with a view to correction, redemption, and healing, not embarrassment or condemnation. After all, "the Holy Spirit is the bond of tenderness between the Father and the Son. Thus, the indwelling Spirit bears the indelible stamp of the compassion of God, and the heart of the Spirit-filled person overflows with tenderness."5

The Spirit's work in our leadership is therefore very freeing. He changes the hearts and lives of people. He touches the human spirit and brings to us awareness not only of our sin, but also of our holy potential. Rebirth in Christ and our ongoing transformation is uniquely the Spirit's work, but it is easy for us leaders to think that these things are primarily *our* work. In truth, however, we are partners with the Spirit in God's transforming work in us and in others. As we enjoy communion with the Holy Spirit, He continually reminds us that *effective leadership comes only as we depend on Him and follow Him.*

THE TRINITY: FATHER, SON, AND HOLY SPIRIT

As we spend time in the Soul Room with the community of the Father, Son, and Holy Spirit, we discover further intimacy with each of these Persons of the Trinity. And we must always remember that the Trinity is in fact three Persons, not an abstract idea.

> Trinity is a conceptual attempt to provide coherence to God as God is revealed variously as Father, Son, and Holy Spirit in our Scriptures: God is emphatically *personal*; God is only and exclusively God in *relationship*. Trinity is not an attempt to explain or define God by means of abstractions (although there is some of that, too), but a witness that God reveals himself as personal and in personal relations.... Under the image of the Trinity we discover that we do not know God by defining him but by being loved by him and loving in return.6

And this Triune God—God the Father, God the Son, and God the Spirit—desires my presence in the Soul Room, and upon my arrival, They greet me with love and acceptance. But how do I respond to Them? Do I tend to emphasize one Person of the Trinity over the others? Which member of the Trinity do I feel closest to? Why? And which Person do I need to know better? Why?

Is it the Father you know best? If so, you probably have a high view of the sovereignty of God. He is in charge. Things never get out of control. But sometimes with that emphasis on the Father, you begin to feel that God is distant, removed, and uninterested in you because, being in charge of the universe, He has so much to do.

Or perhaps God the Son, the Lord Jesus Christ, has been emphasized in your faith journey. Do you feel closest to Him? After all, you have experienced Him as Savior, Lamb of God, and Redeemer; you have received His forgiveness. But if you focus too much on the Son, your God may become more of a buddy than the Almighty King of the universe. You can lose your sense of the awe, the mystery, and the majesty of God.

Or perhaps the Holy Spirit has been most emphasized. You enjoy His presence with you and in you. This focus on the Holy Spirit causes God to feel close, real, and approachable. But with an overemphasis on the Holy Spirit, one's faith can become rather emotional and feelings-based rather than rooted in the historical Christ, the sacrificial and saving death of the Redeemer, and the sovereign rule of the Father.

THE SOUL ROOM COMMUNITY

The love, acceptance, and forgiveness of God is a very relational experience, and as we spend time in the Soul Room with God the Father, God the Son, and God the Spirit, we keep discovering that we know One better than we know the Others. We become aware of the importance of having a solid relationship with Each—and of how prone we are to imbalance, to knowing One at the expense of knowing the Others. Abiding in the Soul Room centers me and saves me from my off-center tendencies. Time in the Soul Room enables me to better understand the nature of my God and brings me to a new place of intimacy in my relationship with each of the Three.

Being in the Soul Room with God the Father, God the Son, and God the Spirit stirs my emotions, warms my spirit, compels me to worship, and increases my desire to let God love me.

THE FATHER, SON, AND HOLY SPIRIT ARE THE WELCOMING COMMUNITY WAITING FOR MY ARRIVAL IN THE SOUL ROOM.

God, I'm not telling You anything You don't already know about me, but sometimes in the rush of life and demands of leadership, I don't make getting to know You more personally the priority that I know it should be and that I want it to be. Life's demands are so loud and relentless. Please forgive me for responding to those demands instead of protecting my time with You. Forgive me for being satisfied with knowing You in such a shallow way. Please give me a renewed desire and greater resolve to deepen our friendship and to connect more regularly and more intimately with You—Father, Son, and Holy Spirit. In the name of that precious Soul Room community I pray. Amen.

Before You Take the Next Step

What point in this chapter was especially meaningful to you? Why?

Which person of the Trinity do you feel closest to? Why?

Which person of the Trinity do you feel furthest from? Why?

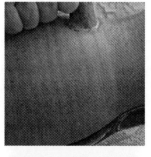

Christ took what was ours
that he might give us what
was his: he takes our broken
humanity and cleanses it
by his self-sanctifying life of
obedience. Now in the Spirit
he gives us back our
humanity cleansed and
redeemed: take, eat,
this is broken for you.
— James Torrance

What Exactly Happens in the Soul Room?

Leadership: Moving from Management to Mystery

You may have a book from this popular series in your home. Millions of copies have been sold, yet 113 publishers turned down the authors. One hundred and thirteen publishers didn't get it; apparently they didn't understand the value of stories. But life is about stories; life is about people, places, happenings, joys, sorrows, hope. And—as you may have guessed—I'm talking about *Chicken Soup for the Soul*. (The series even includes *Chicken Soup for Dog Lovers!*)

Much like these collections of stories, the Bible offers us stories—specifically, God-directed stories within His bigger story—and both the big and the small stories are written for all generations of all cultures in all times. God knows the value of stories. He Himself is writing a story in history, and He invites us to become an integral part of His story. The Bible is a storybook and, therefore, a people book.

In this chapter, we will see what happens in the Soul Room as we look at and enter into God's story, as we examine the convergence of biblical story and our own story and consider how this convergence provides healing and direction for our life. We will also address the tensions that exist in the Soul Room—the tensions, for instance, between management and mystery, between pleasant times and dark times. Clearly, much significant transformational activity happens in the Soul Room.

God, You know the burdens that are weighing *me down. Help me relinquish them to Your perfect care. Help me open myself to the soul-nourishment You long to give me right now. Please help me clearly hear Your voice and understand Your message. I want to hear from You, Father God, and I'd like to see the story of my life from a new perspective, from Your perspective. I also ask You to help me understand more clearly that I am Your beloved child. I request this in the strong name of Jesus Christ. Amen.*

GOD'S CHICKEN SOUP

The Bible is *about* real people and *for* real people. We find in between its covers people born as infants and growing into adulthood, people living in specific places and at particular times, people living with faith in God and others turning their backs on Him. Despite the dominance of story in its pages, we've often made the Bible a book of principles. We've tended to remove the principles from the story and then use them as a straightedge against which we measure ourselves. This is not God's way. In fact, when we meet with Him in the Soul Room, we find God opening the written record and telling us the stories that are found there.

God shares these stories with us because He wants the stories of His people today—your story and mine—to intersect with the stories of His people then. Too often we regard the biblical stories as separate from our stories. When this occurs, Klaus Issler suggests, "we skew our perception of God by reading scripture as essentially a historical account of how God acted in the past, rather than a divine record about people just like us who experienced a normal friendship with God available to contemporary believers as well."[1] It is essential that we identify our stories with the stories of biblical people, for the living God of history past and of history present is the One writing the story. As Christian thinker Dallas Willard warns, unless we identify with these biblical folk, "we will not genuinely be able to believe the

Bible or find its content to be real, because it will have no experiential substance to us.... [The Bible] becomes simply a book of doctrine, of abstract truth about God, which one can search endlessly without encountering God himself or hearing his voice."[2]

The Soul Room, however, is the place where we can encounter God, worship Him, and hear His voice. And it is no accident that there in the Soul Room—occupied as it is by the Father, Son, and Holy Spirit—God's story is continually tended and carefully unveiled. After all, the Triune God guided the writing of the historical record, and this holy record makes it very clear that people matter to God. Consider the people lists in Numbers 1, 1 Chronicles 1–8, Nehemiah 7, Matthew 1, and Romans 16. God wanted the people mentioned in Romans 16 to be remembered as models of faith—that is the key to His story. I doubt that any of us would use these names for our children, but these people of faith mattered greatly to God.

In fact, we see again and again what matters to God as we spend time in His book. History, for instance, has long wanted to know which pharaoh ruled during the time of Moses. What was his name? Well, we have no answer to that question because, in God's salvation story, that detail isn't important. Let's listen in as God tells His story and see what aspects of the story God wanted His people to know and remember. Here is a scene from Exodus 1:

> The King of Egypt said to the Hebrew midwives, whose names were Shiphrah and Puah, "When you help the Hebrew women in childbirth and observe them on the delivery stool, if it is a boy, kill him; but if it is a girl, let her live." The midwives, however, feared God and did not do what the king of Egypt had told them to do; they let the boys live.... And because the midwives feared God, he gave them families of their own. (verses 15-17, 21)

Shiphrah and Puah matter in God's story because they honored and obeyed Him despite the pharaoh's commands. So their names matter to God, but the name of that pharaoh is incidental to Him.

What matters to God becomes clear to me during my time of abiding—my time of quiet—away from the Leadership Room and in the presence of Father, Son, and Holy Spirit. There in the Soul Room, God uses His story to keep me focused on what matters most to Him. If I didn't have access to the Scriptures, I could easily feel that I'm the definer of life and godliness. But there in the Soul Room, as I enjoy fellowship with the Trinity, God opens the Scripture story to me and defines the shape of my life and leadership. Father, Son, and Spirit form my view of life and of the world around me. God really does use His holy and life-giving Word as chicken soup for my soul.

> Too many of us Christian leaders disregard God's story and keep ourselves too busy to commune with the Father, Son, and Spirit.

I often fear, though, that much of the buzz about church leadership today comes more from cultural pressures than from God's pages. Guidelines for leadership formation in the church too often look the same as the culture's guidelines for leadership formation. And that is not a big surprise, actually, since too many of us Christian leaders disregard God's story and keep ourselves too busy to commune with the Father, Son, and Spirit.

I therefore believe it is crucial—for our soul as well as for our leadership—to continually ask ourselves these questions: "Am I enjoying the Bible as a personal love letter crafted and written by God Himself? Or is the Bible just one of many documents that I read? Do I read the news more frequently than the Bible? What is the source of the news I consider most important?" One woman from our ministry offers us—as believers and as leaders—a good and godly goal: "I am learning to turn to the Bible as my first response rather than my last resort."

Furthermore, turning to the Bible when I'm in the Soul Room helps me see how my story and God's ongoing story converge. There in the Soul Room, the Trinity and I connect for fellowship and communion, for my guidance and growth.

THE SOUL ROOM AND THE CONVERGENCE OF STORIES

Alone in the presence of God, I begin to realize that my entry into the Soul Room is not a visit to a historical place or a museum of ancient artifacts. Instead, when I enter that sacred place, I find myself very much involved in current time and in the living community where my story is being written. Furthermore, God's story provides a backdrop that enables me to better understand myself. It is a fresh encounter that invites reflection, an encounter that I look forward to with great anticipation.

After all, the Father is there welcoming me as His beloved child. The Son is there with His nail-pierced hands. The Spirit is there to grant me understanding and empowerment. And I am there in holy celebration, ready with heartfelt confession, and alive with an eager expectation of what God has for me. And among the riches available in the Soul Room is convergence.

What do I mean by *convergence*? Consider the college student who seems to switch majors frequently. She's looking for something that will integrate her mental abilities, relational skills, emotional bent, and vocational gifting. She's looking for convergence. She's looking for that area of study that so kindles her passion that she can give hours, days, weeks, and even years to it with continuous energy—and that will give her a blessed sense of fulfillment as she does. As I like to put it, this student is looking for a life pursuit that involves *enjoyment* effort, not just *endurance* effort.

We can also come to understand convergence when we trace someone's vocational journey. Imagine a man who has moved from job to job looking for a vocation that is fulfilling. He is skilled at many things, but something is missing. When he finally stumbles upon "the perfect job," he suddenly loves to go to work. He finds himself using his talents and abilities more fully than ever before, and his sense of value increases. Now the most exciting part of his workday is when he arrives at the office rather than when he leaves it. Convergence is occurring in this man's life.

When such convergence occurs in the Soul Room, we can make significant discoveries about who we are. We can experience profound gratitude to God, healthy and genuine honesty about ourselves, and our heavenly Father's transforming touch. In the Soul Room, God's formation of my character into Christ's image can be a rich and ongoing reality in my life. Let's look at some aspects of that holy transformation.

Celebrating My Birth Person—When we open the Bible, we can be doing so much more than reading history. I can, for instance, learn much about myself. As I read passages like Genesis 1:26-27, Psalm 8, and Psalm 139, for instance, I can celebrate my birth person. After all, God created me in His image; I am an image bearer of God. I'm not merely a teenager trying to fit in, a newlywed learning what marriage is all about, or a recent retiree settling into a new chapter of life. I'm much more than anything like that. I'm reminded in the Soul Room that, first and foremost, I am an image bearer of God. I reflect who He is, and this fact gives me great dignity. As the psalmist states, the God who created the heavens cares for persons, is mindful of us, and has crowned us with glory and honor (Psalm 8:3-5).

What amazing truths! To think that God was looking in on my mother's womb! In fact, He was actually the One knitting me together, bringing form to my body. I celebrate that I am fearfully and wonderfully made by Him. I'm not an accident in the bedroom. Instead, God has been intimately involved in my life since before the moment of my conception. In a world of people suffering from a poor self-image, I am blessed to be able to celebrate my birth person, and doing so gives me strength, causes me to stand tall, and enables me to walk with greater confidence.

Facing My Sin Person—As we read God's Word and find ourselves more and more rooted in the truth that He has created each of us as a unique and wonderful reflection of His image, we are also led to admit that God's original image in us has been marred by our selfishness and rebellion. I don't look the way God meant me to look; I don't reflect His image the way He originally intended.

This kind of honesty about ourselves is very difficult. It means admitting failure, wrong decisions, selfishness, and pride. All of us know the tendency to deny our sin person. But in the Soul Room, we are free to acknowledge that aspect of ourselves because there the community of God loves and accepts me despite all my sin. Father, Son, and Spirit convict me of that sin, but at the same time they reinforce both their love for me and their commitment to me. My honesty about my sin is met by God's love. My sin is covered by His grace. My guilt is removed by His cleansing. My shame is lifted by His acceptance. And my brokenness is restored by His healing. What an amazing and grace-filled progression! No wonder I have come to realize that revealing myself in the presence of God is not something to fear.

When sin is ignored rather than acknowledged and confessed, however, it cripples us, festers, and eventually destroys us. The impact of sin on us is profound:

> Scriptures underscore the dynamic nature of sin with expressions like "hardening the heart" (compare Psalm 95:8; Hebrews 3:8) and the "searing of the conscience" (1 Timothy 4:2). Paul describes sin as a debilitating power that prevents the will from carrying out its good intentions (Roman 7:18-24). James pictures it as a restless agitation deep within the heart that breaks out in external conflicts (James 4:1-4,7).[3]

In Soul Room solitude, however, we move from being an imposter self to being our real self, from being a hidden person to being the beloved of God. And that's important to the health of both our life and our leadership in the church and beyond. Read what Henri Nouwen learned:

> Over the years, I have come to realize that the greatest trap in our life is not success, popularity, or power, but self-rejection.... Self-rejection is the greatest enemy of the spiritual life because it contradicts the sacred voice that calls us the "Beloved." Being the Beloved constitutes the core truth of our existence.[4]

In the Soul Room, I am reminded of whose I am—the Lord's—and who I am—His beloved. I experience a deepening relationship with the Father. And as we grow closer, I am more comfortable exercising my amazing right as His child to call Him "Papa, Daddy."

In the Soul Room—in the loving community of Father, Son, and Holy Spirit—we experience grace and truth as "a healing combination."[5] Dr. Henry Cloud reminds us that "grace and truth...deal with one of the main barriers to all growth: guilt."[6] He explains:

> Grace and truth together reverse the effects of the fall, which were separation from God and others. Grace and truth together invite us out of isolation and into relationship. Grace, when it is combined with truth, invites *the true self*, the "me" as I really am, warts and all, into *relationship*. It is one thing to have safety in relationship; it is quite another to be truly known and accepted in the relationship.

> With grace alone, we are safe from condemnation, but we cannot experience true intimacy. When the one who offers grace also offers truth (truth

about who we are, truth about who he or she is, and truth about the world around us), and we respond with our true self, then real intimacy is possible. Real intimacy always comes in the company of truth.[7]

Sin blinds, damages, destroys, and, yes, separates us from God and other people. Sin is not to be treated lightly, as though it were a small speed bump in my life or leadership. Consider the last time sin blinded your judgment, made you feel discouraged about your ministry, and weakened your effectiveness as a leader.

Deep confession is characterized by that sense of brokenness as well as by a passionate desire to change and again be a credit to my Master's name. When heartfelt confession occurs, God's cleansing is greater, and His healing is deeper. So, instead of rushing away to get on with life, sit at the cross and let God do deep surgery in your heart. Resist the temptation to hurry on to do something. Instead, let yourself be drawn closer and closer to Father, Son, and Spirit. As one believer put it, "When we realize we are forgiven, we find we can borrow the goodness of the forgiver rather than working to manufacturer the illusion of our own goodness."[8]

Why not take a break from reading right now and reflect on some of these points. In what ways has your sin person influenced your leadership? What influence might the above thoughts about our sin person have on your leadership in the future? Be specific.

Enjoying My "Followership Person"

In the Soul Room, in addition to celebrating our birth person and facing our sin person, we are able to enjoy our "followership person." To understand what I mean by the phrase, first remember that Jesus is the Christ of invitation, the One who says, "Come unto Me." My acceptance of this invitation leads me to the Soul Room. My acceptance of Jesus' closely related second invitation "Come, follow Me" moves me into the Leadership Room. So I define *followership people* as those who have released to Christ the reins of control and are earnestly following Him. I find that many people desire the comfort and release of the Soul Room, but they continue to hold the reins of control in the Leadership Room. Have you found this true in your life? It is definitely one of the holy tensions I continually face.

But let's get back to what can happen in the Soul Room, and I have a few questions for you: Do you like yourself? When you sit and rest, do you feel some contentment or even some joy about being yourself? Or is your acceptance of yourself contingent upon your doing something, being somewhere, or getting something done? It's so easy for our self-image to be wrapped up in the accomplishments of our lives rather than in the presence of God within us, isn't it? That's another reason to regularly spend time in the Soul Room.

In my Soul Room times of worship and fellowship with the Trinity, I experience a real joy. It's not just a joy about the Father, the Son, and the Spirit—although They offer plenty of reason for joy—but that sense of joy in the Soul Room is also a joy about myself.

Now the Lord is the Spirit, and where the Spirit of the Lord is, there is freedom. And we, who with unveiled faces all reflect the Lord's glory, are being transformed into his likeness with ever-increasing glory, which comes from the Lord, who is the Spirit.—2 Corinthians 3:17-18

When God is doing His work and we're cooperating through followership, something happens to our self-image. A song my wife wrote for children captures the basis for that "something." It's called "I'm Special":

I'm special
    Yes, just me
I'm special
    As special as can be
God made me special
    As special as can be
For He made me like Himself
    And it's Him in me I see
If you ask me why I like me so
    I will answer
God made me
    Yes, I know.

God did make us, and He made us to be in relationship, and He offers us a relationship with Himself. And there, in the Soul Room with Father, Son, and Spirit, we experience acceptance that is unconditional, and that is a solid basis for relationship. With that foundation for our lives, we see our mission more clearly and pursue it more confidently.

Mission—and this is a key point—is where I *express* my identity rather than *establish* it. And when that mission involves leadership, whether pastoral or lay, our excitement increases as people come to Christ, connect as community at the cross, and develop a lifestyle rooted in Soul Room time. But when ministry fruit is minimal, we can feel very discouraged. In those times we must remember that the primary basis of our specialness is the love of God. A secondary basis of our sense of specialness is the fruit of our life and our ministry.

Of course the challenges of ministry leadership are constant and relentless. We do well when we let that pressure press us to become faithful pray-ers, lifelong learners, committed followers of our dynamic Lord, and regular visitors to the Soul Room. Then our relationship with the Trinity can become our primary source of joy and inspiration, of blessing and direction. Father, Son, and Spirit are increasingly directing and shaping our lives.

When Soul Room leaders I know move from the Soul Room to the Leadership Room, they talk about their growing friendship with the Father, Son, and Holy Spirit. They talk about their roots sinking deeper into the Sacred Three and how they discover there, with the Three, peace, fulfillment, passion, and meaning for ministry and for life. These people of faith and love of God describe their leadership in terms of their relationship with Him. And they are hardly the first to do so.

Go back with me to the first century when Christians are unpopular. Listen to the Sanhedrin puzzle over the character and leadership of two simple men: "When they saw the courage of Peter and John and realized that they were unschooled, ordinary men, they were astonished and they took note that these men had been with Jesus" (Acts 4:13). Being with Jesus was the key to effective leadership then, and it continues to be so today.

That's why seminary professor Howard Hendricks challenges college graduates with these stirring words:

My greatest fear for you, graduates, is not that you will fail. My greatest fear for you is my greatest fear for myself—and that is that you will succeed... in doing the wrong things—with the wrong means.

You see, I spend a lot of time with people just like you. And what has disturbed me over the years is to find students from schools like this and my own who go out and depend on their giftedness, on their personality, on their education and training, on their experience. In fact, on EVERYTHING except God. To be sure, God will use your training; you've never had one that's better. God will use your giftedness; some of you are gifted beyond description. God will use your experience... because He's the one who gave it to you. He will use your personality...to reach people whom the rest of us could not reach with a twenty-foot pole. But for God's sake, don't depend on it. USE it, but come with that humility that recognizes in every scene and circumstance of your life, "Lord, without You, I can do nothing."9

In the Soul Room, my followership person gains this perspective: I can do nothing without the Lord. Temperament, leadership skills, giftedness, resume, and passions are of value, but they remain of secondary value in the formation and impact of my life as a leader. What is primary is that I love the Lord my God with all my heart, soul, mind, and strength and that I love my neighbor as I love myself (Mark 12:30-31).

NOT AN OPTION!

Are you tempted to say that having regular meaningful alone times with God sounds a little impractical? Maybe you're a salaried pastor who each week has many meetings to attend, if not plan, run, and evaluate. Or maybe, rather than being a paid leader in your church or ministry, you are one of those priceless volunteers, and you have several meetings in each of your forty- to fifty-hour workweeks. As a church leader, you are asked to add even more meetings to that schedule. Whether you are a paid or a volunteer leader, the wisdom, clarity, creativity, courage, and enthusiasm you need for all these meetings must be an outgrowth of The Meeting—of your meeting with the Three in the Soul Room. On that meeting-room door is a sign that reads "Community. Story. Convergence." And those meetings should be considered mandatory!

The Puritans, who had great insight into how the Christian life actually works, knew this. They understood that "communion with God is a relationship in which the initiative and power are with God." Christian professor and writer J. I. Packer adds, "In its narrow sense of our communing with God, communion is a Christian duty; in the broader and more foundational sense…communion is a divine gift."[10] This communion is continuously welcomed and pursued by God, regardless of our performance. That truth is an important one to cling to because many times we Christians compare ourselves with others and end up feeling less than blue ribbon in our communion with God. Or our sins of either the past or the present haunt us, making us feel dirty and unworthy to enter into God's presence. Sometimes we look at other people and believe quite easily that God could really use *them*, but we don't think God could use us at all.

It is in these very moments of uncertainty about what we have to offer His kingdom work that the God who initiates and enjoys communion with us speaks to our creation person and says, "I used all My wisdom when I created you as you are—mind, soul, and body." It is in these moments of feeling unworthy to minister that our sin person is surrounded by the community of Three that extends to us unconditional love, gracious forgiveness, and warm acceptance. Often we're afraid to face our sin person because of what might happen if the onion of our lives is peeled. We also fear that if people really knew us, they would run away. In the Soul Room, however, the God of communion—Father, Son, and Holy Spirit—runs toward us to embrace us and celebrate us (Luke 15:11-24).

As frustrated as we may become about our lack of direction and achievement, the God who is initiating communion with us not only crowns us with glory and honor in our creation person, but He also brings cleansing and transformation to our sin person. He then places on our followership person the mantle of being His ambassador. Do you see that, in the Soul Room, facing oneself—all of oneself—is not a fearful experience of isolation? Instead it is a rich and life-giving experience of God's passionate love and unshakable presence with us. These Soul Room times keep life from being a trying-to-measure-up experience and enable us to know life as a living-in-community-and-following-Jesus experience.

THE SOUL ROOM: MOVING FROM MANAGEMENT TO MYSTERY

In a world that worships management and leadership techniques, the Soul Room is definitely an oddity, for in the Soul Room we encounter mystery. When we meet there with the Triune God, something happens. As James Torrance puts it, "In grace, the triune God personally stands in for us, gives himself to us and draws us into his inner life."[11] Let's unpack this mystery and truth.

> When God pours Himself into the cup of our lives, holy transformation occurs in us and then spills onto the saucer (the lives of those around us) and onto the plate (in our time together).

First of all, who is in the Soul Room is very important, and we can be confident that the Father, Son, and Spirit will always be there to welcome us and commune with us. In a world of broken relationships, the fact that Father, Son, and Spirit will never leave me or turn against me can be very reassuring. We can also be confident that Father, Son, and Spirit will tend the Soul Room well, providing for us whatever we need and opening the Word for us when we're in their presence.

When we are in the Soul Room, we will notice at some point that our experience—that what is going on within us—starts having little connection with the environment and our agenda. Something unique and mysterious takes place. I'm no longer merely with the Trinity; I'm now drawn into sweet communion almost as one of Them. An intimacy—a touching of my mind, a softening of my will, a releasing of my spirit, an energizing of my body—happens. All of this is hard to explain, but joyous to experience. And this divine touch can energize and empower our leadership like nothing this world offers.

However—and as the world is well aware—leadership does call for management. Someone needs to determine why we are meeting, who is coming, how many are coming, what will happen at the meeting, and whether we need tables, chairs, PowerPoint, or refreshments. Being thorough and efficient in these matters is important. Even with all the details attended to and everything in place, though, the gathering might just be people going through the motions. But when we've spent time with God in the Soul Room, He comes into the midst of this well-orchestrated management dynamic and touches people's lives in unexpected and unanticipated ways. When God pours Himself into the cup of our lives, holy transformation occurs in us and then spills onto the saucer (the lives of those around us) and onto the plate (in our time together).

> The Soul Room is a place of genuine communion with the Lord of the universe, the Savior of my soul, and the Spirit who empowers my life.

For example, bitter people cannot be *managed* into asking forgiveness of another. Nonexpressive people cannot be *managed* into becoming more open with their thoughts and feelings. People set in their ways and established in their mind-set cannot be managed into being open to the new and different. Significant steps of lasting life change are not the result of savvy management or insightful manipulation. For lasting change in us human beings, God must break in. He must fill us: the Pitcher pours itself into the cup. And when He does so, mystery takes over. It's unique and divine; it's to be experienced and celebrated. This breaking in of God's Spirit—this mystery of "Christ in [us]" (Colossians 1:27; 2:3)—has an impact that the best planning could never produce.

And this is why our time in the Soul Room is to be anticipated, guarded from the tyranny of the urgent, and cherished as a holy encounter. The Soul Room is a place of genuine communion with the Lord of the universe, the Savior of my soul, and the Spirit who empowers my life. And it's my guess that such sweet communion happened when composer George Frederick Handel wrote the score of *The Messiah* in only twenty-four days. Afterward he said, "It seemed as though all heaven was opened to me." Something happened beyond merely the nuts and bolts—beyond the management of notes and rests—of composing music. And what was that something? Simply put, God was there.

Likewise, God was with Olympic athlete and fellow believer Eric Liddell when he worked out and competed. In Liddell's words—made famous in the movie *Chariots of Fire*—"When I run, I feel His presence." Running for Liddell wasn't merely putting one foot in front of the other quickly. Nor was it arms pumping and eyes focused on the finish line. Instead, for Liddell, God Himself was there in a very real and powerful way. Liddell himself came in touch with the Father, Son, and Spirit, and we can experience that convergence and that sweet, transforming communion just as Handel and Liddell did.

WHEN DARKNESS ACCOMPANIES THE MYSTERY

On occasion, though, transforming communion with Father, Son, Spirit is not sweet. Sometimes as God is forming us, the Soul Room will seem empty and dark. What once was a room of conversation and dialogue can feel like a room of monologue. You speak, and God doesn't seem to be listening. You hear only silence. The Soul Room used to be a place of creativity and energy. Now you find it a place of boredom and weariness. What used to be a place of consolation has become a place of desolation. You may even feel that God has withdrawn His presence.

These times are definitely the difficult legs of our journey—and such stretches are inevitable. We might find ourselves asking, "Is all this a result of some sin in my life?" Consider this possibility and if the Spirit brings some specific sin to mind, confess it and ask forgiveness. However, a dark night of the soul is not always connected to some specific wrong on our part; it isn't necessarily a sign that we have sinned. Instead, the hard times may be God's way of weaning us from spiritual childhood and enabling us to enter spiritual adulthood. After all, His heart's desire is that being in His Presence would completely satisfy us.

To be honest, the Soul Room has been rather dark for me during the writing of this book. God has often seemed silent, if not completely absent. These recent years have, in fact, been the hardest times of my life. Two car accidents involving both my wife and me—accidents that were caused by other drivers—have taken away our stamina and our ability to concentrate. I have found myself questioning my future. I have felt defeated and alone. I know that God is faithful, but I have wondered where He was on those two occasions. This book was placed on hold for a full ten months following our first accident while I sought to regain energy and the ability to concentrate so I could begin writing again.

One month after I actually returned to the writing, we had our second accident. The Soul Room remained a painfully quiet place. I went there, but nothing seemed to happen. What had once been a place of refuge and nourishment, of peace and communion, became a place of utter frustration. I felt great tension between my view of God and my family's painful circumstances. As I sat in the Soul Room, I found myself asking questions about God—"Is He sovereign? Is He faithful? Does He really never slumber or sleep? How could He allow this to happen to us?" In this Soul Room that felt utterly empty, I simply concluded that I would choose to trust Him. I chose to believe that He will be enough. After all, He has always been enough so far, and I'll stake my life on the fact that He will be enough from now on. By His grace, I'll continue to be a followership person.

Choosing to Trust

Let me tell you about my last year at Wheaton College. During the fall semester in Systematic Theology, many of us had become friends with a missionary. Older than the rest of us, he lived with his wife and five children in Chicago and daily commuted to Wheaton. When he grew tired of his long drives, he asked us if we knew someone who needed a roommate. Since my roommate was leaving in the spring, I said, "Well, I need a roommate." It was a remarkable final semester of college for me. Since I anticipated going into ministry, the idea of sharing a room with someone who had already been in ministry for at least twenty years sounded like a good thing. He had also lived on foreign soil. God had used him in wonderful ways both here in the States and abroad. During those months together, we laughed, talked, and shared our faith stories. One night, though, he shared a particularly compelling part of his story.…

My roommate had come to Christ early in life, and he sensed a call to the mission field in his teenage years. Years later, while in his thirties, he suddenly had a new experience with God. It wasn't an "out of body" experience. It's just that something new occurred in his relationship with God that continues to this day. He shared that his life after this experience continued to be profoundly different from what it had been for years before. He also said that it was almost as though he had been born again for a second time at that point. He knew that this was not an accurate theological statement, but he felt that it was an accurate description of his experience with God. He testified to the fact that he was now enjoying a new awareness of God's presence in his life. His story made a deep impact on me.

In retrospect, I believe something went on in this man's life that resulted in a new level of both convergence and communion: his God-given passion converged with the Lord's blessing, and his sense of relationship and intimacy with the Triune God meant sweeter communion than ever before. Put differently, I sensed that a missionary seeking to carry out a task for God had become a missionary living in communion with God and that the task was now the missionary's expression of his love for His Lord.

> I wonder if the Soul Room is too often regarded as an optional rest stop on our quest for efficiency.

In our frenetically paced world where value is often measured by task-efficiency and production, I wonder if the Soul Room is too often regarded as an optional rest stop on our quest for efficiency. More specifically, does your busyness in the Leadership Room keep you from entering the Soul Room? Do your responsibilities in the Leadership Room keep you from experiencing the shalom of the Soul Room? Do the affirming, encouraging people on whom your ministry focuses diminish your need for the Persons of the Soul Room— Father, Son, and Holy Spirit? The Leadership Room reminds us that we're needed and important, but the Soul Room puts us in a place where we can meet those needs in God's power and by His grace.

So what role is the Soul Room playing in your life and leadership right now? Do you faithfully invest time there so that you can abide in God's presence for yourself—for your spiritual health, for direction, and for hope? In your life, is such abiding a frequent experience or a rather unfamiliar occurrence? Is abiding something you do out of a sense of duty? Or is your abiding a natural outgrowth of the relationship you are enjoying, nourishing, and protecting? In the next chapter, I will give you some practical tips for how to abide in the Soul Room and in the story that is Scripture.

IN THE SOUL ROOM, GOD'S STORY TRANSFORMS MY STORY.
THE SOUL ROOM BECOMES A PLACE OF CONVERGENCE AND MYSTERY.

God, thank You for taking the clutter and the guilt of my story and giving me a new chapter to live. Thank You for grafting me into Your story. Thank You that, in the Soul Room, I don't merely have conversation with You, but I come—with an attitude of worship and awe—to enjoy genuine friendship and intimate communion with my heavenly Father, my gracious Savior, and my Comforter and Guide. Thank You that, in a world that offers only insecurity and instability, I have the mystery and therefore the security of Christ in me—my hope of glory. What a gift! What an opportunity for a new beginning! Thank You in the name of the Lord Jesus. Amen.

Before You Take the Next Step

What thought in this chapter has present value for your life? How is this thought helping you?

How special do you feel in God's eyes? Does your sense of being special waver according to your performance? In what ways are you coming to see yourself as special simply because of your relationship with the Father through the Son and by the Spirit?

Describe your own Soul Room experience over the last couple of weeks. Has it been rich and fresh, new and stimulating, stale and difficult, or have you rarely visited that sacred place? As you linger with God now, praise Him and perhaps even ask Him to help you with your Soul Room time.

Do you lean more toward management or toward mystery? It's not either/or, so allow God to develop you in both ways.

*Opening and
lingering in the
Scriptures—
it's not something
I do; it's Someone
I'm with.*

What Do I Do in the Soul Room?

Abiding for Myself:

Building Altars and Being Nourished by God's Word

Some think my ministry of church planting in the Middle East is dangerous. They don't know danger! What was dangerous was growing up trying to live the Christian life, but rarely opening the Bible. That is dangerous!

But when I was a sixteen-year-old party animal and leader in my school, Chuck Miller befriended me. One of the things he taught me was the 2PROAPT method of Bible study. As I began to get daily directions from God through His Word, I was transformed from "school party animal" to "school evangelist." My swim coach had to postpone swim practice on the mornings when Chuck led our Teen Breakfast Club. Most of the team was AWOL and hanging out with him.

God does indeed use His Word to transform us—to nourish our soul, to bring peace to our spirit, and to give direction to our life. With blessings like these waiting, why do we ever miss the opportunity to open the Bible and be with our God? We all know the answers: We get busy, pressure mounts, opportunities increase, and demands multiply. And, often prompting us to choose the good of life over the best, the Evil One shrewdly draws us away from quiet time with God.

Our enemy pushes us further away than we'd planned to go, and we stay away from the Soul Room longer than we'd planned to stay. I'm sure you know what I'm talking about.

QUIET TIME THAT'S TOO QUIET

I have long sought to make it a habit to regularly spend intimate time with the Father, the Son, and the Spirit, but I have found it very helpful to call it my time of altar building. When I called it quiet time, the time often became quieter than I planned. (I fell asleep!) When I called it devotional time, the activity seemed too passive. But when I started calling it a time of altar building, I found myself being active and involved.

After all, an altar is a place of offering something (in this case, myself) to God. An altar is a place of surrender, of releasing control of my life to my powerful, wise, and loving Father. And an altar is a place of sacrifice, of dying to my control, my plans, and my dreams for my life and choosing to trust God's control, His plans, and His dreams for my life.

My inspiration for my altar-building time was Abraham, the first of the Old Testament patriarchs, a friend of God, and our forefather in the faith. I realized when I was a senior in high school that building altars was a lifelong pattern for Abraham. When God appeared to him at Shechem, Abraham built an altar (Genesis 12:6-7). When he pitched his tent east of Bethel, he built an altar (verse 8). After Lot chose the rich Jordan Valley—home to Sodom and Gomorrah—for his family and flocks, Abraham moved near Hebron and built another altar to the Lord (13:18).

Now consider the most memorable altar in Abraham's life. God asked this man of faith to sacrifice his son Isaac as a burnt offering (22:2). In response, Abraham took the son whom he had waited years for, placed him on the altar, and lifted his knife to kill him—and God intervened. Scripture tells us, "Abraham called that place The Lord Will Provide" (verse 14). Abraham had learned to continually present himself to God. As he did so, he discovered again and again that God provides. I also believe that these intentional times of altar building made Abraham a significant man of God. As God tells the story, He frequently acknowledges time when Abraham is in the Soul Room building altars and giving his life afresh to God.

The altar-building lifestyle of Abraham has long influenced my own pattern of living, but what most often moves me to the Soul Room is the simple—and simply amazing—fact that I'm invited there. Father, Son, and Spirit invite me to meet with Them, They wait expectantly for my arrival, They anticipate my coming, and They welcome my presence. And They do the same for you.

That's great, you may be thinking, *but so many things get in the way of my entering the Soul Room. How do I overcome them? And, besides, I'm not sure exactly what to do once I enter the Soul Room. How does one "abide"? And how do I "build an altar" anyway?* Key to answering these questions—a key to the Soul Room—is a unique way of reading Scripture, a tool I call 2PROAPT. Before I introduce that process, let's pray.

Father God, as I consider the words I've just read and then as I read on in this chapter, may I sense afresh the honor and privilege of being Your treasured child. Enable me to push away the events of the last few days, the thoughts of tomorrow, and the schedule for today so that I might discover the richness of being in quiet solitude with You. Free me to let go of my agenda and then allow You to guide me according to Your good desire for me now and in the future. In Jesus' name I pray. Amen.

READING SCRIPTURE

We have been trained to examine whatever we read and form opinions about its message. But rather than having us read for information like that, God desires that we allow the Holy Spirit to use the truths of Scripture to transform our character and guide our life. It is too easy to treat Scripture as mere information to be stored in our mind rather than asking God's Spirit to use His written truth to form the affections of our heart, the structure of our character, and the patterns of our life.

In *Shaped by the Word*, author Robert Mulholland offers significant insight about how God's Spirit can use our formative reading of Scripture to shape our lives. But first he cautions us to read Scripture differently than we do other things. Scripture is not something we are to "exercise control over it by grasping it with our mind"; reading the Bible is not the time to "analyze, critique, dissect, reorganize, synthesize, and digest the material we find appropriate. This mode of reading is detrimental to the role of scripture in spiritual formation."[1]

Consider the alternative Mulholland proposes:

> First, I suggest that your top priority be to listen for God. Seek to allow your attention and focus to be on listening for what God is saying to you as you read this book. Listen for God to speak to you in and through, around and within, over and behind and out front of everything that you read. Keep asking yourself, "What is God seeking to say to me in all of this?" ... You will begin to open yourself to the possibility of God's setting the agenda for your life through the text. ... Second, I suggest that you respond to what you read in this book with your heart and spirit rather than with your rational, cognitive, intellectual dynamics.[2]

Now Mulholland is not saying that we check our brain at the door when we go to read our Bible. He is well aware that God calls us to love Him with all our mind, and Mulholland charges us to "seek to utilize our cognitive, intellectual, rational dynamics to the best of our ability." But he goes on to say this: "We must remember that the injunction to love God with all of our mind comes a little bit farther down the road in Jesus' list; loving God with all of our heart and all of our soul precedes loving God with all of our mind."[3]

I would encourage you to have *Shaped by the Word* in your library. In it, Mulholland makes some significant statements about how to read God's Word. We must, for instance, listen for what God is saying to us, and we must respond with our heart and our spirit. Let me now share with you a tool that embodies much of what Mulholland says about formational reading.

2PROAPT: A Tool for Encountering God in Scripture

In response to a speaking invitation in the early 1970s, I prayed that God would give me a creative tool that would help high-school students experience a richer time in their study of Scripture. I wanted to help walk them into deeper intimacy and interaction with the Father. I wanted their time in the Scripture to result in greater life change. I wanted them to enter in to a transforming dialogue with God. The result was a funny-sounding word that isn't in any dictionary. It's the acrostic 2PROAPT. What do these letters stand for?

P = Pray

P = Preview

R = Read

O = Observe

A = Apply

P = Pray

T = Tell

2PROAPT

Allow me to unpack the meaning of each letter for you.

2PROAPT: A Tool for Us

Pray honestly: Tell God exactly what is in your heart. Let Him know that you are tired, hurried, doing well, upset with a friend, upset with Him, or excited to be meeting with Him in the Soul Room. Tell Him that you love Him. Be honest with your heavenly Father: "God, despite how distracted I am or how discouraged I feel, please speak to me in this passage. I'm listening for You. Unveil what You want me to discover."

This is a time of heart preparation. I often find that music—anything from contemporary praise music to the classic Handel's *Messiah*—helps prepare my heart for a deeper encounter with God, for a time when God's Spirit can minister to me and enable me to better understand Scripture.

Preview the whole rapidly: Quickly read your text all the way through. Whether you are tackling an entire chapter or only a few verses, read through your selection without stopping. Read it out loud. Let what God is saying touch your feelings as well as your thoughts. Read with a heart that asks, "God, what is on Your mind for me?" This is reading in the formative sense.

Read the passage slowly: Here, we read with the goal of gaining insight. As you read, ask yourself, "What is it saying?" Listen carefully for the message of the passage as well as its tone. Notice which words or phrases are repeated.

Observe what the passage says and what it means: Look at the structure of the passage. Notice the context. Identify the subject, the verbs and their tenses, the object, the pronouns, etc. Notice whether God or people are acting. Then step back and ask God's Spirit to focus your attention on the part of the passage that He desires you to dwell on. He may draw you to a phrase, a sentence, or perhaps a few sentences. The Spirit of God will lead you to interact with the words, ideas, and substance of the text. He may lead you to connect with the people in the passage (who is mentioned, what is happening to them, and what they might be feeling). Position yourself in the passage; imagine the sounds, the smells, the facial expressions, and the conversations. Don't try to dissect the whole passage. Instead, ask the Spirit to draw your attention to that portion of the passage that is meant for you at this moment.

Now observe what that portion means. Think about what a specific phrase or verse means. Try writing the passage in your own words. Then ask formative questions like "What does this passage mean to me?," "What does the Spirit want this to mean in my life?," and "What does the meaning of the passage say about my life situations and my inner thoughts and feelings?"

Apply the passage to your life: Prayerfully consider how God wants this passage—what it says and what it means—to influence you. Ask yourself, "What will I do in response to what I have read and understood? When will I do it? With whom will I do it?" Be aware that, at this point in the process, the Evil One steps up his attacks and his attempts to distract us. He is not threatened by our efforts to gather information, but the moment we consider living God's truth, he greatly increases his opposition. Nevertheless, at this point of application—despite Satan's efforts—God transforms our life. When we meet with Him in the Soul Room, He uses Scripture to reshape our heart and mind.

I compare these stages of the 2PROAPT process to taking a picture with a manual camera: First I frame my shot (pray and preview), but then I have to work to get the picture in focus (read and observe). Finally, there comes the moment when the image is clear and in focus, and I am ready to shoot the picture: I am ready to live this passage (apply). Let me give you an example.

I observe that the text of Hebrews 10:24 says, "Let us consider how to stimulate one another to love and good deeds" (NASB). Next I observe that the text means I am to encourage fellow believers to love others and to do good deeds. Then, in applying the text, I think about what I can do to motivate and enable others—as well as myself!—to live a life of love and good deeds. (This sounds like leadership development, doesn't it?)

Let's bring the image into clearer focus. Who exactly are the "others"? I might answer, "Well, everyone, of course." Although that is true, this assignment would be overwhelming. After all, everyone is a lot of people! So I bring the application into sharper focus by choosing a few specific "everyones" whom I will see in the next few days. I take a few moments with God and ask Him which of these "everyones" I should love with His love. As I think about the possibilities, God brings to mind three people whom I will see in the next few days. I write down their names and pray for each one. I ask God what I might do to encourage that person and, next to each name, write down the thoughts that His Spirit brings to mind.

Do you see what is happening here in the Soul Room? God's Spirit is speaking to me through the Scriptures. God is influencing my thoughts and attitudes about the people I will see, and He is giving shape and meaning to my schedule. This is a different approach to time management. I usually just plan my schedule and then ask God to bless it. When we plan our schedule outside the Soul Room, we shouldn't be surprised that it's too full and tends to increase our level of guilt, anxiety, and exhaustion.

Pray for God's enabling power: Ask Him to strengthen you so that you can live according to the truth He's pointed out to you. This is not just another step in the process. This prayer for God's presence and power will enable you to live out His truth. This prayer also recognizes that the Evil One will actively oppose any Soul Room intentions from being carried into the Leadership Room. This praying further protects me from my weaknesses, my tendencies toward procrastination, discouragement, or insecurity. I ask God for sustained excitement, focus, and sensitivity so that, in the Hebrews 10:24 example, I will in the next few days encourage these three people.

> Whenever I read Scripture, I invite God's Spirit to take the clay of my life and shape it. ... The lifestyle of healthy leaders is seamless: Soul Room and Leadership Room merge together.

Tell someone else what God gave you. Just as we remember a story or a joke by telling someone, we will better remember what God shows us if we share it with another person in the normal pattern of conversation. So ask yourself, "Who would be encouraged by what God has given me in the Scriptures today?" Ask God to make you sensitive to the opportunities He will provide for you to share with your spouse, your children, your neighbor, or someone at the store, in church, or on the church board.

2PROAPT. Pray. Preview. Read. Observe. Apply. Pray. Tell.

2PROAPT: A Tool for Us and a Tool for God

This 2PROAPT process reminds us that Scripture is not merely a source of information. It is a tool I use to approach the written Word of God, and consequently 2PROAPT is a tool that He uses for my formation and transformation. So, whenever I read Scripture, I invite God's Spirit to take the clay of my life and shape it. As God works in my thoughts and attitudes through the text of Scripture, my behaviors are changed. I think of it as overflow: God's forming and reforming of me spills over from my mind and heart and into my words, my hands, my feet. I become a living expression of the God who is actively shaping me more into His image.

Work is no longer merely task after task to accomplish. Instead, work is an opportunity for the living God to express Himself and share His love through me. My home is no longer merely a place to lay my head at night. Instead, I am positioned in a family and a neighborhood where my life can be an expression of the living presence of Jesus Christ in the world. God's Spirit leads me from Soul Room formation into Leadership Room influence. The lifestyle of healthy leaders is seamless: Soul Room and Leadership Room merge together.

> God's Spirit leads me from Soul Room formation into Leadership Room influence.

By God's grace, I find a growing desire within me for His fingerprints to be seen all over my life. The Soul Room is not disconnected and detached from the rest of my life. It is the main place where I am grounded in God's truth, transformed by His touch, and energized by His power. It is the place where I build altars to God's goodness and faithfulness and where, on those altars, I once again lay down my life to serve Him. The Soul Room is the control room for my soul, for my life—but it can be so hard to go there, can't it? Let's talk about five obstacles to spending time alone with God—and how to overcome them.

TURNING OBSTACLES INTO CHALLENGES

Altar-Building Challenge #1: "I've Tried Building Altars and I Failed." Let me guess. You once got excited about studying the Bible, you tried it for a while and kept at it for a few weeks, but then you stopped. In your mind, you failed, and you feel guilty about failing. Who wants to go back there?

Well, I've been there too. I've read the Bible, failed to be consistent, and eventually set it aside. (After all, some days those small words on those thin pages read more like the telephone book than the inspired Word of God.) But what I've learned—and this may help you—is to go to the Scriptures with realistic expectations. Oh, I may make a great discovery that brings light and insight to my next seven days, but I don't expect such an experience every time I read and reflect on God's Word.

Also, realize that God doesn't see you as a failure but as a friend. When we enter the Soul Room, we are spending time with a

Friend who knows us well and who sees us as real people who stumble and fail. We have all tried something and then set it aside, but that shouldn't keep us from trying again. (The enemy will tell us otherwise!) After all, God desires that we grow, and nothing is more life-forming and health-giving than reopening the Bible and re-entering the Soul Room. Go ahead and try again! Your Friend awaits.

Altar-Building Challenge #2: "My Life Is Full of Distractions." Do many hands tug at you and many voices call to you? When you try to focus on something, do distractions come from without or does turmoil rise from within? This is a very common—and discouraging—experience that most of us Christians know all too well.

To counter the feelings of loneliness and hopelessness that you may be feeling, become part of a small group in your church. Build altars and practice listening for God in this safe context. Learn from others how they cope with feeling overwhelmed and alone. You'll also hear about the different ways God speaks through Scripture to these friends of His. And you'll have a group cheering you on as you enter the Soul Room to do your own altar building.

Altar-Building Challenge #3: "I Don't Have Time." These days when I ask people how they are, the word I hear more and more is *busy*. Busy. Busy. Busy! We live as if we are running on a treadmill and always on the time clock. My years of pastoral experience have taught me that, as someone has said, we need to come apart and be with the Lord before we really come apart!

Ask God right now to help you take five to ten minutes a day to be with Him. Don't start with thirty minutes or an hour. Be realistic; don't set yourself up for failure. What would be a realistic faith step for you? Let yourself successfully take that first small step: be consistent with a regular brief time with Him.

Altar-Building Challenge #4: "I Cannot Add One More Thing to My 'To Do' List." I know that feeling, but let me share one of the phrases God gave me in the Soul Room: "Prayer is not something I do, but Someone I am with." Read that again: "Prayer is not something I do, but Someone—Father, Son, and Holy Spirit—I am with." Likewise, Soul Room reading with 2PROAPT is not something I do, but Someone I am with. When prayer becomes just another item on my "to do" list, I miss the richness of fellowship with God. Prayer becomes performance rather than communion with my heavenly Father.

But what if my idea of God—distorted by upbringing, experience, or cultural messages—doesn't make me want to be with this Someone? What if I am afraid of God, afraid to be with Him, afraid to listen to Him, afraid of what He might say to me? What if He seems large, distant, severe, or even cruel?

> *Think of Soul Room ... as an opportunity to make a new Friend or get to know Him better...*

If the idea of being with God isn't attractive, I would encourage you to learn more about the God of the Bible and about His unfailing and gracious love. Read Psalm 73 or 136 and discover the ways that God is with us in our pain and struggles. Risk opening yourself to His love so that it can move you from fear of Him to intimacy with Him. Think of Soul Room time not as an added item on your "to do" list, but as an opportunity to make a new Friend or get to know Him better—and may you soon begin to experience it as such.

Altar-Building Challenge #5: "The Bible Is Difficult for Me to Understand. I Don't Know What to Read or Even Where to Sit When I Read." First of all, the place where you meet with God doesn't have to be fancy. Meet with Him in your car over lunch. Meet with Him as you sit in your bed before you rise or as you retire. Or turn a room at home or even your favorite chair into a Soul Room. Just find a place.

Once you have a place, you'll need a Bible if you don't already have one. The New International Version—the one I use most often in this book—aims to be an accurate, idea-for-idea translation of the original languages of the Bible. But you may find the New Living Translation or a paraphrase like *The Message* easier to read. You might enjoy a study Bible that offers notes of explanation along the way—but don't focus on those notes. Remember, you want to listen to God speak to you from the text. The notes are helpful, but secondary. Don't allow them to become primary.

When you begin reading the Bible, you might enjoy Psalm 100, Psalm 23, or Psalm 5. As you read the text, ask questions like "What am I learning about God?," "What is He saying to me about Himself?," and "What am I learning about myself?" Listen for what God's Spirit is saying to you for today.

You may also enjoy a biographical passage. Let yourself get into the skin of the people of the Bible. Imagine yourself walking in Joseph's sandals (Genesis 37-50). Or you may feel the need to know Jesus better. Read the gospel of Mark or John. Ask, "Who does Jesus tell us He is?" and be listening for God to answer.

Plenty of other obstacles can make it difficult to regularly enter the Soul Room and build altars, and obstacles change with time. Don't try to surmount any of these obstacles on your own. Find people in your church whose intimacy with God you admire. Talk with them about what makes it difficult for you to spend regular time with the Lord. Ask how they have coped with similar obstacles in their own journey. And I'll remind you again of my greatest coping mechanism: I focus on the fact that entering the Soul Room to build an altar is not something I do, but Someone I am with.

A PLAN FOR SPIRITUAL GROWTH

In a world of plans—of medical plans, vacation plans, life insurance plans, college savings plans—what is your plan for spiritual growth? What tools will you use? I would encourage you to consider using 2PROAPT. Author Simon Chan suggests: "Spiritual reading presupposes the Bible as God's Word calling us to make a decisive response and thus trains us in a certain spiritual attitude—openness to God, humble listening, willingness to obey. These basic dispositions are the fertile ground from which the seeds of virtue sprout. Unlike ordinary reading, spiritual reading is done to affect the heart, not to gain information."[4]

When you abide in the Soul Room—when you meet Father, Son, and Spirit there—something happens. They welcome you, enjoy communion with you, and unlock the story for you. Father, Son, and

Spirit transform your life, impacting your values, personality, character, dreams, attitudes, and actions. As you regularly approach the altar and offer your life to the story and community of God, you will become more and more the divine original God intends you to be. The way in which God touches you through a particular passage will be unique, and no one else will have the exact same experience with the Holy Community in the Soul Room.

> God uses the process of Soul Room reading to make His Word alive to you and to form His life in you.

Such time in the Soul Room—time spent with a soft heart, the Three, and an open Bible— is absolutely foundational to our life and our leadership. God uses the process of Soul Room reading to make His Word alive to you and to form His life in you.

I am now living in the Middle East where I have been involved in planting the first Christian church ever among a large Muslim people group. Before God called us to this ministry, there were no Christians here, nor were there any missionaries. As I met with the very first Christian from this people group, I simply taught him what I had been taught: to read Scripture and apply it to my life— 2PROAPT. That first Christian has now started the first-ever church by teaching the same simple yet powerful process. In the Muslim country where I live, people who once hated Christians are being transformed by the love of Jesus as they are reading the Bible, applying it to their lives, and being born again.

IN THE SOUL ROOM AND AS I USE THE 2PROAPT PROCESS,
I EXPERIENCE AND ENJOY A LIFE-TRANSFORMING
FRIENDSHIP WITH GOD.

Let's close in prayer.

Lord God, *I do understand the importance of Soul Room time, the importance of being with You and of reading—and living out—Your Word. Please help me make regular time for such communion with You. I can only imagine the riches You have for me... After all, in our world of the artificial, You never do or speak that which is false. In our world of the routine, Your love is fresh and Your mercies are new every morning. In our world of confusion and darkness, You bring clarity and light. In our world of competition, You bring community. In our world that demeans life in so many ways, You give dignity, purpose, and value. In our vast world of many different kinds of places, You are with us always, offering the one place of true refreshment and peace, divine hope and direction. Almighty and wonderful God, I thank You. Grow me as Your leader in the name of the Father, the Son, and the Spirit. Amen.*

Before You Take the Next Step

How did this chapter encourage you to spend time in the Soul Room?

Which of the altar-building challenges do you struggle with most? What way of overcoming this challenge might God be providing for you?

You would benefit by identifying now a few windows in each of the next seven days when you will be alone with God. What would be a faith step for you? Ten minutes per day? Twenty minutes per day? Remember that God uses the process of Soul Room reading to make His Word alive to you and to see His life formed in you.

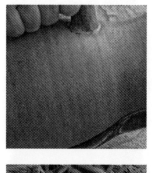

*You are probably
a follower of Jesus
today because
someone prayed
for you.
May you do the
same for many,
many others.*

What Can I Do in the Soul Room to Help My Friends?

Abiding with God for Others:

Interceding with a Big-Picture Perspective

God, would you destroy a city if there are fifty righteous people in it? Will you really sweep it away and not spare the place for the sake of those fifty righteous people?

All right. If I find fifty righteous people in the City of Sodom, I will spare the whole place for their sake.

Father, I hate to bother You again, but suppose there are only forty-five righteous people. Will You destroy the whole city because of five people?

No, I will not destroy it.

God, I'm sorry, but suppose there are forty righteous people.

For the sake of the forty, I will not destroy it.

Father, I hate to be a pest, but what if there are thirty righteous people?

I won't destroy the city.

Will You destroy the city if there are twenty righteous people?

No, I will not.

God, please don't be angry with me, but suppose there are only ten righteous people.

For the sake of ten, I will not destroy it.

Vital to Abraham's Soul Room time and the altar building he did there was prayer. Yes, he prayed for himself, but as this paraphrase of Abraham's discussion with God in Genesis 18 shows, Abraham also prayed and pleaded with God for others—what I call "abiding for others."

> My name is Samuel, and I'm a prophet in Israel. It's been a hard day. I am really crushed that the people of God have demanded an earthly king. I have made plain to them the sin of asking for a king other than the Lord their God.
>
> I told the people, "Do not be afraid. You have done all this evil; yet do not turn away from the Lord, but serve the Lord with all your heart. Do not turn away after useless idols. They can do you no good, nor can they rescue you, because they are useless. For the sake of his great name the Lord will not reject his people, because the Lord was pleased to make you his own."
>
> And I, Samuel, made this promise to this straying people: "As for me, far be it from me that I should sin against the Lord by failing to pray for you." (1 Samuel 12:20-23)

Samuel had a passion for pleading with God for the people; he had a passion for abiding for others.

> I'm the impetuous one. Too often I speak before I think. You probably know my name already. Now I'm a prisoner in chains and surrounded by soldiers. It's not the easiest place to sleep, but I had dozed off—only to be awakened when someone hit me. I heard the voice say, "Get up!" and I did. To my amazement, my chains fell right off me. Now I'm told to put on my clothes and sandals. I wrap my cloak around myself and follow the speaker, who looks like an angel of God. This is all very unreal, but I follow anyway. Soon we have passed the guards. The iron gate leading out of prison opens before us, and I realize I'm free.
>
> I know immediately where to go. Mary, the mother of John Mark, is a woman who prays, and I'm sure she has been praying for me. I'm excited to get to her house. I arrive, hear some noise from inside, and knock on the door. The servant who comes to answer the door is so stunned that she doesn't even open the door, but instead she runs back to the crowd inside with the news "Peter is at the door!" I keep knocking on the door, which folks finally open. I tell these faithful friends what happened, but I don't stay long. I'm so grateful, though, that these people were willing to abide in the Soul Room of God for me and plead with God for my release, for my life. (See Acts 12.)

Pleading to God for others is kingdom work. But too often in churches today, pleading with God for others is seen as the job of only a special few. It is not emphasized; it is not taught as a foundational pattern and fundamental passion of daily life for all believers and therefore all Christian leaders. And consequently the church is weaker. One wise man of God put it this way:

> God's intense longing to bless seems in some sense to be graciously limited by His dependence on the intercession that rises from the earth. He seeks to rouse the spirit of intercession that He may be able to bestow His blessing on mankind. God regards intercession as the highest expression of His people's readiness to receive and to yield themselves wholly to the working of His almighty power.[1]

In this chapter we will consider the privilege and Christian duty of abiding for others. We'll address questions like these: When do I abide? What compels me to abide and intercede for others? How am I to pray for others? What can I do to develop a more seasoned and insightful prayer life?

In this chapter, I will tell some stories about intercessory prayer from my life and ministry. I don't mean to imply that I am a prayer giant. I am not. Nor do I mean to imply that prayer is easy and that the outcomes are always wonderful. Prayer is difficult work, and the visible outcomes are not always what we expect. But before I share these prayer stories, I want to tell you about some of the "filters" that I use in praying. These have opened my heart to people (those who acknowledge the Lord as God as well as those who don't), fueled my concern for them, and impacted what I do in the Leadership Room. Prayer is powerful, and that is why I hope that, together, we may grow in our ability to offer honest prayers for our own life and heartfelt intercessory prayers for others. And may our Soul Room praying have a positive impact on our Leadership Room living and leading.

Majestic God, redeeming Christ, responsive Holy Spirit, may I be very aware of Your presence as I read this chapter. You know where I am emotionally, physically, mentally, and spiritually—and where I need Your touch. I thank You for Your care, and I ask You to please stimulate my mind, warm my heart, and release my will to be responsive to You and to Your desires and dreams for me for today and for tomorrow. I pray this in the name of the Sacred Three. Amen.

Let me share with you the following thoughts about intercession from Oswald Chambers, thoughts based on Romans 8:26,34—"The Spirit intercedes for the saints in accordance with God's will....Christ Jesus...is at the right hand of God and is also interceding for us."

> Do we need any more arguments than these to become intercessors—that Christ "always lives to make intercession" (Hebrews 7:25), and that the Holy Spirit "makes intercession for the saints"?...
>
> Beware of getting ahead of God by your very desire to do His will. We run ahead of Him in a thousand and one activities, becoming so burdened with people and problems that we don't worship God, and we fail to intercede.... God continually introduces us to people in whom we have no interest, and unless we are worshiping God the natural tendency is to be heartless toward them. We give them a quick verse of Scripture, like jabbing them with a spear, or leave them with a hurried, uncaring word of counsel before we go. A heartless Christian must be a terrible grief to our Lord.
>
> Are our lives in the proper place so that we may participate in the intercession of our Lord and the Holy Spirit?[2]

Chambers also makes this observation: "Our relationship with others is maintained through the work of intercession, where God works His miracles."[3] So am I establishing and strengthening community primarily by being *with* the people I lead or by interceding *for* them? The answer may be "both," but I personally have found that when I intercede for people, God convicts me of my wrong attitudes toward them and increases my compassion for them. This becomes powerful glue for forming and maintaining relationships.

The very topic of intercession may raise some questions for you. Let me address a few of them.

WHEN DO WE ABIDE FOR OTHERS?

We are free to abide for others *anytime, all the time, and at particular times*. The Spirit continually brings people to mind for whom we can pray, and we need to do just that. We might be walking, sitting in a meeting, or having a meal and be bringing people into the powerful presence of God at the same time. We can abide for others in the middle of the night, while driving to work, or after talking to a person on the phone. We can also set aside meaningful time to enter the Soul Room and be with God, not just for ourselves, but to present particular friends and situations to the Father, Son, and Spirit. As John Calvin said, "We must repeat the same supplications not twice or three times only, but as often as we have need, a hundred and a thousand times…. We must never be weary in waiting for God's help."[4]

WHAT PROMPTS US TO ABIDE FOR OTHERS
AND INTERCEDE FOR SPECIFIC PEOPLE?

Richard Foster offers a partial answer when he reminds us, "If we truly love people, we will desire for them far more than it is within our power to give them, and this will lead us to prayer. Intercession is a way of loving others."[5]

> *The quality of my life and the fruit of my ministry are due largely to the faithful prayers of others.*

We often intercede quite naturally and easily when crisis strikes. Perhaps he was in an accident, her husband walked out on her and the kids, he has been sick for a long time, a doctor is running tests to see if she has cancer, or he has lost his job. The situation prompts us to pray.

At other times, we abide for people because we realize that such intercession has been the key to our spiritual transformation and that, by God's grace, this transformation enhances effective leadership and ministry. James teaches very clearly that the prayers of righteous people—righteous because of Christ's blood—are powerful and effective (5:16). And I can attest to that truth. The reason I am who I am today is because people have pleaded with God for me throughout my life. Some prayed for me before I was born. Others have prayed for me since I was a young child. The quality of my life and the fruit of my ministry are due largely to the faithful prayers of others. I'm guessing that the same is true for your life. In fact, you may be reading this book because people have been pleading with God for your continual spiritual growth and your effective leadership in Him.

Not surprisingly, our ability to intercede for one another like that is often influenced by the level of our connection with them. I've found that, as God moves relationships from acquaintance to friend to more intimate friend, my abiding for them increases. I also know that I need to intentionally place time in my schedule to plead with God for His people.

In my ministry to youth at Lake Avenue Congregational Church in Pasadena, California, for instance, our summer staff was alone with God every morning from 9:00 to 10:30. We built into our schedule this time in the Soul Room to praise God, to be refreshed, and to do 2PROAPT formational reading. We encouraged each person involved to take the last part of this time to intentionally abide and pray for others. Some thirty years later this pattern still marks the lives of many of those people. May we follow their example!

What Do We Pray for When We Abide for Others?

Do you often find that your prayer is repetitive and focuses only on someone's physical health, another person's financial troubles, or the next church event? These are vital prayers, but we can do more in our intercessory prayer. The following filters help me to see people from God's perspective and to pray more broadly and passionately for them.

Also remember that essential in any time of prayer is not only speaking but also listening. We need to stop talking and be quiet in God's presence. We need to listen for whatever God wishes to bring to our mind.

Let's now consider some specific thoughts about prayer and some guidelines for intercession that can help you plead for other people. I'll also share some prayer stories along the way.

1. What Scripture might I pray for a particular person? Choose a passage and pray that text for the person you have in mind.

While I was working on this chapter, I called a close friend and heard her words of hurt, discouragement, and struggle. It was a pain-filled and very difficult conversation. The following morning God led me to Psalm 121.

I lift up my eyes to the hills—
*   where does my help come from?*
My help comes from the Lord,
the Maker of heaven and earth.

He will not let your foot slip—
*   he who watches over you will not slumber;*
indeed, he who watches over Israel
*   will neither slumber nor sleep.*

The Lord watches over you—
*   the Lord is your shade at your right hand;*
*   the sun will not harm you by day,*
*   nor the moon by night.*

The Lord will keep you from all harm—
*   he will watch over your life;*
the Lord will watch over your coming and going
*   both now and forevermore.*

I prayed the words of this psalm for my friend. For instance, I knew that the hills represented a formidable challenge to the psalmist, and I knew what challenges my friend was facing. So I prayed something like this: "Father, I lift my eyes up to the hills, to those enormous obstacles that my friend just can't get over. This day, Lord, may she ask where her help comes from and discover afresh that her help comes from You, the Maker of heaven and earth. May she find hope in the truths that You will not let her foot slip, You will never fall asleep, You watch over her, You provide shade to protect her from the burning rays of the sun, and You provide protection over her life. Wherever she moves today, may she have an awareness of Your watching over her. May she know Your presence not merely during this time of crisis, but throughout her life. God, bring refreshment to her today through Your presence. I pray in Your name. Amen."

Praying Psalm 121 for my friend lifted some of the weight I had felt in my empathy for her. It also raised my confidence and conviction that God would see her through this difficult time. The following evening I phoned to see how she was doing. During our conversation, I told her that I had prayed Psalm 121 for her. I encouraged her to read it that night. Praying Scripture for a particular person and even praying it for ourselves focuses and enriches our prayer time.

2. What power or passion is directing that person's life?

Is the person I'm concerned about being borne along by the loving kindness and grace of God? Is he soaring on eagle's wings, confident in the sovereign grip of God on his life? Or does adding a new accomplishment to the resume, having a baby, graduating from college, or some other pursuit have her excited about life? Of course a strong resume, a college degree, a marriage, and parenting all have real value, but we must regard these as mere vehicles through which God's love and grace flow to us. They are not to be ultimate goals in life. Too often, however, earthly things become the gasoline in the tank of our life. That's why, as we listen to God and pray to Him for our friends, it is helpful for us to consider what power or passion is currently moving those friends through life. May our prayer be that they will be fueled by the rich news that Christ is the Giver of life and of life abundant. Matthew 6:24-34 gives words to this kind of prayer.

A brief aside. One of the challenges of leadership and making disciples is to let both phone and face-to-face conversations with people prompt us to enter the Soul Room for intercession on their behalf. Many times I move on too quickly from conversations and later forget them, or I merely worry about the possible course of a person's life. In both cases Soul Room praying is a better alternative.

Let me share a story about a woman who had been coming with her husband to the large church where I served as one of the pastors. She called and talked with me about her deep concern for her husband. She had recently come to faith in Christ. Her husband had not, but he was seeking God. He didn't, however, want anyone to push him or shove him to Jesus.

This woman explained that her husband had expressed significant respect for me, and she wondered if I could connect with him in some way. She knew the connection needed to be natural, not plotted. We agreed to pray and trust that some Sunday between services we might run into each other even though ours was a congregation of over twelve hundred people.

As I was in the Soul Room, pleading with God for this man, I thought about the fact that he had already enjoyed great success in his vocation. He had a very influential position in the business world, everything was going great for him, yet something was gnawing at his soul. I knew he needed God.

The following Sunday, to my great amazement, I ran into this couple as I was leaving the sanctuary on my way to teach a class. I had never before met the man, and I only barely recognized his wife. But in the course of our conversation, I told him I would enjoy getting to know him. I asked if they would like to have lunch together sometime. (She had shared earlier that the lunch would go much better if she were present. He wasn't very comfortable in a one-to-one situation.) He agreed to have lunch, we set up a time, and I enjoyed a lunch with his wife and him. I was elated when, about four or five weeks later, this man came to faith in Christ.

Now think about where ministry to this man began. Notice the roots of the kingdom fruit, of his salvation. Don't miss where God was at work preparing me to lead. All this happened in the Soul Room as I spent time, almost daily, praying for this man and his wife. Then, at lunch, I—now in the Leadership Room—was able to talk to him about how Jesus Christ impacts a life and makes it richer. Following his birth into the kingdom, I continued to pray for him faithfully for months—and I wish you could have watched him blossom!

3. What priorities shape that person's calendar? Who or what determines that person's schedule?

I've spent a lot of time with men in my years of ministry, and I often hear them talk about how committed to their family they are. Sometimes when I've heard that statement, I've asked the man to take out his calendar and show me his schedule for the previous two weeks. When he does, I comment, "You know, your schedule over the last two weeks doesn't show that you're very committed to your family." And he has to agree.

In our pressure-cooker culture, schedules are out of control. That's why I will pray about the calendars of those people for whom I am interceding. And the best way I know how to pray is based on the three priorities for believers Jesus outlined in the Upper Room:

- *Abiding* Are they making time to abide with Jesus for themselves? Are they creating space for God? Is meaningful 2PROAPT formational reading a growing part of their weekly schedule?

- *Loving one another* Are they with their family in a nurturing and relational role, or are they present in body alone? Are they making time to be with and care for others in the body of Christ? Are they active in a church? Are they contributing to a 2PROAPT small group where they share what God has given them in their own 2PROAPT formational time? Do they hold one another accountable for abiding in the Soul Room? for being engaged and effective in the Leadership Room of their lives?

- *Bearing witness* Are they disgusted with or being drawn to ungodly people in a compassionate way? Are they praying for and relating to specific people whom they desire to see come to Christ? Have they asked you to pray for these friends?

These priorities—abiding, loving one another, and bearing witness—are to be the framework for our schedules. In John 15, Jesus keeps clarifying these priorities so that they can guide our thinking and our praying.

Imagine, for instance, praying for a student who is going off to college. She faces many new experiences—dorm life, new friends, living away from home, a totally different schedule, and greater freedom than she has probably ever had. What values will shape her daily and her weekly schedule? That issue is always crucial, but it is especially essential during this season of life when vital life and leadership patterns can form. So this critical issue can give substance to our prayers for her.

Now, in another example, join me in praying for a particular woman in my church. As you do, notice the insight God gave me as I prayed for her through the filter of the Upper Room Lifestyle—the three priorities of abiding, loving, and bearing witness. This vivacious Christian woman, married with children, asked me if we could talk. We set up a time with another woman from the church, and I sat with her and listened. In my prayer-preparation for this upcoming meeting, God often led me to pray this "three priorities" filter for the woman. Then, when we met, she shared her uncertainty about her faith in Christ. She also talked about the significant amount of guilt she felt, her many activities in the church, and her deep weariness and fatigue. Then I asked this woman to share her "coming to Christ" story. She had met the Lord years earlier, but she was lacking assurance of her salvation. We had a great time looking at Scripture and praying for her to know with confidence that she was indeed God's child.

But where did we go from there? Did we celebrate her new confidence in Christ and leave it at that? No, because I had prayed for her, I was concerned about her lifestyle. I recognized that her walk with God—like yours and mine and every other believer's—needs to be rooted in the Soul Room with the Father, Son, and Spirit who are writing her story. So I talked with her about her times with God, which she said were occasional at best. I could see how much she needed to cultivate a steady pattern of interaction with God in the Soul Room.

She mentioned, "I don't know where to read," so I gave her a copy of my book *Now That I Am a Christian—Volume One*. I encouraged her to carve time out of her busy schedule to enjoy being with God. I urged her to be realistic about her starting point. Was she ready for ten minutes a day? Was ten minutes every other day a better "next step" for her? I asked specifically, "What faith step could you take toward being alone with God and allowing these studies to walk you into a closer relationship with the Father, Son, and Holy Spirit?"

I wish you could have seen what happened in her life over the next few months. I watched her countenance brighten and her confidence grow. One time she came running up to me and said, "You know, I am certain I am God's daughter, and I'm falling more in love with Him. And because of my refreshing relationship with Jesus, I think I'm a better wife and mother." Her greater intimacy with God in the Soul Room was making her into a healthier, godlier person who was able to serve well in the Leadership Room.

Can you see that her time in the Soul Room impacted her life in the Leadership Room? Likewise, the Leadership Room where I had sat with her for that first appointment had been impacted by what had happened ahead of time when I had entered my Soul Room on her behalf.

4. How is this person doing in the various aspects of life?

God has created everyone in five dimensions—physical, intellectual, social, emotional, and spiritual. (I prefer this sequence because it moves from the outward and most visible aspects of life to what is inward and invisible.) As I'm praying for people, I often ask God questions and then listen for Him to give me insight. Let me show you how I might use this "total-person filter" to pray for a man named Bill.

How is Bill *physically*? How is his health? Does he seem energetic and bright-eyed? Or does he seem sluggish, tired, and worn out?

How is Bill *intellectually*? Is he aware of what's going on in the world around him? Is he involved in some kind of ongoing learning? Is he hungry to know more and more about who God is?

How is Bill *socially*? Does he have friends? Are they casual friends or close friends? Does he do things with others? Does he enjoy being with his wife? Do others seek out Bill's friendship?

How is Bill *emotionally*? Does he freely express joy, wonder, excitement, warmth, or love? Or do I sense anxiety, shame, or discouragement? When Bill enters a room, does the atmosphere brighten, or does tension arise?

How is Bill *spiritually*? Is worship a vital part of his life? When he talks about his life, does he mention God? Does he ever bring up Scripture in conversation? Do the people of God seem to matter to him? Do I sense an eternal perspective on life or a narrower, "right now" orientation?

Whatever filter you use to pray for people—praying Scripture for them, praying about the power or passion that is directing their lives, praying about the priorities that guide their decisions and influence their schedules, or praying about the total person—the time you spend in the Soul Room on behalf of others will alert you to opportunities in the Leadership Room and provide you with greater wisdom in those Leadership Room encounters. Let me share with you some real-life stories to illustrate how this Soul Room/Leadership Room connection might play out.

- I remember once sitting and praying through a list of high-school students. Often I simply say the person's name to God and then sit quietly, listening for what He might be saying to me about this person. After a few moments, I go onto the next name and listen again. On this particular occasion, having said the name of a particular eleventh-grade guy, I realized that I hadn't seen him for quite a while. I also found that I didn't have much to pray about for him because I didn't have recent news about him.

  Then I realized that, this very afternoon, I was going to be on his high-school campus. Although I was well aware that the student body numbers over two thousand students, I asked God to help me run into this young man during my "holy hanging around." Well, I was not even seventy-five yards onto campus when who was walking straight toward me but the fellow I had prayed for that morning. It was great to see him. He stopped, we reconnected, and I asked many questions. (Leaders must have holy curiosity.) After several minutes, we parted. I then took a few steps out of the flow of students to talk with God: "You're too much! Thank You! Thank You that, because of the Soul Room time earlier today, my involvement in the Leadership Room was so much more effective, so much more alive with Your presence, so much more significant."

- On another occasion, I was talking to Joe and Karen, a nice couple new to our church who had yet to form any real connections with us. I enjoyed talking with them, but in my prayer for them later, I wondered if they were being drawn in emotionally to the fellowship. *Is church merely a series of events to which Joe and Karen go, or is it a community they're becoming a part of?* In my pleading with God for them, I noticed in my mind's eye that they tended to leave church very quickly after the service was over. I didn't sense that they were becoming connected to the congregation. That day when I was in the Soul Room, God nudged me to call a particular couple in the church and see if they would reach out to Joe and Karen, befriend them, and perhaps invite them to dinner sometime in the next couple of weeks. Later that day when I phoned this caring couple, the wife said that she and her husband would be delighted to have Joe and Karen over for a meal. This caring couple's dinner invitation marked the beginning of Joe and Karen's dynamic involvement in the church.

- Paul and Betty are a fun couple with lots of energy, but when they spoke to each other, I sensed a lot of heat in the communication, and I noticed that Betty tended to dominate. As I prayed and pleaded with God for this couple, I sensed that something underneath—like a burr under the saddle—was causing conflict and needed to be removed. So I prayed, "God, I don't know how You'd like to remove that burr, but I'm willing to be the one who prays for them." In the course of the next couple of weeks, Paul shared with me about that burr in their saddle. I told him, "Let's believe God to pull out the burr."

Only a few weeks later, the three of us were together, and I was amazed to see what God had done in their marriage. A lingering injury—that burr under their saddle—had been a trophy on the mantle that often came up in their arguments. I was grateful to see that trophy taken down and discarded.

Also, as the three of us met, I found myself praying: "Thank You, God, that ministry is not just about preaching sermons or leading Bible studies. It's about the Spirit of God transforming people into the image of Christ. I desire to work with You when I am in the Soul Room pleading with You for others. Thank You for the privilege of partnering with You in ministry." In the Soul Room, God is the Pitcher filling my Cup, and what He pours into me flows into the lives of others (Saucer/Plate).

• As I pray, the Lord focuses my attention on Lori, a dear girl who is struggling in high school. Not very fluent in her speech and apparently embarrassed about herself, she is something of an outsider. She doesn't have many friends in the youth group, and I wonder if she has any at school. God really burdens my heart for Lori.

I pray for her: "Lord, which high-school girl could reach out to Lori, befriend her, and be a vehicle through whom Christ could express His love?" God brings Carolyn to mind, so the following Sunday I ask Carolyn, "Do you know Lori?" When she answers, "A little," I suggest, "Do you have the same lunch hour that Lori does? What if one day a week you had lunch with her and drew her into your circle of friends? Please pray and see if God leads you to take this faith step. Maybe God would even want you to invite her to join you and your friends at a football game." (By the way, I called this way of leading "channeling" long before New Age philosophy popularized that term. Led by God, I channel or connect one person to another.)

Well, I was elated when Carolyn started praying for Lori and then, later, really reached out to her. If I had taken a picture of Lori before Carolyn's kindness to her and compared it with a picture after they began to connect, the change would be obvious. Lori's countenance was brighter, and her physical presence was stronger. Something dramatic had happened in Lori's life. And where had it begun? Not during a talk, not at an after-football-game social— although I thank God for good talks and wonderful socials! The change in Lori actually began in my Soul Room when I was pleading with God for particular people and He brought Lori to mind.

In the Soul Room, I pray in agreement with whatever the Spirit brings to my mind. Have you ever noticed that, while you are praying, God brings certain ideas to your mind? Some of these ideas need to percolate for a while, but others invite our immediate response. Sometimes, when I'm not intentionally praying, God will bring to my mind something that triggers prayer—and that statement reminds me of my dear and godly wife Cathy.

Cathy is a real sweetheart. So much of what I have become is because of her love and prayers for me. She is a woman who really abides for others. She is also very sensitive to the promptings of God's Spirit. Listen to one of her stories:

> In my profession as an elementary performing-arts teacher in the public schools, I was part of a good-sized music faculty. We traveled together through life's joys and tears, excitement and disappointment, rewards and despairs.
>
> A few years ago our school district met its financial problems by downsizing in some areas, and the music department was one of them. This caused an entire year of emotional and professional distress for some of the music teachers. Although I was not in the group of teachers being reassigned or laid off, I was constantly offering prayer, comfort, and counsel to those who were. During this period some people struggled with anger, bitterness, confusion, and complaining.
>
> Toward the end of that school year, I arrived at my large elementary school to find the music faculty there in deep anguish. One of the prime performing-arts teachers, a young man I had known for a long time, had been asked to change his teaching position. This young man, whom I will call Ralph, was a Christian with a special love for elementary children, and the kids were greatly attracted to him. But he was being asked to move to secondary music so that another elementary music teacher could keep her job. It seemed a noble step, but was it God's purpose for Ralph? As we all talked, I began to pray internally for Ralph, who was confused and disturbed.
>
> The teaching day proceeded, we did our jobs, and Ralph and one of the other teachers went to another nearby school to finish out the day there. I finished my teaching day, loaded my car, and started for home. I was tired, distressed, and still praying for this situation. While sitting at the second stoplight, I heard the Spirit of God say clearly, "Turn around, go back, and pray with Ralph."
>
> My initial response was "Oh! I have been praying, Lord, and I'm tired."
>
> "You prayed *for* him, not *with* him. Turn around and go pray with Ralph." This was the Spirit's clear word to me.
>
> So I turned around, went to the other school, and found Ralph. As we talked, two other music teachers joined us—individuals who had been in

the early-morning conversation at the first school. Ralph was still feeling great pressure to take the high-school music position. My statement to him was "You must not take this position because of the pressure to do so. You must be led by God."

He confessed that he was still confused, so I asked if we music teachers could pray for him. I did not know for certain the spiritual status of the other two teachers, but we all prayed for Ralph's decision and for him to be sure of God's leading.

After our prayer time, Ralph said that he felt at peace about taking the new position. I later learned that one of the other teachers who had joined us in prayer was a Christian who had been neglecting her walk with the Lord. She was convicted by God's Spirit that day, went home, and spent time confessing her negligence to her Lord. This confession time resulted in her writing two letters of apology to administrators asking forgiveness for her bitterness and critical tongue during the year.

As Cathy's story illustrates, when you are praying for people, be sensitive to the insights and obedient to any directives God gives you. Remember that the issue is not how many people you pray for, but what God is saying to you about the people for whom you do pray. Remember Scripture's teaching that you and I are in great company when we're abiding for others and pleading before God's throne for them.

In the same way, the Spirit helps us in our weakness. We do not know what we ought to pray for, but the Spirit himself intercedes for us with groans that words cannot express. And he who searches our hearts knows the mind of the Spirit, because the Spirit intercedes for the saints in accordance with God's will. (Romans 8:26-27)

Christ Jesus... is at the right hand of God and is also interceding for us. (Romans 8:34)

Because Jesus lives forever, he has a permanent priesthood. Therefore he is able to save completely those who come to God through him, because he always lives to intercede for them. (Hebrews 7:24-25)

Being in the Soul Room—being alone with God and abiding for others—is a Pitcher/Cup experience that the Lord uses to form us into the leaders He wants us to be. In the Soul Room—as we spend time abiding for others as well as for ourselves—God pours Himself into us, shapes our character, increases our insights into people and situations, and develops our leadership abilities. Soul Room time is always time well invested. As someone has said, "Prayer doesn't prepare me for the battle. Prayer *is* the battle." Would you join me in praying the following prayer?

WHEN I ABIDE IN THE SOUL ROOM FOR OTHERS—AN ACT THAT HONORS GOD—HE GROWS COMPASSION IN MY HEART AND INCREASES THE FRUIT OF MY LEADERSHIP.

God, I thank You for the people in my life who have gone to the Soul Room to pray for me. So much of who I am today is because of the people who have invested meaningful time in the prayer closet on my behalf. I ask that the godly discipline of praying for others would occupy primary space in my daily and my weekly schedule. In the Soul Room may I celebrate Your blessings, intercede for others, listen for the insights You give, obey the directives You issue, and give thanks for those who pray for me. I pray this in the name of the Father, Son, and Holy Spirit. Amen.

Before You Take the Next Step

What has prompted you to abide—to plead with God—for others? If possible, share two or three specific examples.

What insight from this chapter makes you more fully appreciate the importance of abiding for others?

A passage from Scripture, a passion apparent in a person's life, the priority that seems most important to him/her, an evaluation of how he/she is doing physically, intellectually, socially, emotionally, and spiritually—these four guidelines for intercession can help us pray for people. Which of these four do you want to draw on now as you pray for people God is putting on your heart?

As you plan the week ahead, what two or three times will you set aside to abide for others?

*[The church] is so
dear to our Lord
that He purchased it
with His own blood.
— Chuck Colson*

What Is the Church?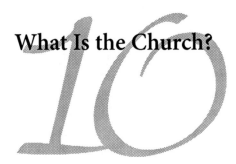

Learning to Live in Committed Community

When someone says to you, "Tell me about your church," what do you say? Before you read on, think about your response. In fact, to really benefit, take out a piece of paper and write down your ideas.

Now imagine asking first-century church leader Paul the apostle about the church in Rome. What do you think he would say? Let me offer what might have been his response:

> I commend to you our sister Phoebe, a servant of the church in Cenchrea. I ask you to receive her in the Lord in a way worthy of the saints and to give her any help she may need from you, for she has been a great help to many people, including me. Greet Priscilla and Aquila, my fellow workers in Christ Jesus. They risked their lives for me. Not only I but all the churches of the Gentiles are grateful to them. Greet also the church that meets at their house. Greet my dear friend Epenetus, who was the first convert to Christ in the province of Asia. Greet Mary, who worked very hard for you. Greet Andronicus and Junias, my relatives who have been in prison with me. They are outstanding among the apostles, and they were in Christ before I was. (Romans 16:1-7)

And Paul goes on to mention more than twenty additional names! Clearly, when Paul thought about the church, he thought about specific people. When he wrote about the church, he wrote about specific people. So I believe that when someone asked Paul about the church, he talked about the people. We do well to learn from his example.

Sometimes, however, when I talk about "the church," I'm referring to the church universal—to God's people around the world throughout time. It will be a marvelous day when all of us are brought together in glory. But other times when I talk about the church, I mean the local expression of kingdom work—the local church in Rome, Galatia, Paris, Chicago, or Memphis. God clearly calls each one of us to be committed to such a local body of believers. In chapters 10-14, we will address what it means to be a participant, a person of influence, and a leader in the all-important local congregation of believers.

NOT A BUILDING, NOT PROGRAMS, BUT PEOPLE

When we read Romans 16:1-16, we see all the details Paul knew about the church—about the people—in Rome. When he mentioned individual men and women, he often recalled their specific salvation story. He was aware that some had come to Christ before he had. He knew that others had gone through hard times.

When you prepared your response to "Tell me about your church," did you think about particular people and their stories, or did you talk about ministry programs? Did your description sound something like "We have two worship services on Sunday morning, a gifted pastor, an excellent youth program, and a great worship band"? Unlike Paul, when we talk about the church, we often talk about the *what* of ministry programs rather than the *who* of the people who comprise the church. Or we talk about the location of the building and the adequacy or inadequacy of the facilities rather than the faith of the people who fill that building week after week. Are ministry events important? Absolutely! Are buildings helpful? Without a doubt! But neither of these is the church. Christ did not die for events or buildings.

In this chapter, we will see that our talk about events often reveals a gap between our knowledge that the church is people and our actual, everyday approach and attitude toward the church. We will also discuss five challenges that inevitably arise as people live together in committed faith communities.

Lord Jesus Christ, thank You for loving Your church. As I read these pages, please increase my love for the local congregation. You know where I've been injured by the church, and I ask You to bring healing so I can love more freely. I also ask You to give me a willingness to allow Your vision for the church to become my vision. And, Lord, may the leadership in Your church be formed and guided by You, the Lord of the church. In Jesus' name. Amen.

WHAT IS THE CHURCH?

The church is people for whom Christ died and rose again (1 Corinthians 15:1-10). When I see the people receiving Communion, I see the church. When I see people being baptized, I see the church. When I see people loving widows and orphans in the name of Jesus, I see the church. When I see the building, I don't see the church unless it is occupied and I'm looking specifically at the people. The building without the people is not the church; it is just a building. I am very grateful for buildings and the opportunity to plan events and hold gatherings in them. Events and gatherings are very important, but I must never forget that these are merely vehicles to help us Christians connect with one another. Events won't go to heaven. Buildings won't go to heaven. Only people will.

THE CHURCH IS PEOPLE—
BUT DOES OUR TALK ABOUT EVENTS REFLECT THIS BELIEF?

My friend and mentor of many years Richard Halverson made this significant observation.

> Christianity was birthed in Galilee as a relationship.
> It spread to Greece and became a philosophy.
> It spread to Rome and became an empire.
> It spread to Britain and became a culture.
> It spread to the United States and became an enterprise.[1]

We in America must leave behind our church-as-enterprise approach to ministry, return to Galilee, and lead a church that truly is about relationships. It is too tempting and often much easier to measure the effectiveness of ministry by the size of the enterprise rather than by the transformation of individual lives and the richness of the community's fellowship. And don't misunderstand me. I get very excited about numerical growth as well as the growth of believers, about quantitative as well as qualitative growth. What a joy to experience both!

In my own ministry, even with the excitement of a high-schoolers' breakfast club growing from twenty to three hundred or a small college group becoming a gathering of five hundred students, my focus must continually be on the people. I am aware that many leaders believe this in their heart, but often in their implementation, they drift from being centered on people.

Consider, for instance, the questions that are usually asked when an event is over. Listen to how the event is evaluated.

- How was the worship?
- How was the message?
- How was the attendance?
- How was the skit?
- Was the PowerPoint presentation effective?
- Was the announcement for the upcoming concert done well?
- Did we sell many tickets for it?

Seldom do we ask "people questions" after an event—and if we do, those questions tend to be at the end of our list. Wouldn't it be great if we first asked questions like "Was Bill there? How did his history test go?"; "Was Sue there? Did she get her part-time job?"; or "Were Mr. and Mrs. Johnson there? Did they close on the purchase of their home? Have we volunteered to look after their two-year-old on their moving day?"

Imagine if, after an event, leaders discussed questions like these:

- With whom did you have a conversation?
- How was [each person by name] doing?
- What can we do to encourage [again, specific people are named]?
- With whom did you pray?
- What Scripture did you share with someone tonight?

Of course, after we've asked these "people questions," it is definitely helpful and important to ask "program questions." However, I have found it valuable to focus on the "people questions" immediately after an event and to talk about the event dynamics later. This order of discussion keeps the focus clear: the church is about people. (I also believe that it's easier to remember program details longer than people details.) Furthermore, people celebration improves morale, while program discussion merely improves the effectiveness of gatherings. But it's not an either/or situation; the discussion of both people and program is essential. The challenge is keeping the people the primary focus.

CELEBRATE FIRST; FINE-TUNE LATER

I learned the hard way an important leadership lesson about timing one's evaluations. We were celebrating the Lord's dynamic expressions of His grace and love on a Sunday night immediately after a senior-high retreat. We had lots of laughs as we talked about all that God had done in students' lives that weekend. Then—and, I would quickly realize, much too soon—I asked, "What could we have done to improve the weekend?" Many good suggestions were made, but slowly the evening went from bright to dark, from being a joyous celebration to a burdensome evaluation. We didn't spend enough time celebrating and savoring the wonders and mystery of what God had done. We jumped too quickly into trying to make the retreat better. Ouch!

We who are in leadership must focus on what is primary: What did God's Spirit do in people's lives? What did His Spirit do in us leaders? We must focus on celebrating the people stories and God's transforming work in their lives. Later, we can evaluate the nuts and bolts of the event—but not for at least a few days. We goal-oriented folks too often rush to evaluation, and, driven by the let's-improve-the-event dynamic, we miss the joy of seeing God touch lives and transform people.

This same lesson about what to ask and when applies not just to special ministry events but also to Sunday-morning worship and teaching times. In our discussion time after a worship service, for instance, do we consider what God was saying to us and calling us to do? Or do we immediately evaluate whether we liked or disliked the service? We are too easily drawn to evaluation rather than to celebration, reflection, and application.

THE CHURCH IS PEOPLE

God the Father, whom we gather to worship, is about people. Jesus, who died for our sins, is about people. The Spirit, who calls us into God's family, is about people. Therefore, we who are leaders in the church must be about people. Chapter 11 will address how to deal with the holy and often significant tension between focusing on people and being responsible for an event. But right now we're going to turn to 1 Corinthians and learn more about the church. When the church of Corinth was in great conflict, see what picture God gave them to help them define who they were and how they were to live.

> The Church Is People
> Purchased by the Blood of Christ,
> Positioned in a Body,
> and Learning to Live in Committed Community.

> The body is a unit, though it is made up of many parts; and though all its parts are many, they form one body. So it is with Christ. For we were all baptized by one Spirit into one body—whether Jews or Greeks, slave or free—and we were all given the one Spirit to drink....

> God has arranged the parts in the body, every one of them, just as he wanted them to be. If they were all one part, where would the body be? As it is, there are many parts, but one body. The eye cannot say to the hand, "I don't need you! " And the head cannot say to the feet, "I don't need you!" ... Now you are the body of Christ, and each one of you is a part of it. (1 Corinthians 12:12-27)

In 1 Corinthians 12, Paul taught that the church is people arranged, by God's grace, in a body. Though God says that the church is a body, the church at Corinth was struggling to live and work together as a single, unified body. Believers in Corinth were loyal to different leaders, they excused flagrant immorality, they didn't value the sanctity of marriage, and they witnessed or participated in conflicts between social classes. The believers in Corinth were anything but a well-functioning organism; the church was not functioning as Christ's transforming community.

Scripture makes clear that living as a Christian involves being enfolded into the body of Christ, into a local community of Christ-followers. Though we come to Christ alone, we grow in Christ together. The Head of the body, Jesus Christ, plus a single body part do not comprise a functioning body. Furthermore, we who call ourselves Christians need one another. And I guarantee that living as an integral part of the body of Christ will be one of the most formative experiences of your life. You will also find it a challenging place to experience and express God's grace to one another.

In light of these truths, consider these comments about the church:

> We cannot play at community development—it is essential to who we are and profound enough in its implications to keep us pursuing it until it climaxes in that great communal celebration of Lamb and Bride.... Community is a way of life. We don't like to think of being responsible for others. I like not being my brother's keeper. Nor do I want any other having responsibility for me. Dependency is on the most feared list today. Self-disclosure is relegated to the professionals whom I pay to listen. Vulnerability and weakness are dangerous. Commitment is too binding and controlling. It is easy to settle for a counterfeit or substitute because of the cost to us of pursuing real community. We must not settle for small-group times that are as good as the garden club or the local Alcoholics Anonymous meeting. Community is distinctly Christian.[2]

In our culture today, a committed community is indeed unique. It stands out as different; it is not the norm. The image of the body Paul used definitely carries with it the countercultural idea of commitment to fellow believers. Let me explain.

Imagine getting out of bed on Monday planning to start the day with a tennis match. On the way to the court, your right arm decides not to join you. It just doesn't feel like playing tennis. Can you imagine how frustrating—and ineffective and inefficient—this would be? Yet so often we Christians treat our commitment to the church—to the people of a particular congregation—just as carelessly as your right arm treated its commitment to a game of tennis. We are at church if it's convenient for us, if we like the program, or if the timing fits with what we already have planned. But a body simply cannot function well if all the parts don't show up ready to do and be what God designed them to do and be.

Therefore God remains passionate about wanting to see His church function as a healthy body with Christ as its Head. God intends for His eternal values, His loving and selfless attitude, and His kingdom desires to guide the functioning and facilitate the effective working together of each part. Again, the church is people learning to live in a committed community. Today, because of widespread family-of-origin injuries, because of all-too-common throw-away relationships in our culture, and because of seemingly omnipresent dysfunctional relationship patterns, the church may be the first truly committed community many people ever participate in. The church therefore becomes the tangible means by which God both displays His glory and reinforces that He is the One who heals broken people and enables healthy living. The church is a showcase for God's craftsmanship in community building, and that display brings hope to both individuals and the world.

THE INEVITABLE CHALLENGES OF
LEARNING TO LIVE IN A COMMITTED COMMUNITY

The church was not an afterthought in God's plan for salvation (see Genesis 12; Ephesians 1 and 2; Colossians 1; Revelation 1 and 5). The church stands at the very center of His eternal purposes: "Through the church, the manifold wisdom of God should be made known to the rulers and authorities in the heavenly realms, according to his eternal purpose which he accomplished in Christ Jesus our Lord" (Ephesians 3:10-11). And we must agree that God exercised His wisdom when He designed the church. Despite these divine origins— and you already know this—the church can be a demanding place to live and work. After all, learning to live in committed community does not come naturally or easily to us. Let me share five challenges you will probably face as you live in a committed community and engage in developing disciples of the people of God you meet there.

Challenge #1: *I came to Christ, not to a community.* When we approach the cross, we go alone, but then the Father, the Son, and the Holy Spirit welcome us into their kingdom community through the blood of Christ. But when our gaze moves from the cross, we notice all the others who have also come. We see the church. Unfortunately, though, many of us never heard about the church when the gospel was presented to us. We were primarily invited into a "God and me" relationship, not into a "God and us" community. But, as Chuck Colson points out, "according to the Scripture, Christianity is corporate. This is why we speak of the body with its different parts, the community of the redeemed, the holy nation and royal priesthood—or, as Carl Henry calls it, 'the new society of God's people, the new society of the twice-born.'"[3]

Community is one thing in theory; it's another thing to live it out. Case in point. I remember meeting with some wonderful, prayerful parents of senior-high students. After I stressed the importance of the youth group being a body, of our learning to laugh with, cry with, support, and encourage one another, one of the fathers approached me. A man of significant spiritual stature and biblical understanding, he made this statement: "Chuck, I don't know you very well. I don't know if I want to be committed to you." Internally, I died. What was I going to say, much less do? This man was resisting God's design—the church as committed community. With a lot of fear, a voice of compassion (I hope), and according to the nudging of the Spirit (I trust), I said, "I realize we don't know each other like best friends do, but when it comes to your being committed to me, God hasn't given you an option."

Because of their lack of understanding about God's design for their lives in the church, these teenagers and their parents—all of whom had committed themselves to Jesus—now needed to make a second decision, almost like a second conversion: they needed to commit themselves to the church, to Jesus' people.

John Stott further emphasizes the importance of our functioning in a committed community:

> One of our chief evangelical blind spots has been to overlook the central importance of the church. We tend to proclaim individual salvation without moving on to the saved community. Our message is more good news of a new life than of a new society....
>
> This vision of a renewed human community has stirred me deeply. At the same time, the realities of the lovelessness and sin in so many churches are enough to make one weep, for they dishonor Christ. Yet increasing numbers of church members are seeking the church's radical renewal. For the sake of the glory of God and the evangelization of the world, nothing is more important than the church becoming God's new society.[4]

When we share the gospel in an attempt to reconcile people to God and make disciples, we must clarify that God's salvation involves a cross *and* a community. Leaders who integrate spiritual formation with the development of their leadership skills will best be able to extend—and teach other people to extend—an invitation into God's kingdom *and* His community.

Challenge #2: *Do I belong?* Some of us may be tempted to think that other believers have a greater right to belong to the body than we do: "I am a lowly foot, not an important hand. I haven't volunteered for any position, I don't come from a Christian background, and I don't even feel like I belong." Could any of those thoughts be yours?

If so, please stop right here. Realize that, as a Christian, you are an essential part of an organism that God designed and that He intends for you to be part of. We need to choose to honor God as the Designer of the body—the church. You and I belong, not because of any function we perform, but because of God's design and His choice to include us in the body. I belong because of Him, not because of me. Period.

So, even though you are a rather private person, even though you are more of an introvert than an extrovert, in God's grand design you both belong to and are vital to the health and mission of the body of Christ. Read that truth again: in God's grand design, you both belong to and are vital to the health and mission of the body of Christ.

Godly leaders must therefore embrace and affirm every person who is part of the body. Finding themselves part of a community may be very new and uncomfortable for some folks, and even though they long to be accepted, they may not trust that they truly belong in the church. The Lord will use a godly leader's affirmation and encouragement to provide His people with a sense that they belong in His family.

Challenge #3: *Am I needed?* Do you realize that something important would be missing if you were not connected to the body? Every single part is special. Every single one makes a unique and important contribution to the life of the body. Unfortunately, too many Christians believe that they can only contribute significantly when they have a position or title, when they are performing well, or when they are accomplishing tangible things for the kingdom. Only in such circumstances do they truly know that they are needed.

Again, God uses His people to correctly answer the question "Am I needed?" when others ask it. Your smile, your presence, your listening ear, and your words of encouragement may not be noted on any organizational chart, but these expressions of kindness are absolutely essential to the healthy functioning of the body of Christ. At times you may have a significant role in the organization, but even when you don't, you are—like every person you lead—essential to the health of the organism. Imagine how a human body would be diminished if a knee were missing or if there were no elbow. A believer's presence in the body is always needed—and leaders need to remind their people of that truth.

Challenge #4: *Do I need you? Do I need others?* We in America assume that rugged individualism is a positive, if not a godly, character trait. Hand in hand with this way of thinking is the idea that saying "I need you" is a sign of weakness or inadequacy. We too often live as if we have little need for others, and if we do let on about any need, we make sure that the needs we share and the people we share them with are very few. And that's one reason why being a connected part of a community scares people. It goes against the grain of our American identity, our individualistic approach to life, and it diminishes our privacy.

But body parts that are separated from the rest of the body are not healthy either in their function or in their life. A body part that is isolated from the rest of the body will not stay healthy. Some people, however, fear that being in community means losing one's uniqueness. These people don't realize that unity does not mean uniformity—a truth I've often had to teach.

One time, for instance, I traveled to Pittsburgh with three college students from our ministry in California. At one of our later sessions, I addressed the unity/uniformity issue by introducing my ministry companions. One was a scientist—a graduate student at Cal Tech. Another was a comedian, and whenever he entered a room, everyone knew he had arrived. The third was a very easy-to-get-along-with person whom everyone loved to be around. These three students were hardly photocopies of one another! We leaders need to make it clear that involvement in a committed community does not negate or override a person's unique identity. Instead, community enriches and further develops each person's uniqueness. In godly community, we also learn to glorify God rather than self.

Finally, saying that we need another person is not a sign of weakness, but of wisdom. God's Spirit desires us to lead in a way that enables others to admit their needs. We—and those we lead—can acknowledge personal needs more freely when we choose to respond to God's plan for His people and to trust that He always is and always will be present with us. And God can indeed transform our attitudes and behaviors, free us to say, "I need," and bless us through those who help meet those needs.

Challenge #5: *Do I need to accept God's arrangement of the parts?* Do you ever find yourself thinking, "I'm glad that guy knows Christ and is part of His body, but did God need to position him so close to me?" All of us who name Jesus as Lord and Savior are members of the body of Christ. And if you are honest, there are some members with whom you are very comfortable and others whom you sometimes feel you could probably do without. You may also feel that you need only a few friends—and that you'd prefer to choose them yourself. Bottom line, you struggle with God's arrangement of the parts of His body.

Don't feel alone. I have often found myself debating with God about His wisdom in arranging the parts the way He has. Let me share a personal example. One day, as I stepped out of my car in the church parking lot, a woman who lived near the church property saw me— and this was a regular occurrence. Quite elderly, she called out to me in a loud, shrill voice, "Oh, Pastor Miller! Pastor Miller!" I wondered, "What should I do? Do I play deaf and walk faster? Do I stop and acknowledge her? Do I walk faster but at least have the courtesy to turn and wave?" Occasionally I stopped and talked with her, and every time I did, God used her to deeply humble me because she would always say to me, "Pastor Miller, I pray for you every day." I would be so convicted about my uncaring heart toward her.

Now, I love to have people pray daily and earnestly for me, but in my fallen humanity and because of my sinful, judgmental attitude, I would prefer that other kinds of people than the hollering church neighbor pray for me. Yet God used this precious woman to convict me of my sin nature during the six years I served on that church staff.

I learned to see that parts of the body that are very different from me nevertheless make significant contributions to my life. I also grew as I learned to more fully trust and appreciate God's arrangement of the parts in His body.

Over the years, in fact, I have very much appreciated the way God has placed many different men near me in the body of Christ. My life has been greatly enriched by the men God has had touch my life and ministry. My father, though a wonderful Christian from whom I gained much, was not a verbally affirming man, and he had little interest in sports, which have always played a big part in my life. But when God arranged the parts of the body of Christ, He provided me with lifelong fathers and brothers in the faith who have affirmed me, corrected me, and joined me in both playing and talking sports.

Similarly, when my wife and I first became parents, God used His people to help us out. At the time I was pastor of Christian Education and Youth, and the entire summertime youth program loomed in front of us. I found myself asking, "What are we going to do?" That was when a special woman, who had been praying for us, gave us a call. She had talked to her husband and teenage children and, as a family, they had agreed that she needed to move in with us for a few days until we were able to get our feet on the ground and my wife could recover a bit from her long and difficult labor. Was I ever thankful for God's arrangement of the parts in His body, the church!

Discovering the richness of the different people-parts in the body of Christ often occurs in spontaneous and unexpected ways. Our openness to seeing that richness, however, is often the result of prayer time spent in the transforming presence of our Father. Pitcher/Cup time changes how I see and respond to the people in my Saucer and Plate.

WHAT IS YOUR FEELING ABOUT THE CHURCH?

To be effective and godly leaders, we must clearly identify our personal view of the church because our perspective will impact both our attitude toward the people in our church and our way of ministering to them.

Before you ask God to help you honestly evaluate your view of His body, remember that there is no perfect church. (Someone has wisely said that if you find the perfect church, don't join it or it will no longer be perfect.) Now consider how you think about your church. Is it primarily a place where you are free to do your own thing for God without any accountability? Are you excited about being part of God's body, but you don't want to be committed to the entire congregation of unique individuals—some very likable and others less so? Or are you learning to let God grow His church and honoring the Holy Spirit as the source of the church's very life and breath? And in your ministry are individuals strengthening and deepening their connection with other parts of the body? Again, the church is people, purchased by the blood of Christ, positioned in a body, and learning to live in a committed community.

So yield to God the Potter's work on the clay of your life and welcome the fingerprints of Him who is all wise. Also remember that God did not design the church to be an appendage to your life. He intends the church to be a dynamic community where you are being formed for His glory and being fitted into the life-giving body of Christ as a servant leader. God's church is also the community with whom you go in mission in response to Jesus' Great Commission. May God therefore greatly increase your love and your passion for His body, the church.

**SERVANT LEADERS WILLINGLY TAKE THEIR PLACE
IN THE BODY OF CHRIST AND LEARN TO LIVE IN
COMMITTED COMMUNITY WITH THEIR FLOCK.**

Lord, the watching, hurting world longs for community, and You are the Creator of genuine and life-changing community. Is it any wonder, then, that the devil attacks the church?... The church is people, and, Holy Spirit, help me understand more clearly Your vision for the church. Foster in me the willingness to participate wholeheartedly in the life of Your body. May I be honest about the sin I find in my attitudes and behaviors toward my brothers and sisters in the Lord. Grant me the desire to allow You to grow me beyond where I am today. Heal my wounds, increase my commitment, and raise my excitement about my local church. I pray in the name of Jesus, the Head of the church. Amen.

Before You Take the Next Step

In light of what you've read in this chapter, share something about the local
church that excites you and something about it that frustrates you.

Which of the five challenges that come with living in committed community has
been most difficult for you? Why do you think that's the case?

Remembering that the church is people, spend some time in prayer praising God
for your church. On another day, share with God your areas of concern.

*We must be the people
of God before we do
the work of God.*

Is the Church a Family or a Business?

Integrating the Holy Tension Between
Healthy Relationships and Effective Organization

Sometimes when I go to church, I sense real excitement about the organization. I hear about elders, deacons, committees, calendars, mission, programs, and strategy—yet I find myself wanting to hear that I matter as a person, that I'm more than just another worker who can help implement a strategy. Other times when I go to church, I feel personally cared for. I sense that I, as an individual, am important, that my presence is welcome and appreciated—and the experience is life giving. Perhaps you have experienced these tensions we face in the church—the tension between organization (job descriptions, flow charts, tasks, and goals) and organism (relationships, intimacy, sharing life together).

So is the church a business *or* a family, a corporation *or* a community, an organization *or* an organism? Or is the church business *and* family, company *and* community, organism *and* organization? In building healthy churches and developing spiritual leadership, why does this issue even matter?

In this chapter we will look at the church as both business and family, corporation and community, organization and organism. As we gain focus and find integration in this world of polarities, we will learn more about how to both make disciples and develop healthy and growing leaders. I will also present a new format for board leadership and planning meetings that is based on a first-century example. This format provides a fresh approach to effective meetings.

Lord of the Church, I come to You seeking *understanding and insight about what Your church is and how the church—how Your church—can function most effectively. Show me what I can do so that Your glory will be displayed more fully within it as well as beyond it. Please use this chapter to stimulate significant thinking and meaningful lifestyle changes. I pray this in the name of the Head of the church, Jesus Christ. Amen.*

The Condition of the Church Today

The church today is facing a leadership crisis. Frequently, we hear pastors express concern over the need for more leaders. Too many leaders, paid and unpaid, seem discouraged and tired, and they are throwing in the towel. Listen to Eugene Peterson as he speaks based on his own pastoring experience:

> North American religion is basically a consumer religion. Americans see God as a product that will help them to live well, or to live better. Having seen that, they do what consumers do, shop for the best deal. Pastors, hardly realizing what we are doing, start making deals, packaging the God-product so that people will be attracted to it and then presenting it in ways that will beat out the competition. Religion has never been so taken up with public relations, image building, salesmanship, marketing techniques, and the competitive spirit.[1]

Sadly, the organizational model is a dominant influence in the church today: pastors are evaluated by governing boards, and churches are chosen by worshippers. This model has meant losing pastors but supposedly developing leaders. But hundreds of Christians no longer have a shepherd, a pastor with whom they are in a close relationship. Instead, pastors are leading congregations the way CEOs lead businesses, and the cost is high in terms of both clergy and lay-leader burnout. But as Jim Peterson, an international vice president with the Navigators observes, "It is true that there is a business side to church affairs. There has been ever since Acts 6. But the business side cannot be the controlling factor."[2]

Dr. Richard C. Halverson elaborates on this point:

> It makes a difference *how one thinks about the church*. Thinking of it as an organization *dictates one way of going*…thinking of it as an organism demands a totally different *modus operandi*. When the organizational aspect is primary—*size of membership, building and budget are decisive* … and measurable. When its organic nature is primary—*quality of life, attitudes, relationships are decisive*… and they do not yield easily to measurement.[3]

But "meaning cannot be measured. … Measurement is an extraordinarily useful tool. … But measurement is simply one artifice among many that cannot capture the essence of what makes our lives and organizations worthwhile."[4]

Going Back to Our Roots:
The Countercultural First-Century Church

The early Christian church stands in sharp contrast to our misguided approach to church as organization. The world of the early believers was the ruthlessly evil Roman Empire:

> The cultured citizens of the Roman Empire passed their leisure sitting in amphitheaters howling with delight as lions destroyed human life or as human beings killed one another in the arena below.… Life was cheap. A man could kill his slave if he was unhappy with some little bit of service which the slave performed. Parents could abandon a baby in the gutter or the garbage if the birth was unwanted. Violence and hostility were everywhere.[6]

Against the harsh backdrop of Roman brutality, something happened in Jerusalem: "a community of love, a little microcosm of the Roman Empire bound together in the love of Jesus Christ" was born.[7] The New Testament reports about this miracle, saying that people were devoting themselves to God and one another:

> All the believers were together and had everything in common. Selling their possessions and goods, they gave to anyone as he had need. Every day they continued to meet together in the temple courts. They broke bread in their homes and ate together with glad and sincere hearts, praising God and enjoying the favor of all the people. And the Lord added to their number daily those who were being saved. (Acts 2:44-47)

A little later in the life of this organism—the church—Paul addressed the people of God in Ephesus. The apostle wanted the believers to understand who they were. He wanted them to have a clear understanding of organism:

> God placed all things under [Jesus'] feet and appointed him to be head over everything for the church, which is his body, the fullness of him who fills everything in every way. (Ephesians 1:22-23)

Paul was very clear about this important fact: "You are a body, and Christ is the head." Ephesians 2:21 says we are being "fitted together" (NASB) as the household of God in which the Spirit of God is alive and active.

This matter of being "fitted together" was a concern for Jesus Himself. Do you remember Jesus' last prayer in the Garden of Gethsemane? Do you remember His central request?

> I pray also for those who will believe in me through [the Eleven's] message, that all of them may be one, Father, just as you are in me and I am in you. May they also be in us so that the world may believe that you have sent me. I have given them the glory that you gave me, that they may be one as we are one: I in them and you in me. May they be brought to complete unity to let the world know that you sent me and have loved them even as you have loved me. (John 17:20-23)

Jesus asked His Father to grant unity to His body, the church.

And that prayer was right on target. The New Testament account of the church is a story about a community of people learning to love one another and to be people of God in very ungodly societies so that the world would know that God sent Jesus.

WHY ORGANISM MATTERS: THE BIBLICAL MODEL

The church as organization gives us a measurable bottom line, yet the tension between organism and organization is very real and continual. The tension between intimacy and strategy is constant. The tension between inner journey and outer journey—between Soul Room and Leadership Room—is a daily reality. What can we do to develop churches that can handle this tension? How do we serve as godly and effective leaders in the church? And how do we develop leaders who become Pitcher/Cup...Saucer/Plate people? What is God calling to us to do?

To gain insight about these tensions, we must revisit the issue of how the Christ-life develops. Again we hear from Eugene Peterson:

> The Christian life develops organically. It grows from a seed that's planted in the actual soil of our muscles and brain cells, our emotions and moods, our genetic code and work schedule, the North American weather and our family history. It isn't imposed from without. It isn't monitored and regulated by a religious bureaucracy. God the Father, Son, and Holy Ghost isn't a consulting firm we bring in to give us expert advice on how to run our lives. The gospel life isn't something we learn about and then put together with instructions from the manufacturer; it's something we become as God does his work of creation and salvation in us and as we accustom ourselves to a life of belief and obedience and prayer.[8]

The church is Life sharing life. The church is God's doing, not ours. It is God's present and ongoing creation, and it continually confronts us with mystery. The church is an organism, a body, that is alive; an organization is not. Business management expert Peter Drucker says, "An organization, a social artifact, is very different from a biological organism."[9] The dictionary definition of *artifact* indicates something man-made. When we talk of the church, though, we are talking of something that is God-made and has life within it. Because of this life within the organism that is the church, there is definitely a need for organization.

ADDRESSING THE ORGANISM/ORGANIZATION TENSION: CHANGE CAN HAPPEN

The church is a body alive, and it is learning to respond to its Head, Jesus Christ.

> The church is not to be a conglomeration of individuals who happen to agree on certain ideas. It is bound together as an organism in a bodily unity. It is true that a body is an organization but it is much more than an organization. The essence of a body is that it consists of thousands of cells with one mutually shared life....
>
> *It is the sharing of life that makes a body different from an organization.* An organization derives power from the association of individuals, but a body derives power from its sharing of life. (emphasis added)[10]

So how do we deal with the tension that exists between organism and organization, between life and structures? Do we completely throw out organization, program, strategies, and goals?

First, I don't see resolution of the organism/organization tension as an either/or proposition. Instead, I see the resolution coming in the form of a godly process that is both/and. The key is the correct sequence: it is about Soul Room first and *then* Leadership Room—as the following description of a ministry planning meeting illustrates.

Believing that our programming must grow out of the intimacy with God that we enjoy as we abide for ourselves and for others in the Soul Room (Pitcher/Cup), we enter the Soul Room together. In that room, we experience the community of Father, Son, and Spirit, and we focus on a passage from Scripture. We face our own sinfulness, including our sinful attitudes toward others. Then, together, we plead with God—we intercede—for the men and women in our care and for whatever is going on in their lives. As we linger in God's presence for others, the Spirit grants us discernment as to how we might respond in ministry to those individuals. We begin to sense what the Spirit would like to accomplish in particular individuals as well as in the group as a whole. My growing concern for specific people becomes the foundation of the plan for a meeting, a series of gatherings, a retreat, some talks, etc. Still in this lingering-with-God process, we begin to pray for the events for which we are responsible, the events we gathered to discuss and plan. Then we close in prayer, ready to leave the Soul Room and move into the Leadership Room.

Consider all that has happened in the Soul Room. In that time of both inner transformation and community formation, we—together—encountered the living God, lingered in Scripture, spent time abiding for ourselves and for others, and prayed for the ministry. We came together as the people of God before we started doing the work of God.

When a leadership planning gathering begins with the event to be planned, without the leaders first being the people of God in collective communion with Him, the atmosphere and outcome can feel rather driven and mechanical; the diversity of opinions and desires often squelches any sense of intimacy or community. When we do the work of God without collective Soul Room time, people may feel overrun by the opinions, ideas, and strengths of others in the Leadership Room. Polarities can remain strong, often bringing division rather than community.

But when we are first and foremost the people of God in the Soul Room, we begin to appreciate and respond to the unique creation each member of the group is. Rather than merely getting a ministry task done, we feel like a team, and together we long to see the living God do His life-changing work in the lives of those people for whom we prayed and are planning.

I can't emphasize strongly enough that the key to handling the tension between organism and organization, of inner life and outer life, is keeping the rooms in the right sequence. I must enter the first room first, and the Soul Room—the place of inner communion with God where my inner life and character are nourished and formed by His Spirit—is first.

> *We must focus on being the people of God before we do the work of God.*

Here I listen and respond to God; here I intercede for people and ministry; here I gain discernment for them and for myself. The focus is God, not any agenda. We must always enter the Soul Room prior to entering the Leadership Room. We must focus on being the people of God before we do the work of God.

The church and the disciples it grows are robust when organism and organization become trusted friends. The health of the Pitcher/Cup relationships and its overflow into Saucer breathes life into the body and provides insight and energy to the mission and organization of the church (Plate).

THINKING THE WORLD TOGETHER: A NEW PROCESS FOR MINISTRY

Despite the dire situation that has resulted from making the church as organization the priority over church as organism, I am proposing a new process for developing spirituality and leadership. And the key is described by the rich phrase "thinking the world together."

Before exploring that phrase, we need to recognize the limitations and inadequacy of polarities. In the Western world, we are committed to analytical thinking, so we tend to be comfortable thinking about people and things in terms of polarities. Some of these polarities are objective/subjective, fact/feeling, information/experience, introverted/extroverted, and, yes, organism/organization.

But Parker J. Palmer, a respected writer and a master teacher, offers this valuable insight on polarities: "We look at the world through analytical lenses. We see everything as this or that, plus or minus, on or off, black or white and we fragment reality into an endless series of either-ors. In a phrase, we think the world apart."[11] We tend to have either organism people or organizational people. Rather than coming together, these two groups tend to live in their own spheres. Therefore, they—we!—think the world apart.

But if organism people and organizational people were given the opportunity to enter the Soul Room and listen to God, He would form in them respect for one another and a readiness to listen to those who think and see differently. As these two groups sit together in the Soul Room, God transforms them into a supportive community. They begin to draw upon the strengths and thoughts of one another, thus thinking the world together. Palmer continues:

> Niels Bohr, the Nobel-Prize-winning physicist, offers the keystone I want to build on: "The opposite of a true statement is a false statement, but the opposite of a profound truth can be another profound truth."
>
> With a few well-chosen words, Bohr defines a concept that is essential to thinking the world together—the concept of paradox.[12]

Paradox is an uneasy word for people who like control. It is a discomforting word for an organizational structure. Leaders must learn to live with paradox. For instance, the world of education as we know it is filled with broken paradoxes—and with the lifeless results:

> We separate head from heart. Result: minds that do not know how to feel and hearts that do not know how to think.
>
> We separate facts from feelings. Results: bloodless facts that make the whole world distant and remote and ignorant emotions that reduce truth to how one feels today.[13]

But God did not create us as either/or people, but as both/and people. We are, for instance, people of solitude *and* community. When we live at the extremes of any such polarities, the life that might have been is radically diminished. That's why I love to see developing leaders who are neither organism *or* organization, but who are sequentially organism *and* organization. They are learning to live in the excitement and tension of mystery and management. This brings glory to God; this matches His design.

Think about the creation story and in your mind watch the Father step back from each of His creative days and conclude that it is good. Notice, too, how these days demonstrate organism-life and organization-structure. On the sixth day, for instance, God created humanity. Concluding "It is very good," the Lord calls both Adam and Eve to be in relationship with Him (*organism*) and to give them *organizational* responsibility for His creation. It is not either/or. When we are responding to God and living a godly process of Pitcher/Cup …Saucer/Plate, we will be thinking the world together and knowing new degrees of effective and fruitful ministry.

Okay, you say, *thinking the world together sounds good. But how would I do this? How can my life be a "thinking the world together" life? Even more than that, how can the leadership gatherings that I lead have a "thinking the world together" design?* Let me answer first with an example from the early church and then with a plan for a leadership gathering in the twenty-first century.

LIVING OUT PITCHER/CUP…SAUCER/PLATE: A WAY OF "THINKING THE WORLD TOGETHER"

- Elders have gathered for their monthly meeting. Is it an evening of organism or organization?
- Small-group leaders have gathered to discuss the next six months of meetings. Is it organism or organization?
- The trustees have gathered to consider the finances. Is it organism or organization?
- A family is talking about their summer vacation. Is it organism or organization?

Or, in all these cases, might it be organism *and* organization?

I'm sure you're not surprised that I think these gatherings are opportunities for both organism *and* organization, and the Pitcher/Cup …Saucer/Plate metaphor will help us see that more clearly. Let's review the image, and then I'll help you see it in a biblical passage.

Pitcher. Imagine a pitcher of fresh, cold water. As refreshing and life-giving as it can be, that water is of no value unless someone picks up the pitcher and pours it. Like a pitcher, God contains that which gives life, but we don't have to wait for anyone to prompt Him to share what He contains. God Himself is the great Initiator, and He desires to continually pour the pitcher of Himself into my life and yours. The pitcher represents all that the Three are and all that They desire to pour into our lives—grace, forgiveness, love, wisdom, counsel, direction, dignity, value, and more.

Cup. Think of your life as a cup. Your cup may be almost filled to the top—with busyness, tension, tiredness, and emotional weariness or with joy and contentment. Your cup may be full of dirt and grime, or you may feel that your cup is cracked and that what it contains is leaking away. Whatever the case, the key to the cup of your life is the supply of life you are receiving from the pitcher. As God pours Himself into the cup of your life, refreshment comes, the dirt of sin and failure is removed, and you enjoy a continually renewed sense of value and purpose in life. This Pitcher/Cup process is about organism and life. It is about mystery and communion with God.

Saucer. The cup of your life does not stand alone. You have family and friends, and you connect with people in your neighborhood, your church, and your place of work. The saucer represents your network of people connections, those people you are in relationship with via phone, e-mail, or face-to-face. The Three tip the pitcher and pour Themselves into the cup of our lives. They keep pouring so that what God is doing within your life spills over onto the saucer—spills into the relationships of your life, relationships that God has initiated by His love and sovereignty and for His glory. This Pitcher/Cup …Saucer/Plate process is all about organism, life, and community.

Plate. The plate represents the events and gatherings of your life that require some level of planning and organization. A plate might be dinner with your family, time with your small group on Tuesday night, or your efforts to plan a party for your wife's birthday. A plate might be leading an elders' meeting or preparing a sermon. The event—the plate—receives further divine spillage that originated in the pitcher, filled the cup to overflowing, and spilled over onto the saucer and now onto the plate. Notice—and remember—that the Pitcher is the source of all of this. The key to the event is the Pitcher, the Three-in-One pouring all of Their essence into our lives. The

Pitcher/Cup...Saucer/Plate process develops an awareness in us that God initiated that event and is intimately involved. This Pitcher/Cup ...Saucer/Plate process involves organization, but that essential element is the final step.

We move from organism/relationship (Pitcher/Cup...Saucer) to organization/event or ministry (Plate). When we do so, we begin to see that events do not exist merely for their own sake. We recognize them as gatherings intended to both affect and express the life of the organism—the church, the body of Christ—as we impact the world through our mission.

PITCHER/CUP...SAUCER/PLATE IN THE EARLY CHURCH

In Philippians 2:25-30, Paul spoke of Epaphroditus as "my brother, fellow worker and fellow soldier." The words "he is my brother" speak of relationship, friendship, and intimacy with another—definitely a Pitcher/Cup...Saucer phrase. "He is a fellow worker" suggests shared tasks: there is work to be done, and we are a team—definitely a Pitcher/ Cup...Saucer/Plate phrase. "He is a fellow soldier" implies being in battle together. The Evil One is at work in this world, and we who follow Christ are involved in a Pitcher/Cup...Saucer/Plate battle. The Evil One attacks individuals (Cup), relationships (Saucer), and gatherings of God's people (Plate). No wonder Paul and Epaphroditus needed to be soldiers together!

The leadership relationship of Paul and Epaphroditus was three-dimensional. Notice, however, the sequence of their relationship: Paul began with organism and then moved to organization. The crisis of polarities was gone. God was honored in the soul of each individual, in the relationship of friends, and in the organizational tasks of their lives. Dynamic transformation occurs because organism and organization operate together in the proper sequence.

PITCHER/CUP...SAUCER/PLATE:
A NEW PROCESS FOR 21ST-CENTURY LEADERSHIP MEETINGS

So, you're wondering, *how would Pitcher/Cup...Saucer/Plate work today? Already our meetings run too long. Are you going to add more items to the meeting's agenda?* Well, yes and no.

I am proposing that we begin our meeting time as an organism, that we allow the pitcher of God's Word to be poured into our lives individually and collectively so, together, we experience the fresh presence of God before we approach the organizational agenda. After all, many people arrive at leadership meetings physically and emotionally spent, distracted and burdened by concerns from their day. So they may approach this gathering as just another organizational meeting that requires bottom-line decisions. In the business world, they have not been trained to think about organism and organization, much less to live the worlds of organism and organization sequentially. Furthermore they have often been just casual friends focusing on organizational responsibilities and tasks rather than learning to be fellow workers with God in the life of the organism and organization.

Finally, if I were to look at the agenda of your committee meetings, I would be able to tell rather quickly whether those gatherings are growing Epaphroditus-like leaders or are merely typical organizational experiences. So allow me to suggest a Pitcher/Cup...Saucer/Plate agenda for any **committee, leadership**, or **planning** meeting.

Leaders: Being the People of God

Pitcher/Cup. At the beginning of any leadership gathering, we intentionally spend time with a passage of Scripture for our own personal growth and encouragement. We prepare our hearts and set aside time for God to pour His Spirit and His Word into our lives. It brings us connection to God and focus within our souls.

Imagine God pouring Himself into the cup of your life, causing all of His goodness to overflow into your relationships, out of the cup and onto the saucer. This happens in our meeting when we leaders allow time for each person to share what we noticed in the passage. We simply ask, "What did God say to you through His Word that was meaningful?"

For this reason, I like to select a psalm or some other passage that touches on the character of God. I want every one of us at that meeting to be refreshed in our understanding that God's loving kindness is immense and far more than adequate for whatever challenges we face, whether personal or corporate.

After we have shared our insights into the passage and talked about how God used it to bless and encourage us, we then share personal prayer requests with one other. I might ask, "What is something specific in the next seven to ten days of your life for which I can pray?" A prayer request gives the rest of us a built-in opportunity to follow up later. The result is wonderful divine spillage: pitcher pouring into our cups, our cups overflowing onto the saucers. Instead of being merely a decision-making place, this committee can become an emotional home. After all, something happens within me when I hear people pray for my particular requests. I don't feel that they're only interested in my skills or even my spiritual maturity.

Now, having *been the people of God* (sharing Scripture and praying for one another) we move to *doing the work of God*. So we pray for the people whom we are leading. We pray by name for these people, and we give thanks for each individual and lift their requests to God. With this prayer time, we are both being faithful to Scripture (1 Samuel 12:23) and reminding ourselves that the decisions we wrestle with during the meeting are, bottom line, about people. The reason we're here is because of specific people whom God loves and has called us to serve. Then, because of what's going on in the life of the organism—the church—we need to have some organizational discussion and possibly make some organizational decisions. So we move from Pitcher/Cup...Saucer to Pitcher/Cup...Saucer/Plate.

Leaders: Doing the Work of God

At this point of the meeting, we move to plate by talking about past events, financial reports, dreams for the future, and ministry updates. Upcoming events need attention, and certain other action items need to be addressed. But as we do the work of God, He pours His goodness into the cups of our lives, which then spills over onto the saucer—the relationships around the table—and finally spills over to the events taking place in the body—the plate. The work of God we have prepared ourselves to do in the Soul Room may involve events or gatherings of some kind.

This sequence of Pitcher/Cup...Saucer/Plate keeps us mindful of what is central: communion with God and community with one another, all of which is organism. God's presence will then be manifest and magnified in significant events that have been prayerfully and meaningfully organized. Careful organization contributes to the work of ministry and to the health of the body. Remember, it is not either organization or organism; it is both/and.

I'm convinced that the organizationally focused model that is dominant in the American church may be more efficient, but not effective. Are more lives being more profoundly changed? Are more people coming to our Lord? Are lives being more deeply rooted in God's love and hope? Are we making more and stronger disciples? Are we more and more a family in love with the Lord and with one another? I don't think the organizational model alone produces these fruits.

TELLING A PITCHER/CUP…SAUCER/PLATE STORY

By God's grace, the Pitcher/Cup…Saucer/Plate process can and does work in our day, as the following story from a friend of mine illustrates. We spent years together encouraging and praying for each other. Here is how he expresses it:

> I've served on the board of Forest Home, a large Christian conference center in Southern California, over the last thirty years. Early on, we were meeting seven times a year as an operational board to address the many hands-on concerns and needs of the ministry. It wasn't uncommon for our meetings to begin with dinner and end at 11:00 or even midnight. These meetings could be very intense and very draining.
>
> At the same time, I was part of a small group with Chuck Miller at my home church. There I learned the value of men gathering, sharing Scripture together, praying for one another.
>
> After being on the board a few years, I became chairman. In that role, I sensed the need for our board to live out some of the same patterns I had learned in the men's small group. I suggested that we begin our board meetings in groups of three or four, share a personal prayer request, and actually pray right then with one another. Sometimes we began with a passage of Scripture.
>
> My suggestion was met with mixed reactions. Some had never done anything quite like this, and I could see that they were a little nervous about the idea. Others said that they couldn't imagine adding something new to a meeting that already went too late. I pressed the issue, and we took the time to share and pray. Immediately, our gatherings began to end earlier— 10:00 p.m., sometimes even 9:30 p.m. We were still addressing all of the agenda items, but there was a different spirit among us. Even when we disagreed, there was greater unity and more camaraderie.
>
> Today, nearly thirty years later, this pattern [for board meetings] continues.

We old-timers know this change of ways was an important milestone in our ministry together.

Wherever and however you are leading, remember that God loves to do new things. Also know that He is honored when leadership is first organism and then organization.

GOD IS HONORED WHEN LEADERSHIP STRUCTURES ARE FIRST ORGANISM AND THEN ORGANIZATION.

Lord of the Church, increase my desire to bring You glory and to nurture others in the Soul Room and Leadership Room of my life. I ask Your grace for the organizational leadership demands and decisions that I face. And may the kingdom of God break into every place where I serve. I ask this for God's glory and in our Lord's name. Amen.

Before You Take the Next Step

As you were reading about organism and organization, what did you find helpful, encouraging, and/or instructive? Be specific.

With which side of the organism/organization polarity do you find yourself more at home? In what way might God be inviting you to grow in that aspect of this polarity in which you are less comfortable?

Take a moment to have fun with the Pitcher/Cup…Saucer/Plate metaphor. How would you describe yourself in terms of this image?

The church must
intentionally and
continuously cultivate
organism soil and
organizational soil.
The choice of which
to treat as more
important will greatly
influence the health of
the leaders and the
fruit of the ministry.

Is Leadership Always Exciting and Draining, Rewarding and Disappointing?

Cultivating Healthy Leaders in Ministry

Have you ever heard of a church that didn't need more leaders? Churches, fellowships, and ministries constantly need leaders, people to take responsibility and help God's work happen. Some pastors look at their small congregation and say, "We just don't have enough leaders." Others look at their large fellowships and say, "We're so large that we don't know the people well enough to discern whether or not they are qualified for leadership."

In any church, many of the laity have important leadership roles in the marketplace where they have been entrusted with significant and weighty responsibilities. Of course they could do much to strengthen some of the organizational aspects of their church's ministry. But those brothers and sisters may not have a solid awareness of the Soul Room. So what do we paid leaders do? How do we respond to our need for leaders in view of the apparent lack of spiritually qualified people?

As I address that issue in this chapter, I will compare and contrast two images of leadership: Lifestyle Leadership and Positional Leadership. I will talk about how to first develop organism and how to then develop organization without draining the organism of its life. I will also share how this process protects us from burnout and helps us keep our Soul Room and Leadership Room focus.

Father, thank You for the opportunity to be a leader in Your name and by Your power. You know all the pressures I feel as a leader in Your church: I need Your power. Please be with me as I read this chapter; refresh and nourish me. Also, please grant me understanding and passion regarding the sequence of Lifestyle Leadership and Positional Leadership. I ask this in the name of the Lord Jesus Christ. Amen.

ORGANIZATIONAL LEADERSHIP: WHAT DO YOU SEE?

When you hear the word *leadership*, what images and ideas come to mind? I think the dominant perspective from which we view leadership is the organizational one. So let's take a look at organizational or what I call Positional Leadership. Here's what I see:

- A person with some organizational responsibility; usually has a title
- A person with a program role who is responsible for making certain things happen before and during group gatherings
- A person with a big personality who is very engaging and often funny
- A person with up-front communication skills who can help people relax and create a desire in them to participate more frequently or wholeheartedly
- A person with dreams and the ability to take initiative
- A person who knows how to listen and resolve conflicts
- A person with decision-making power and position, perhaps responsible for budgets and policies
- A person who is in a position over other people

These aspects of organizational leadership are essential to the work of God's kingdom, and such Positional Leadership is a vital component of kingdom work. The pastoral epistles themselves teach the urgency of Positional Leadership. However, considering leadership only from this perspective is limiting. We need another point of view. Before I define it, let me show it to you in the life of Jesus.

JESUS CONFRONTS OUR EXPECTATIONS

Let's once again join Jesus at the Passover meal just prior to His cruci-fixion. The disciples—Christ's leadership team in training—have gathered in the Upper Room. Jesus wants to eat this Passover with them before He suffers and dies. Needless to say, the mood is somber and serious especially after the Lord mentions that the betrayer is present at the table. Shocked, the disciples wonder who the traitor could be.

Despite the significance of Jesus' announcement, a festering issue begins to surface once again among the Twelve. The disciples are having another dispute, a little skirmish about the organizational chart. Listen to Christ's response:

> A dispute arose among them as to which of them was considered to be greatest. Jesus said to them, "The kings of the Gentiles lord it over them; and those who exercise authority over them call themselves Benefactors. But you are not to be like that. Instead, the greatest among you should be like the youngest, and the one who rules like the one who serves. For who is greater, the one who is at the table or the one who serves? Is it not the one who is at the table? But I am among you as one who serves." (Luke 22:24-28)

The disciples' narrow view of leadership—a view from the organizational perspective—has made them very insensitive to the significance of this Passover celebration. Responding to His disciples' power struggle, Jesus makes clear that there are two different para-digms of greatness, two different understandings of leadership. Christ says, "I'll begin by telling you how the culture determines greatness: those with positional power lord it over the others."

Then we watch Jesus confront the Twelve's unspoken assumptions about leadership. Jesus continues: "Now let me tell you how I determine greatness. First, you are not to be like the Gentile kings. Instead, the greatest among you should be like the youngest, and the ruling one should be like the one who serves. We all know that the ones who sit at the table are greater than the ones who serve them. But is that the way you've seen *Me* lead?

"We've been living life together for a number of years. We've been in homes together, walked along the road together, fed thou-sands on the hillside, watched a paralyzed man walk, and much more.

You have acknowledged that I am the Son of God. You know My position and power. However, you've watched Me lead from a posture of serving, not from a position of power and greatness. My leadership is the lifestyle of a servant; I don't use my position to dominate others. I am building a new community that will be characterized by a new kind of leadership. As you step into this leadership, you need to be aware not only of organization, but also of organism."

Organism Leadership

Join me as we observe an organism or what I call Lifestyle Leadership environment. Here's what I see:

- A capable person coming alongside someone who is struggling, providing support, and bringing prayer, Scripture-based hope, and much-needed care

- A grateful person speaking from a heart of compassion rather than from a resume ... communicating that the present moment is primary, not memories of what was done in the past

- Younger people being loved and served by older people—a Christlike act as these people of position and power wait tables rather than sit at table

- A person with graduate degrees and significant professional accomplishments being called by her first name—a sign that she is helping to build a healthily diverse community as she serves

- People displaying a God-given desire to really get to know you and being much more excited about hearing *your* story than about telling their own story

- The young and less fortunate—who have longed for someone to come alongside them with words affirmation and expressions of encouragement—blossoming under the personal care of people with experience and position in the world

- Someone smiling and extending a hand to encourage a discouraged person and motivate that person to try again

Based on the items we see on this list, what did Jesus understand about leadership that we just might have missed? Jesus our Lord regarded relationships—especially relationship with Him—as primary. Jesus said, "Come, follow Me," but consider other ways He could have fulfilled His earthly assignment. He could have, for instance, founded a school for rabbis and trained the next generation of Israel's leaders. He could have tried to connect with the political structures of His day and influence policies and decisions. But instead He started with twelve people from everyday life, and He lived a lifestyle of serving them and others, a countercultural lifestyle in which all twelve participated.

Very aware of the culture's organizational model for leadership, Jesus boldly declared that the disciples were not to be like the political leaders of their day. Jesus was aware that His circle of followers held some unquestioned cultural ideas about leadership and about relationships between older and younger, between ruler and servant. Jesus turned these categories on their heads when He said, "I am among you as One who serves" (verse 27). The Twelve definitely hadn't expected that comment!

Now let's fast-forward and, with Jesus, enter the twenty-first century to take a look at its approach to leadership. First, what is the bottom line for effective Christian leadership today? Is it our resume, our longevity, our position, our power, our temperament, or our skill set? As helpful as these factors may be in clarifying organizational mission and programs, Jesus will not allow these factors to be the bottom line for leadership in His ministry. After all, He spoke about leadership to the church of every century through His lifestyle (washing feet) and His words ("I am among you as One who serves").

So what about leadership today? Do we lead by serving? Or have we allowed our job title, our training, our passion, or our resume to distract us from waiting tables? Are we focusing instead on Positional Leadership? What a different approach Positional Leadership—leadership from above or up front—is from what the Lord Jesus describes: "For even the Son of Man did not come to be served, but to serve, and to give his life as a ransom for many" (Mark 10:45).

Lifestyle Leadership is godly leadership after the Lord Jesus' example. And this kind of leadership can be lived out in any situation, in any culture, and at any time. This Lifestyle Leadership defines my foundational role (servant) and my inner security (God's child) whether

> *Lifestyle Leadership defines my foundational role (servant) and my inner security (God's child).*

I am with one person, a hundred people, or thousands. I believe that when the church of Jesus Christ is captivated by His call to servanthood (and this will happen to individuals who abide in the Soul Room) and as the church is led by the Spirit into the Leadership Room, genuine Lifestyle Leadership—a leadership that serves—will usher in a new quality of life and of community in the church. I believe the church will then enjoy a new degree of influence in the world.

SEEING LIFESTYLE LEADERSHIP MORE CLEARLY

The church today is too often quick to recruit Positional Leadership and too slow to develop Lifestyle Leadership. We forget that the mark of the love of God is servanthood, and Jesus certainly modeled that through His lifestyle. In fact, as Eugene Peterson put it, "The Word became flesh and blood, and moved into the neighborhood" (John 1:14, MSG).

I do see two leadership pictures in Scripture, but one is definitely primary and the other is clearly secondary. These pictures influence how I train and develop leaders. The primary picture is that of Lifestyle Leadership, while the secondary picture is that of Positional Leadership. In the Upper Room, Jesus demonstrates Positional Leadership (He is the Son of God) that is expressed through Lifestyle Leadership (He is the Servant of God). In the last handful of hours before the Crucifixion, Christ wanted His leadership team to clearly understand how to live and carry on His ministry, and He showed them.

Remember Luke's account of the Leadership Room tussle among the disciples on the night before Christ's crucifixion? The gospel writer John provided more details when he reported Christ's show-and-tell demonstration of Lifestyle Leadership. Christ first lives out that lifestyle in front of the disciples, and then in John 13 and 14 He talks with them about it. There Christ speaks of His intimate and treasured relationship with His Father. Then we again see Jesus' lifestyle of servanthood as He pours water into a basin and washes the feet of His disciples. He leads by Lifestyle Leadership, not Positional Leadership: He doesn't pull rank; He serves. And Jesus wants His disciples to pattern their leadership after this act of service and love. He makes clear that their love for one another will reveal to people that they are His disciples (see John 13:35). Their genuine and active love for one another will attract people first to them and then to new life in Jesus Christ.

Jesus more fully defines Lifestyle Leadership when He speaks of the three priorities in John 15. In this blueprint for Christlike leadership, Jesus makes clear that kingdom impact occurs through the abiding, the loving-one-another, and the bearing-witness lifestyle of servant leadership—and this leadership happens effectively only as we live or abide in the Scriptures and in the presence of God's Spirit. Intimacy with God and with the Word of God is vital for healthy leadership. Jesus calls this "abiding in Him and in His words" (John 15:7). Clearly, the foundation of godly leadership is our Soul Room relationship with the Three. God's process for forming leaders begins with Pitcher/Cup.

Having called His disciples to abide in God and the Word of God, Jesus then commands them to love one another in the same incarnational manner that He has loved and cared for them. Continuing this lifestyle of committed community that He has lived among them—loving one another—is Priority #2 for His disciples then and now.

Next Jesus offers a warning: "As you protect your relationship with the Sacred Three in the Soul Room and then share Soul Room love with one another, this world will not like you. How will you respond to its rejection? I want you to talk about Me and our relationship. Point to the community of God-lovers to validate our relationship. I want others to believe in Me because of you" (see John 15:18-27). Priority #3 is bearing witness to Jesus Christ. (You can revisit these priorities in chapter 5.)

At this point the recently arguing disciples experienced Lifestyle Leadership as the Son of God washed their feet. They heard Lifestyle Leadership explained in Jesus' discussion of the three priorities:

Priority #1 — Abiding in Christ

Priority #2 — Loving one another

Priority #3 — Bearing witness to Christ

Christ both modeled and taught this process by which the Spirit would empower the disciples to turn the world upside down.

Lifestyle Leadership takes priority and precedence over Positional Leadership. Both are essential, but they must be approached in the proper sequence, as the following chart illustrates.

COMPARING AND CONTRASTING
LIFESTYLE LEADERSHIP AND POSITIONAL LEADERSHIP

Lifestyle Leadership	Positional Leadership
Organism	Organization
Pitcher/Cup... Saucer: You connect with people through relationships	Pitcher/Cup... Saucer/Plate. You connect with people through events. You bear responsibility for programs and budgets.
Informal and relational	Formal and structural
Asks, "With whom am I connecting and how are they doing?"	Asks, "How were the events? Are the programs sensitive to and meeting the concerns and needs of the people?"
Functions at all times and in all places	Functions at certain times and in particular places
Is a constant role	Is a situational role

Six More Insights

1.   Lifestyle Leadership is the ongoing **base** from which Positional Leadership is exercised. Regardless of one's position, the foundation for godly influence is always that person's lifestyle rooted in a relationship with Christ. We never move beyond or above Lifestyle Leadership.

2.   Positional Leadership too often takes on the goal of the **organization** rather than the passion of the **organism**. As essential as budgets, program planning, and the development of job descriptions are, these can easily lead to a focus on the what of ministry rather than the who of ministry. The focus needs to be the people.

> *Positional Leadership must always be rooted in Lifestyle Leadership.*

3.   Positional Leadership must always be rooted in Lifestyle Leadership. Do you know the people? Are you **among** the people? Are you praying for particular people? Do the people know you? Do they know how to pray for specific aspects of your life?

4.   Lifestyle Leadership **enfolds**, befriends, and leads people to Christ and the lifestyle of the Upper Room. Lifestyle Leadership always welcomes new people into the circle of friends, for such relationship is the soil where people grow and future Positional Leaders are developed.

5.   As Lifestyle Leadership people mature, they gain the opportunity to be in Positional Leadership. Their vibrant, **godly lifestyle** is the primary recommendation for them to be in Positional Leadership. Too often we place people in leadership positions because of their financial know-how or interpersonal skills even though we are aware that their intimacy with God is thin or their commitment to loving one another is meager. As a result, two cultures of people serve on leadership committees and boards, and that often means relational divisions and difficulty making decisions.

Occasionally when I talk to pastors, I ask, "Who are the spiritual people on your leadership board? Who are the people who have a passion for God?" Only rarely do they say that every member has a growing intimacy with God. That answer tells me that board members serve from different heartbeats or passions, and unity will be difficult to achieve. Overflow from Lifestyle Leadership should be the primary reason for asking someone into Positional Leadership.

6.   Positional Leadership **enlists** Lifestyle Leaders to partner in specific activities that God might use to transform individuals and the community of Christ. Positional Leaders and Lifestyle Leaders must work together.

WHEN LIFESTYLE LEADERSHIP DEVELOPMENT IS SIMPLY ASSUMED

What personal price do we pay when the development of Lifestyle Leadership is treated casually and carelessly? What is the cost to us collectively when Lifestyle Leadership development is given less attention and is simply assumed to be happening?

We lose the soil in which Positional Leaders are grown. We imply that it is okay to be busy and not necessarily transformed and growing people. We diminish the Lifestyle Leadership crop from which to choose new Positional Leaders, and the result is a leadership less spiritually mature and less sensitive to God's Spirit. We also bring secular patterns of our culture into kingdom leadership.

We starve the souls and exhaust those we place in positions of leadership. Leaders can begin to feel bitter and used. When the time comes for them to leave Positional Leadership, they often distance themselves from the church because their community relationships were not tended or further developed during the time they spent in the organizational areas of responsibility.

We end up communicating that the real influencers are those in Positional Leadership, and this message desecrates Christ's design for the church. In the body of Christ, the healthy functioning of every part is essential for God's glory, their good, and God's mission in the world.

We discourage, if not injure, our Lifestyle Leadership people by making them feel second-rate. When those in Positional Leadership are esteemed as the church VIPs, we create a two-tier culture and diminish relational camaraderie as well as the energy and impact the church could have in the world. An emphasis on Positional Leadership may also create a cultural climate of competition and lessen our cultural distinctive as the people of God. The secular mind-set of "How long will it take me to climb the rungs of the ladder to eldership?" can set in. I remember one man asking me, "I've been in this church since its founding. Why haven't I been asked to be an elder?"

We make spirituality an option for some to choose rather than a normal pattern for every believer. The Upper Room lifestyle is not something to fit in if you and I have the time or only if we're longing to be a positional leader in the church. The Upper Room lifestyle reflects the passion of our Lord for His church and for everyone in the body of Christ.

Again, I can't emphasize enough that both Positional Leadership and Lifestyle Leadership are essential. It is not either/or, but both/and. Yet the organism (Lifestyle Leadership) must be foundational and seen as primary in the development of the church body and its programs and ministries. Future leaders grow in the soil of Lifestyle Leadership; Positional Leadership (organization) is a place where that Lifestyle Leadership is expressed. But Positional Leaders must continually ask themselves, "Who am I nurturing?" and not just "What decisions do we need to make tonight regarding the budget or upcoming programs?" Positional Leaders must always remain rooted in Lifestyle Leadership. Their attitude must be like that of Christ Jesus: "I am among you as one who serves" (Luke 22:27).

GROWING LIFESTYLE LEADERS

As you well know, pastors and leaders are always in need of spiritually healthy, committed leaders. The issue of how to develop leaders is no small concern, and this challenge is further complicated by the pressures of our culture, frequent job relocations, and people often leaving one congregation for another.

But let's consider this issue from a slightly different perspective. Rather than asking "How do you develop leaders?" I prefer the questions "What can we do to develop Lifestyle Leadership soil?" and "What can we do to attract people to the Upper Room lifestyle?" That, after all, is the key to forming and transforming Lifestyle Leaders.

Now of course I'm not saying that creating such cultural and programmatic change is easy. Actually, change is usually quite challenging, and it can threaten people and programs. People are busy, and they're threatened by the prospect of leadership: "I'm doing so much, and I don't know if I can add anything else to my schedule." Positional Leaders who feel the need to protect their program turf can also feel threatened by change.

In the next two chapters, however, I will address this matter of needing more leaders by answering the question "What can we do to develop Lifestyle Leadership soil?" You'll join me in five church environments. I will describe a situation, encourage you to reflect on what you would do, and then share with you what God led me to do. These five ministry opportunities vary, ranging from junior high through adult and addressing different needs (from dealing with cliques to church planting). You will see how cultivating Lifestyle Leadership soil is foundational to developing healthy leadership for your ministry. In fact, much of the message of this book finds its implementation in this issue of cultivating Lifestyle Leadership soil.

LIFESTYLE LEADERSHIP IS THE SOIL OUT OF WHICH
POSITIONAL LEADERSHIP GROWS AND BEARS FRUIT.

God, the cultural voices of leadership and organization are so loud and overwhelming. They can easily drown out the voice of Your Spirit. In our culture, position precedes everything. But in Your Word and in Your way, serving precedes everything. Bring me to Your feet and make me responsive to the Upper Room lifestyle. In the name of the Lord Jesus Christ, the kind of servant leader I desire to be, I pray. Amen.

Before You Take the Next Step

What idea in this chapter especially caught your attention? Why do you think you were drawn to it?

What Lifestyle Leader(s) do you see in your church? What does this leadership style tell you about them?

In what specific ways is your Lifestyle Leadership currently touching other people?

Think about a group you are a part of, but in which you do not have a Positional Leadership role. In what ways are you offering Lifestyle Leadership in that setting? Think creatively about other ways you could offer Lifestyle Leadership. It's easier than you think.

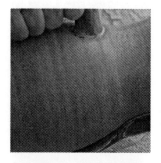

So much noise, so much pressure, so many distractions characterize twenty-first-century life. By God's grace, the Soul Room, the Leadership Room, and the seven intentionals will help you develop your ministry now and sustain it for the long haul.

Lead Youth? I Can't Wait!
Lead Youth? What Was I Thinking?

Developing Healthy Leaders in Youth Ministry

Ministry is about stories, and in my four decades of serving God and people, I have my stories to tell! In fact, I'm going to use some of them as case studies in the next two chapters as I invite you to consider Lifestyle Leadership as a way to address the demands of ministry, whether to junior-high, senior-high, college, singles (Gen-X), or adult groups. In addition to telling two of these stories in this chapter, I will also present what I believe are seven key aspects of leadership development.

First, though, a disclaimer. As I share these stories celebrating God's transformational work in people's lives, please don't think I'm claiming to have some spiritual Midas touch that makes everything I do turn to gold. Over the years I've experienced plenty of dark times. There have been moments of misunderstanding and being misunderstood, and some of the seeds I've planted over the years didn't seem to take root. I'm grateful for the times God graciously blessed my efforts. These experiences illustrate the way He faithfully forms leaders for His kingdom work.

Father God, You who are loving and wise know my heart. You know if I need You to fuel my excitement about church, to minister to me in my tiredness, to free me from my sense of being trapped in an organization, or to touch me in some other way. So I yield myself to You—and I ask You to help me see in Your church opportunities to cooperate with You. Holy Spirit, break into my life and the life of the church I attend in such a way that the organism will breathe greater freshness and God-presence within the organization. Hear my prayer, O Lord, in the name of the Father and the Son and the Holy Spirit. Amen.

STORY #1:
CAN JUNIOR-HIGH STUDENTS BECOME EXCITED ABOUT JESUS?

Early in our ministry, my wife Cathy and I served as lay junior-high sponsors of the Sunday-night youth group at Fourth Presbyterian Church in Washington, DC. We began with ten students who had little excitement about Jesus and who considered church an endurance contest.

Our initial goal was simply to get to know them. We wanted them to become a community of genuine friends who responded positively to our Lord. Encountering resistance, I spent much time in the Soul Room praying for these ten people, and I noticed that two of the girls seemed to have the softest heart-soil toward God. So, after much praying for them and then after joking and laughing with them, I shared an idea: "Girls, I sense that you think the Bible is boring, but I find it exciting. So I'd like to do an experiment with you. Let's see if I can help you discover the excitement and value of the Bible."

To my joy and amazement, they agreed. After school, we shared laughter, popcorn, Coke, and—from a popular paraphrased New Testament—John 4, the story of Jesus and the woman at the well. After about five quiet minutes for personal reflection, each of us shared things we noticed about the woman, about Jesus, and about how this story of the woman, the water, and the well related to our lives. Then I focused on the "Jesus water" and the difference it makes in our life.

Before we closed, I asked the girls to pray for me in some very specific ways, and then I asked how I could be praying for them in the next seven days. After we prayed for one another, I could hardly believe my ears when I heard, "Could we do this again? This was fun!" And our second meeting was as positive as the first.

In my Soul Room of abiding for others, I prayed for these girls and their friends. During my prayer and discussion times with Cathy, God gave us both the desire to have a party for the Sunday-night group and to have them invite their friends—and God did grand things that night. More than sixty students came. We had to send out for more refreshments and prizes. We struggled to maintain a healthy sense of order with their high energy and craziness. From the management side, the night was a disaster. From the relational side, it was a smashing success. Praise God! But now what?

I continued to meet with the two girls. We were falling more in love with Jesus and continuing to pray for their friends. Within four months we had around ninety students coming to the socials. This prepared the way for a junior-high retreat. So I was asking God, "What should be the focus of the weekend talks? Our group consists of many fun seekers, some resistant Christians, and two excited and growing Christians. What, Lord, do You want to say and do in their midst?" I knew that Jesus needed to be lived, seen, felt—and then described by godly, sensitive, real people.

So, on a snowy Friday evening, we boarded a bus and headed for The Mimslyn Inn in Luray, Virginia. We sledded, built snowmen, performed skits, sang praises to God, ate scrumptious meals on linen-covered tables, and warmed ourselves by roaring fires. We made new friends (many of whom are still in touch with one another more than forty years later), listened to testimonies, and dreamed about the difference Christ can make in our life. And we leaders prayed and prayed.

When I presented the opportunity for people to receive new life in Jesus Christ, the response was overwhelming. When I presented the opportunity for Christians to follow Christ more obediently and passionately, the response was equally strong. As we drove home on Sunday, nearly all of the fifty-eight junior-high students had expressed a desire to follow Christ or to follow Him more closely. More than thirty-five were new Christians. Thank You, Lord! And now what?

What message would you share—and continue to share—with these rambunctious seventh- and eighth-graders? What opportunities for growing in Christ would you provide them? What structure would you develop to spiritually nurture both new Christians and the open-to-growing church kids?

STORY #1: WHAT GOD DID IN THE LIVES OF JUNIOR-HIGH STUDENTS

Junior-high students were falling in love with Jesus, and thirty-five of them were new followers of Jesus. The three questions I just asked you were crucial to determining the path of this ministry.

1. *What **message** would I share and continue to share?* I wanted these students to know that the Father, Son, and Holy Spirit give life. I wanted them to be excited about developing a life-giving relationship with Jesus Christ. The students needed to hear again and again that God gives eternal life (John 17:3)—and that this eternal life begins now.

> We wanted to help these hungry-to-grow junior-high students develop the lifestyle pattern of abiding in Christ and in His Word.

I also wanted to answer the questions "How do you nurture a relationship with Jesus?" and "What is God—Father, Son, and Holy Spirit—really like?" The students needed to hear about and experience the Father's love—a personal love for them that is steady, will never leave them, and offers security in their crazy, upside-down, who-knows-what-might-happen-tomorrow world. I wanted to teach and re-teach the lifestyle priorities of abiding, loving one another, and bearing witness.

2. *What **opportunities** should we provide as a follow-up to this retreat—and why would I choose those?* Junior-high Sunday school, multigenerational worship on Sunday mornings, and social gatherings to which they could bring their friends and have genuine fun—all these needed to continue for the students new in Christ as well as those who were coming more alive in Him. However, we wanted to help these hungry-to-

grow junior-high students develop the lifestyle pattern of abiding in Christ and in His Word. We wanted to teach them how to sit alone in God's presence with an open Bible and experience His Spirit touching their thoughts and their lives. We wanted them to discover what we already knew—that such Pitcher/Cup time is key to a vibrant, nourishing Christian lifestyle. But we had no program for helping them develop the lifestyle of abiding, no forum for them to share in community what was happening when they were alone with God in the Word, and no place where they could know accountability for their commitment to Jesus.

3. *What **structure** would we develop that would nurture new believers as well as hungry-to-grow students?* We needed to establish an ongoing gathering where the students could come because they were part of the team desiring to abide in Christ and His Word, so we birthed the "Team Meeting." There, students talked each week about their personal communion with God through Scripture. I wanted this sharing of Scripture to become normative in the life of a Christian and in the life of a group of Christians. (We too often leave such talk to the people who speak and teach from the front!) This meeting time would be an opportunity for students to abide in the same passages, share what God was teaching them from the Scriptures, and be held accountable for their abiding during the week. As they did so, they began to experience the mystery and wonder of God's Spirit transforming them individually and as a group.

God used Team Meetings to shape a nurturing community of people who held one another accountable for growing in their faith, a community of people who prayed for, cheered for, and supported this growth in one another. This structure was the foundation on which all the other aspects of the ministry were built. This lifestyle nurtured emerging leaders and influenced the entire junior-high ministry. The students' attitudes and excitement about Jesus created a different dynamic in Sunday school, Sunday-morning worship, and every junior-high gathering. Furthermore, over the next six years, scores of other junior-high students came to faith in Christ, and these students moved on and had a tremendous impact in the senior-high ministry.

The junior-high years of big mood swings and emotional insecurity get a lot of bad publicity. Can God really transform these students? A phone call from a nearby junior-high principal answers the question. He said, "Over the last two or three years, our faculty has watched our student body change for the better because of your influence. We are a better school because of what is happening in their lives. So the faculty is asking you to speak to them at a teachers' training meeting to help them better understand junior-high students." God transforms anyone of any age who is willing to respond to Him.

STORY #2: WHAT DO YOU DO ABOUT HIGH-SCHOOL CLIQUES?

My wife and I, with our two preschoolers, arrived in California to begin our new ministry in a wonderful church that God had used for His kingdom for many years. One of my responsibilities was to lead about ninety senior-high students attending five local high schools. I got to know them by attending their Sunday-night youth group, doing some "holy hanging around" at the high-school campuses, and seizing whatever opportunities I could find or create.

After laughing with them, asking questions, and joining them in doing things they liked to do, I began to get a sense of the social and spiritual climate of this group. I also benefited from the significant time I regularly set aside to be in the Soul Room, abiding in prayer for these senior-high students.

It didn't take long for me to notice that this high-school group was filled with cliques. Some students were clearly insiders while others were just as clearly outsiders. Some kids were cool, and others simply weren't. The group had done everything that other evangelical-church youth groups were doing—Sunday school, socials, outreach events, mission trips—but they had experienced little community. Some of the juniors had not talked to other juniors since entering the group as freshmen—and they were proud of that fact! I discovered a great deal of deep pain in this youth group, so I was especially encouraged when I saw some camaraderie begin to develop. Yet I was well aware of the few highly resistant students, and I found myself praying, "God, what am I going to do? What do You want to do here to replace these cliques with authentic Christian community?"

Now imagine stepping in to lead this senior-high group. What would you do? What message from the Bible would you consistently share—individually and collectively—with these high-school students? What opportunities for growing in Christ would you provide them? What structure would you develop to foster Lifestyle Leadership soil in a group of students divided by cliques?

STORY #2: WHAT GOD DID TO BREAK HIGH-SCHOOL CLIQUES

Once again, praying and asking God to help me answer the questions I just asked you were crucial steps in determining the path of this high-school ministry.

1. *What **message** do I share?* I passionately desired these senior-high students to see that God—Father, Son, and Holy Spirit—is amazing and marvelous. I wanted them to encounter His love and then realize that He dreams bigger dreams for them than they could ever dream for themselves. I wanted to communicate that Jesus is not just our ticket to eternity. He is the Lord who brings meaningful change to our lives now, who calls us to love one another, and who helps us bear witness of Him and His love to those who don't yet know Him.

   My priority was a gathering that would foster the students' Soul Room encounter with God, enabling them to meet alone with Him and then later share their discoveries with others.

2. *What **structure** would we develop that would nurture new believers as well as hungry-to-grow students?* I knew we must provide numerous gatherings for students, but my priority was a gathering that would foster the students' Soul Room encounter with God, enabling them to meet with Him alone and then later share their discoveries with others. So I let the students know that I was there to laugh, play ball, and crack jokes with them, but I made it clear that I was also there to lead them into the lifestyle Christ desired for them. I knew that Sunday school, socials, retreats, camps, and caring for others would all help grow a godly lifestyle, but I wanted a unique opportunity for those students who were hungry for God.

So I invited these students to be part of a team that would learn to sit in God's presence and enjoy Him, that would fall more in love with Christ through the lifestyle of the Upper Room, that would learn to hear God's Spirit speak to them from Scriptures, and that would willingly be held accountable to others for making time to be alone with God and for being His light on their campuses.

This team opportunity needed to be the central and most important youth-group activity, more important than the upcoming missions trip, the next retreat, Friday's social, or even Sunday school. From this team gathering, leaders would emerge who would influence the larger group and its other activities. In these team gatherings, we would continually nurture the students' sense of God's call on their lives and His loving requirements for their lifestyle.

3. *What **structure** would we need to develop or change to provide students an opportunity to abide, love one another, and bear witness?* What structure would facilitate the Pitcher/Cup...Saucer/Plate process? In past high-school ministries, leaders desired the students' attendance at gatherings, their willingness to help with special projects, their learning to be good stewards of their money, and, at times, their memorization of Scripture. The message had been loud and clear: "We want you to grow, and we will help you by giving you tasks. You will grow through the ministry of doing." As helpful as those activities may be, something crucial was missing: a time and place that fosters the individual's relationship with God. It is all too rare to find in youth ministry a structure that encourages teenagers to make a team commitment to both meet alone with God and gather with one another regularly to share their lives and their Soul Room discoveries. Relational accountability for day-to-day communion with God in Scripture needs to be central, but it is often overlooked in most youth ministry in America. In terms of our metaphor, Pitcher/Cup is neglected.

So, after a few weeks of praying and interacting with the high-school students I'd been getting to know, I began to see that we needed to have a day for declaring our desire to live the lifestyle of the Upper Room. We needed to declare our commitment to abiding in Him, loving one another, and bearing witness to His goodness. So we needed to develop a structure, a forum, that gave students the opportunity to become that kind of a community.

In the case of the junior-high ministry, we had no structure to start with, so we added something new. In this high-school situation, though, God led us to change the existing Sunday-night structure. Renaming it Team Meeting, we designed it for those students whom God prompted to make a commitment to the Upper Room lifestyle. We also worked hard to be sure that those students who weren't ready to make such a commitment didn't feel like second-class citizens. In fact, those who participated in the Team Meeting prayed for those who weren't yet a part of it. In those meetings, we developed Lifestyle Leadership soil, we encouraged a core of students to care for the large group, and God raised up healthy leaders for the ministry.

To launch this program change, we scheduled a Day of Declaration. Beforehand, we provided a covenant describing the Upper Room lifestyle of abiding, loving one another, and bearing witness. We asked students to think and pray about making this commitment.

A number of students on that Saturday of Declaration looked at Scripture that addressed, among other things, community. We witnessed students who hadn't spoken to one another for two years suddenly talking and even praying together.

A team was forming that committed themselves to reading and reflecting on biblical passages, and then gathering on Sunday night to share what God had given them as they studied the week's selections. They became a community who celebrated God's blessings in one another's lives and, during the week, prayed for one another as well as for students in the group and school friends they longed to see become followers of Christ. They asked God to bring the freshness of Christ through them to all of the youth-group gatherings.

This setting proved to be an effective structure for the tending of Lifestyle Leadership soil, and we saw students grow in their faith and bear fruit. We watched a ministry that had once rejected newcomers become a ministry that sought out and embraced newcomers. We even developed a breakfast club for students to bring their school friends to. But I told them, "Whatever you do, don't bring a friend if what I'm going to speak on is contradicted by your lifestyle. Remember, when I speak at breakfast, I'm just going to be explaining your lifestyle to them." These high-school students brought friends— and lots of them. Friends who had never been inside the door of a church joined us. Friends who had no use for Jesus Christ came to breakfast. And our students watched these friends come to Christ.

Do you think we would have seen these same results if we had just added to the schedule another meeting called "outreach" or even "Bible study"? That approach hadn't worked in the past. After all, these students needed to learn that the Christian life is not about meetings, but about tending their relationship with Jesus—and they did. Their abiding shaped and transformed their relationship with Him. They let God so work in them individually that suddenly they were open to being a community together. They wanted their lives to tantalize friends so they would listen to and embrace this Jesus that they were getting to know better. They wanted their personal and community life to impact their culture.

One of the results of God's work in that senior-high group was to develop servant leaders, some of whom moved into Positional Leadership within as well as beyond this ministry. Due to their Positional Leadership roles on their high-school campuses, I was often invited to speak at baccalaureates. I will never forget a college student saying, "The evening after you spoke at the Arcadia High School baccalaureate, I gave my life to Jesus Christ." How thrilling that news was—and her new life as a follower of Jesus could be traced back to that day of declaration when a group of senior-high students had said, "Yes, I want to love God back through the lifestyle of the Upper Room. I desire to live the Pitcher/Cup... Saucer/Plate process." In the following years, the lifestyle of these teens continued to impact scores of their friends, their parents, and, in time, their own children.

SEVEN LEADERSHIP INTENTIONALS
FOR DEVELOPING THE LIFESTYLE OF THE UPPER ROOM

Whether you have served as a Christian leader for many years or are just beginning, I want to share with you a few of what I consider non-negotiables for ministry; I call them "intentionals." These are things we must be very intentional about when it comes to cultivating the lifestyle of the Upper Room. Some of these intentionals occur in the Soul Room; others, in the Leadership Room; and some in both. Each of these universal intentionals is a timeless ministry directive for all peoples and all generations.

LEADERSHIP INTENTIONAL #1: Abiding for Myself (Soul Room)

> If you abide in me, and my words abide in you, ask whatever you wish, and it will be done for you. — John 15:7 (esv)

I must continually nurture my intimacy with God by spending intentional time in the Soul Room. In fact, when I first enter the Soul Room, my personal communion with God matters more than anything else, even more than the ministry. Basking in the presence of God; enjoying friendship with the Father, Son, and Holy Spirit; discovering the vastness of God yet His personal love for me; learning to listen to Him; confessing my sins; experiencing forgiveness and healing—all of this plus much more occurs during my Soul Room time of worshipping the Lord. This Upper Room communion energizes me; Jesus' Upper Room priorities focus me. The life and grace of God in me and through me can tantalize teenagers and attract them to Him. The propellant for my own life and ministry must be the amazing grace of God and His personal presence alive in me. My motivation for life and ministry must find daily refreshment and restoration in the Soul Room presence of Father, Son, and Holy Spirit. Nothing compels me to live the priorities of abiding, loving one another, and bearing witness and to lead more effectively than having worshipful communion with God as I abide in the Soul Room for myself. The pressures of life and leadership make this Intentional #1.

LEADERSHIP INTENTIONAL #2: Abiding for Others (Soul Room)

> Moreover, as for me, far be it from me that I should sin against the Lord by ceasing to pray for you… — 1 Samuel 12:23 (esv)

I was passionate about becoming a friend to junior-high and senior-high students so that, as a friend, I could introduce them to my best Friend: the God revealed in the Scriptures. I knew that their meeting the Lord would make students new creatures in Christ, give them a solid foundation for their lives, and help them become healthy people, effective leaders, and strong members of the church and community. My Soul Room time of abiding for others—of praying for my students—fueled this passion in me.

As I prayed for teenagers in my care, I asked God to open their hearts and eyes to the relevancy of Christ to their lives and to draw them to discover Him afresh in the pages of Scripture. The Bible needed to come alive for the students in both groups. From this common lifestyle soil would emerge leaders, people of godly lifestyle and therefore godly influence. (For further thoughts on how to abide for others, revisit chapter 9.)

LEADERSHIP INTENTIONAL #3: Developing a Structure for Lifestyle (Leadership Room)

> They devoted themselves to the apostles' teaching and to the fellowship, to the breaking of bread and to prayer.... Every day they continued to meet together in the temple courts. They broke bread in their homes and ate together with glad and sincere hearts, praising God and enjoying the favor of all the people. — Acts 2:42,46

The Upper Room lifestyle of abiding, loving one another, and bearing witness must become the structural paradigm of the students' lives and of the ministry. For me, these three concentric circles listed in John 15 serve as the starting point from which a godly life is lived and all ministry programs develop. We are to see every other aspect of friendship and ministry in relation to developing this Upper Room lifestyle in the students.

So, to all junior- and senior-high students, I presented John 15 as the common lifestyle for everyone, not as the specialty lifestyle of a few. I continually prayed with great anticipation that more and more students would commit to this Upper Room lifestyle of abiding, loving one another, and bearing witness and would see the Lord impact their lives through the Pitcher/Cup…Saucer/Plate paradigm. Furthermore, healthy soil produces the fruit of committed students and godly student leaders—and to God be the glory!

**LEADERSHIP INTENTIONAL #4: Asking Meaningful Questions
(Leadership Room)**

> What do you want me to do for you?…Who do people say I am? [and]
> Who do you say I am?…What do you want?…Simon, son of John, do you
> truly love me? — Jesus in Mark 10:51; 8:27,29; John 1:38; 21:16

A healthy leader is a servant leader who asks meaningful questions.
Read the Gospels. Jesus is a master at asking effective questions.
Questions cause thinking, create dialogue, and show interest in the
one questioned. With questions we may seek information or counsel.
A well-phrased, well-timed question is priceless. Yet the questions we
ask in ministry must rise out of the heart-compassion for people that
God is developing in us in the Soul Room. The answers we receive
provide further insight for how to pray for the people.

LEADERSHIP INTENTIONAL #5:
Creating Space for "Holy Hanging Around" (Leadership Room)

> The Word became flesh and blood, and moved into the neighborhood. —
> John 1:14 (MSG)

I must be passionate about creating time and space in my schedule
for "holy hanging around." The church exists as church gathered and
church scattered, but it's all too easy to become consumed with
church gathered. We leaders want people to come to our place, but we
rarely make time to visit their worlds.

Notice in Scripture that the Master created space for holy
hanging around. You would find him at the boat docks talking with fishermen, celebrating at a wedding feast, and conversing with a woman at
a well. He lived out among the people, building relationships, offering
insights, and seizing opportunities to share God's love and truth. The
same must be true of us in the twenty-first century. Our leadership must
extend beyond the church campus. It must include going, doing, and
holy hanging around in places where the students are. In those places,
friendships are built, questions are asked, laughter is shared, and affirmation can be extended, and you will find yourself more motivated to
enter the Soul Room on behalf of these people. There in the Soul Room
with the community of the Sacred Three, you will share the holy-

hanging-around experience and pray for those you were with or will soon be with. Schedule times to go where the people are. It is not an option; it must be normative for all leaders, pastoral and lay alike.

LEADERSHIP INTENTIONAL #6:
Modeling the Process (Soul Room, Leadership Room)

> Don't let anyone look down on you because you are young [or for any other reason] but set an example for the believers in speech, in life, in love, in faith and in purity. —1 Timothy 4:12

The Upper Room lifestyle—abiding, loving one another, bearing witness—outlines God's priorities for our life, so I must model for students the Pitcher/Cup...Saucer/Plate process that fosters that godly lifestyle. After all, students are looking for models more than they are looking for information: "Don't tell me; show me." Furthermore, it has been rightly said, "It can't happen through you until it is happening in you." So I want the students to clearly see that I am living the same process of Pitcher/Cup...Saucer/Plate that I am encouraging them to live. I need to model that this process draws me to God, determines my schedule, and influences my relationships. This life-giving process sustains leaders for a lifetime of ministry and grows lasting fruit.

LEADERSHIP INTENTIONAL #7:
Remembering—Always—That the Ministry Is God's, Not Mine

> What, after all, is Apollos? And what is Paul? Only servants, through whom you came to believe—as the Lord has assigned to each his task. I planted the seed, Apollos watered it, but God made it grow. So neither he who plants nor he who waters is anything, but only God, who makes things grow. —1 Corinthians 3:5-7

In the press of praying, planning, and executing ministry, we leaders can find it all too easy to feel that everything depends on us. We forget both that God is sovereign and that only He can transform a human heart. Granted, God uses us as vital players, but He is working above, under, around, and, yes, through us—in ways we cannot even imagine—to bring about what He desires. This intentional reminds us that God is in charge, and it also keeps us focused on the fact that, even as we manage our ministry responsibilities, we must be looking for the moments of mystery when God's Spirit breaks in and surprises us. Management can never do the supernatural; at best, management can help create an environment where God can work. So don't get lost in the details of programs and management and miss the wonder of God breaking in to transform your life and the lives of the people in your care. Through the years I've seen God break in and touch lives beyond what I could have imagined. To Him be the glory! Great things He has done—and continues to do!

THE LORD'S WORK IN THE LORD'S WAY

> If we aren't doing His work in the Spirit by His methods, we're doing it in the flesh by our own methods. The Lord's work done in the Lord's way will have the Lord's supply. – Dr. Lois LeBar[1]

In ministry to students, I am certainly involved in the Lord's work, and I know I don't want it to be my work. I want it to be Jesus' work, but what would be the Jesus way to develop these students and these ministries? (I use the phrasing "to develop these students and these ministries" to keep the priority and the focus on the students, not on designing and keeping a program going.) The Bible shows us:

- *The Jesus way is a way of integration.* Today almost all the descriptions of positions in ministry focus on a particular specialization (children, youth, worship, small groups, etc.). It is assumed that the applicant is living an integrated lifestyle of abiding, loving one another, and bearing witness. Churches hire for specialization because they assume integration, and this is a fatal assumption. The Jesus way of integration may, however, lead to specialization, but ministry job descriptions must reflect the two components in this sequence: integration and then specialization.

- *The Jesus way is a way of incarnation and connection.* "The Word became flesh and made his dwelling among us" (John 1:14). Jesus models personal relationship and intimate friendship.

- *The Jesus way is a way of invitation.* He says to us, "Come to me" and "Come, follow me" (Matthew 11:28 and 4:19). These gracious invitations address my inner condition (I'm tired and worn) and my outer condition (I need direction, and I desire to live a life that matters for the kingdom). After some sixty-plus years of knowing Jesus, I can verify that receiving these invitations every day is a tremendous honor and the source of amazing energy.

- *The Jesus way is a way of priorities.* And those priorities are abiding, loving one another, and bearing witness (John 15). Abiding in Christ provides me an ongoing source of energy. Loving one another results in a community of friends who have a relationship with God and are committed to living the same priorities that I am. Bearing witness points me to a mission field for life. These priorities provide the blueprint for my years on this earth.

- *The Jesus way is a way of process summarized in the Pitcher/Cup …Saucer/Plate metaphor.* God pours Himself into me and forms me into His image. During this process, His life in me spills out on other people, those who are excited about Jesus and those who are not. These relationships involve me in the everyday events of marriage, family, friends, church, work, neighborhood, and world. This involvement provides me with ways to connect to people and be a kingdom influence in their lives.

The Lord's work, done in the Lord's way, requires Lifestyle Leadership soil. When we do ministry God's way, He will bless with godly leaders as well as fruit for His kingdom.

HAVING DREAMS FOR MINISTRY IS ONE THING.
BEING INTENTIONAL IN MINISTRY IS ANOTHER.

Dear Lord, thank You for the model of growing leaders that Your Son gives us. He took twelve ordinary men, many of whom probably didn't see themselves as leaders, and radically changed their lifestyles. We still speak of these men centuries later— not because of the position they occupied, but because of their godly character and their lifestyle of commitment to Christ. Thank You for that example and for calling me to know and serve this Jesus.

Enable me, Lord, to see ministry as cultivating a soil that will grow people who are continually transformed by Your grace. Use my life to touch with Your love the people I live among and the people I lead. In the name of the Father, Son, and Holy Spirit I pray. Amen.

Before You Take the Next Step

What insight from this chapter particularly resonated with you? What statement in this chapter affirmed you in some way? Explain.

Which of the seven Leadership Intentionals is most firmly established in your life? Why do you think that is the case? Which intentional is least established in your life? Again, why do you that's the case?

Reflect on your life journey and ministry experience. List some instances of God's grace and faithfulness to you. Whom might you encourage with one of these stories?

What is one statement from this chapter that you will share with someone else in the next few days?

Jesus makes us get
rid of life as agenda
and take up life
as adventure.
— Leonard Sweet

Are Adults Really Teachable?
If So, What Do I Have to Offer Them?

Developing Healthy Adult Leaders and Healthy Adult Ministries

Having invested many years of my life and ministry in both youth and adults, I'd like to share some general observations. Youth live with fewer responsibilities; adults are gripped by the tentacles of responsibilities. Youth have energy to burn; adults are hunting for some energy to burn. Youth are flaky; adults are more responsible and grounded. Youth are willing to try new ideas; adults are often stuck in their ways. The belief system, lifestyle, and values of youth are still being formed; the belief system, lifestyle, and values of adults are often cemented. Youth live for the moment; adults are often driven by the moment, but they are concerned about the future. Youth think little about the consequences of their actions; adults are often living with such consequences. Youth often see a big world and a capable God; adults often see a big world and a less capable God. Youth often change more quickly, but not as permanently; adults often change more slowly, but more permanently

I made these observations—and I could go on!—as I led a college group (young adults), a church plant (people ranging in age from the cradle to the sixties), and a singles group (ages 23 to 35). As I share these three real-life stories from my leadership journey, you'll meet the group as they were when I first met them and then see the work God did in their lives. Let me point out that the seven timeless Leadership Intentionals for ministry also guided me in these areas of ministry as I worked to be sensitive to the culture and the generations of those to whom I was ministering (see chapters 15 and 16):

#1: Abiding for Myself (Soul Room)

#2: Abiding for Others (Soul Room)

#3: Developing a Structure for Lifestyle (Leadership Room)

#4: Asking Meaningful Questions (Leadership Room)

#5: Creating Space for "Holy Hanging Around" (Leadership Room)

#6: Modeling the Process (Soul Room, Leadership Room)

#7: Remembering—Always—That the Ministry Is God's, Not Mine

Lord God Almighty, Maker of heaven
and earth and Designer of the human lifespan, I come to You as an
adult praying for adults. When we're adults, life can weigh heavy,
time margins can seem nonexistent, the voices crying to us can be
deafening, and the responsibilities can seem ever increasing. Lord, as
I abide in You, may I know the security only You can offer, the
wisdom and discernment only You can give, and the hope of Your
ongoing transformational work in my life. Grant me compassion and
insight for the adults among whom I live and lead. I ask this for the
glory of God and in the name of Jesus Christ, Your Son. Amen.

STORY #3: A COLLEGE GROUP WITH NO MAGNETIC NORTH

We arrived in Pasadena in 1968. Our nation was caught in the throes of Woodstock and Vietnam. Campuses were aflame with anger and protest. It was a time of sex, drugs, and "do your own thing." Yet God, in His grace, raised up the Jesus People movement. It was a challenging time for our country, for college students, and for Christians.

I found myself pastoring a small group of twenty to twenty-five students, most from Pasadena Community College, Cal Tech, Occidental College, and the University of Southern California. They knew Christ, but being the body of Christ as collegians was foreign to their experience. They were overwhelmed by the demands of college and the impossible-to-ignore cultural distractions—and thus found it hard to hear and respond to God's voice in the midst of all that was swirling around in their world.

I prayed, "God, what is on Your mind for these people? What are You already doing in them? How can I cooperate with You?" The time I spent in the Soul Room praying for them was heavy going. I sought God's direction and asked for insight, yet I often found my mind wandering. At Sunday-night open houses, I simply listened to the students, asked them questions, got to know them, and showed interest in their lives. I wanted to be with them in the Leadership Room as a servant, a listener, and an encourager. This time I spent with them needed to be an extension of my consistent praying for them in the Soul Room. Yet I often found myself feeling puzzled and challenged. I asked God how they as individuals and as a group could find their magnetic north in Him.

How would you develop Lifestyle Leadership soil among these college students? What message would you share and continue to share with them? What opportunities for growing in Christ would you provide them? What structure would you develop to spiritually nurture them during this challenging season of their lives?

Story #3: What God Did in the College Group That Had No Magnetic North

The college group had a regular Sunday-night gathering, but we didn't have a very clear sense of its purpose. Was it a social time? Was there to be any touch of gospel or suggestion that God was there? Was it a "come if you feel like it" time, or should we foster a sense of commitment? The questions I just asked you were crucial to determining the path of this ministry.

1. *What **message** would I share and continue to share?* As I prayed for this group of students, God began to show me that they needed to understand that life with Him involved more than just attending church. They needed to know Jesus as Savior and Companion, to know He's there when we feel terrific, alone, or discouraged, when we celebrate, or when we are standing at one of life's crossroads scratching our heads. God also wants His life in us to cause us to become someone we never imagined we could be.

These were just some aspects of the message the students needed to hear. And at the heart of the message was how intimacy with God transforms our character and attitudes, positions us in a community of growing Christians, brings us a rich and fulfilled life, and enables us to make a significant difference in our culture. God calls us to a lifestyle of intimacy with Him and His people and to the mission of sharing His hope and love in a lost world—and He raises up healthy leaders from this lifestyle.

2. *What* **opportunities** *should we provide so that students can grow in this lifestyle of intimacy with God, this lifestyle of abiding, loving one another, and bearing witness?* The desire for this kind of opportunity led us to change Sunday nights from a come-when-you-want gathering to a time of sharing with one another what we had discovered of God's presence as we had studied Scripture during the week. I invited the students to join an experiment, saying, "Here's how I need you to pray for me this week." I also invited them to pray for one another during the week. We would reconvene the following Sunday to ask questions like "How was your week? How was the history test? How's your roommate? How's your soul? How's your relationship with Jesus? How are those friends of yours I've been praying for?"

Our Sunday nights provided us a magnetic north both individually and as a group. Busy, young adults were beginning to grow. God was forming them into His image. This weekly gathering also transformed how the students came to worship on Sunday morning, why they came to socials, and whom they brought with them. It also changed our Sunday-morning class from being an endurance contest to being a place where the students expected to encounter God.

3. *What* **structure** *would we develop so that students could grow in this lifestyle together, not as isolated individuals, and to experience community in a world that is fractured by anger and hostility, bitterness and condemnation?* The college students were responding to Christ's invitations "Come to Me" and "Come, follow Me." They understood and were committed to abiding in God and His Word, loving one another, and bearing witness. They now had a weekly gathering time when they could share what God was giving them

in Scripture and be held accountable for the Pitcher/Cup... Saucer/Plate lifestyle process. Healthy Lifestyle Leadership soil was cultivated among these students and in this structure. This soil was the place where healthy leaders and a healthy culture grew.

Four years later, when we were preparing a college camp for 140 collegians, I raised a question with the senior pastor: "These college students are really responding to what God wants to do in their lives. May I challenge them to consider offering God the two years after they graduate to go anywhere on the face of the earth Jesus might lead them." He said yes. Grateful and excited, I decided I would simply ask, "Are you open to God's calling you to take the first two years after college to go anywhere in the world with the gospel of Christ?"

I still remember that evening. I asked the students to pray and consider the challenge. I made it clear that I wasn't inviting them to earn a gold star or my approval. I merely asked them to be open to the Spirit's nudge in this direction. Of 140 students at college camp, 105 stood up and said, "God, we're available."

Over the next year "The 105" met together once every six to eight weeks. Students who attended college out of the area came home for those four-hour weekend gatherings. We spent time in worship and prayer for our lives. Then I brought in a big globe and students prayed for countries on the side of the globe they could see. When we turned the globe, students prayed for other countries. This was the same group that began with no magnetic north, but then they discovered a lifestyle of intimacy with God.

As people abide in the Soul Room, God transforms them, and they become dynamic influencers in the Leadership Room. The paradigm of Soul Room/Leadership Room and the Pitcher/Cup... Saucer/Plate process provide for qualitative *and* quantitative growth. In three years time, I was speaking not to twenty or thirty, but to 200 or 250 students every Sunday morning. In four years, more than 280 students were participating in small groups where they shared their abiding (the Pitcher/Cup times). It is a myth to think that if you have quality, you can't have quantity—or that if you have quantity, you can't have quality. After all, God is Lord of the process.

Story #4: Pastoring a Church Plant

Several couples had been meeting for a few months on Sunday mornings, dreaming together about planting a church, and these forty adults invited me to become their first pastor.

The church founders wanted to start small groups right away. I had no argument with the idea, but I did have questions. What would be the purpose and structure of these groups? Would small groups be one among many competing options that our church would provide for people, or might these Koinonia groups become the true heart of the church? Could these Koinonia groups be a place of nurture for each person serving in Sunday school, on the worship team, as an usher, or in any other ministry area?

Well-meaning servants in the church get burned out when they aren't spiritually nurtured, when they don't belong to a community that offers encouragement, prayer, and accountability. So I wanted these founding members of the church—especially those involved in ministry—to experience the nourishment and strength that small groups offer. I also thought that, on occasion, a Koinonia group could serve together in some particular ministry role. Most important, I believed that this kind of small group would develop Lifestyle Leadership soil that would grow healthy leaders.

In the Soul Room, God and I had some significant conversations about this small-group ministry. Then, in the Leadership Room, the church founders and I talked and prayed together: "God, what are we hearing You say to us? What would bring You glory? What is key to building healthy community? God, show us Your will."

What are critical questions you would ask in this church plant opportunity? How would you develop Lifestyle Leadership soil among these adults? What message would you continue to share with these believers? What opportunities for growing in Christ would you provide them? What structure would you develop that would foster a lifestyle of abiding, loving one another, and bearing witness through the Pitcher/Cup…Saucer/Plate process?

Story #4: What God Did in the Church Plant

Planting a church is both an honor and a real leap of faith. Church plants are exciting, interesting, stretching, challenging, and—ideally—ordained and shaped by God.

1. *What* **message** *would I share and continue to share? What passion did these people, who wanted to establish a new and vibrant church, need to sense from my life and from my lips?* I talked to them about Joshua 1 and God's passion that "this book of the law shall not depart out of thy mouth; but thou shall meditate therein day and night" (verse 8, kjv). What an Old Testament picture of abiding in Scripture and in God's presence!

We see that when the nation of Israel entered the Promised Land, the men from the two-and-a-half tribes east of the Jordan were to leave their wives, children, and livestock and go with the other nine-and-a-half tribes to help them conquer the land. What a great picture of community! Those two-and-a-half tribes would be in the new land to support and stand with their brothers in the Lord. There, in that foreign place, they would—through their communion with God and in their community with one another—display the radiance of the God whose presence they followed!

Now consider Joshua 3 and 4. The children of Israel take rocks from a riverbed and build an altar. Why? Something happened here that they will tell their children and that their children will tell their own children. Telling one another what God has done in their lives is the lifestyle of the Upper Room lived out in communion, community, and commission. The passion of God's heart—that people become a community through their communion with Him and "that all the peoples of the earth might know that the hand of the LORD is powerful and so that you might always fear the LORD your God" (Joshua 4:24)—became the passion of the Israelites, and it must become our passion and lifestyle as well. That was my message for the church plant.

2. *What* **opportunities** *should we provide so that members of this church plant can grow in the lifestyle of abiding, loving one another, and bearing witness?* Small groups are often just another entrée on the smorgasbord of a developing church. They are just one of many offerings from which to choose. You like worship? Do worship. Like teaching? Do teaching. Like ushering? Do ushering. Like

women's things? Do women's things. You get the picture: there is something for everyone. We grow church bodies that have great diversity but few unifying traits. We haven't really built a unity—a community. We haven't approached the church as people in community called by God to the lifestyle of the Upper Room. Seldom do we collectively stand at the cross in communion with God, then—as individuals—grow into being a community, and finally go out into the world together in mission.

I wanted our Koinonia small groups to be a place where people could grow in the godly lifestyle we were preaching and teaching about. The groups would usually meet for eight weeks—the first week altogether and the other seven weeks in smaller groups and in different homes. By joining these groups, people expressed a longing to grow in intimacy with God and understood that growth involves a Pitcher/Cup…Saucer/Plate lifestyle. Participants came together weekly to share what God was teaching them in their Soul Room time with Him—what He was showing them in the passages everyone had been abiding in that week.

What does God do through this kind of small-group process? He forms us into His image—inwardly into Christlikeness and outwardly into a community. God Himself—Father, Son, and Spirit—lives in a community after which we are to model our lives. And, as small-group members scatter into the marketplace, they know the love-support and prayer-support of those in their group.

3. *What **structure** would we develop so that people who have been attending the new church could become godly leaders?* As people attending the church expressed a desire to participate in ministry or leadership, we affirmed their desire and, as their spiritual leaders, we wanted first of all to show genuine concern for their life, their soul-nurture, and their intimacy with God. We wanted to be a one-door church. Let me explain.

Before anyone served or led in any church program, we wanted that person to be involved in the abiding-community experience of Koinonia—living the lifestyle of abiding, loving one another, and bearing witness through the Pitcher/Cup…Saucer/Plate process. Koinonia was not one of many items on our smorgasbord of ministry options; it alone was the main course. It was not just for a few, but for everyone hungry for God. Small groups are where God forms individuals into His image. There the lifestyle that grows servant leaders is nurtured and strengthened. The fruit of this ever-growing relationship with God spills over into ushering, leading worship, working with youth, or doing any number of kingdom jobs. But first and foremost we set out to be a church of a common lifestyle.

Through Koinonia, we saw people respond to Christ's invitations "Come unto Me" and "Come, follow Me." Adults were growing in abiding in Christ, loving one another, and bearing witness. Healthy Lifestyle Leadership soil was cultivated among these adults hungry for God. This structure would be the center from which would emerge the leaders and the culture of this church plant. Small groups foster the intimacy with God for which we're designed, and it was thrilling to watch God bless this design.

Now this single door to church leadership may seem inflexible and exclusive, but listen to the story of a newcomer to our church plant. When he and his family began to visit our church, I invited him to meet with me that week. As we sat down together, I saw a look of concern on his face. I said, "My hunch is you think I'm here to enlist you to serve in one of our ministries." He confirmed my suspicions and explained that he had served as youth leader, Sunday-school teacher, and elder at his former church—and he was burned out.

I made this weary servant a promise: "I guarantee that no one will ask you to do anything in our church until you tell me you're ready." You should have seen him relax. He was amazed. I continued: "I would like you to consider one thing, though. I'm concerned about God restoring your soul and your wife's soul, so I'd like you to pray about being in Koinonia. I think that if you were to abide in God's Word and be part of a caring community, your relationship with Christ would be renewed and refreshed. At our church, we want members to be the people of God before they do the work of God."

He and his wife joined the group my wife and I facilitated. I watched freshness return to their love affair with the living God. Eighteen months later he felt ready to serve in a ministry in the church.

Some years after I had left the pastorate of that church, I ran into one of the original elders. I was pleased to hear him say, "Chuck, I want you to know all the structures you built are still in place. We are grateful." His statement meant that Koinonia groups—that people abiding in the Scriptures and loving one another—were still the basic design for this congregation. Process matters.

STORY #5: REACHING GEN-X SINGLES

A young-singles group had been without a pastor for six months. A friend asked if I might be open to serving in that position part-time—and I said, "No thanks." A few months later, he asked if I might speak at their Thursday-night meeting, their main weekly gathering. I agreed and had a wonderful night of interacting with between thirty-five and forty twenty-something singles in a private home in Newport Beach, California.

After that meeting, the leadership asked if I would fill in until they found a part-time pastor. I prayed, spoke with the Three about the possibility, and finally agreed to provide part-time pastoral leadership for three months by speaking Thursday nights and meeting with the leadership team weekly.

That leadership team was comprised of very capable men and women, all college graduates willing to give time and energy to this ministry. I wanted them to be together in the Word. I wanted the Spirit to use our time together to provide them with soul renewal and mental refreshment. So we walked through 1 Thessalonians and studied leadership. We prayed for one another when we were together and during the week.

One night I handed a group directory to each team member. After time in the Word and prayer, we then prayed for every person in the directory—nearly one hundred people. We prayed ten names at a time. Sometimes we merely mentioned a person's name before God. Other times, one of the leadership team prayed in greater detail because he or she knew the person. I encouraged these leaders to take notes as people prayed. I wanted them to get a sense of who was in the group and where the group was at. (I still remember being surprised when later one of the leaders said to another, "Why did we waste so much time tonight praying for all those people?" Yes, there were some on the team who still needed to learn about Lifestyle Leadership!)

Early on, when I stayed late on Thursday nights and met individuals for lunch, I began to get to know the members of the group. I asked questions, I learned life stories, and I listened for joys and discouragements. I was talking with bright, attractive up-and-comers, yet their stories of family-of-origin pain, marketplace struggles, and dating heartbreaks tore my heart.

My times in the Soul Room on their behalf were heavy going. I often found myself grieving as I prayed for these young adults. I asked God, "What would You like to do here? What is Your plan for these special people? God, I'm listening. Please show me."

What message would you share? What opportunities for growth would you provide? What structure would you provide to cultivate Lifestyle Leadership soil and nurture people spiritually?

Story #5: What God Did Among the Gen-X Singles

Many singles today have been deeply wounded in the marketplace, by the culture's commentaries, in relationships with members of the opposite sex, and by members of their family of origin. These people need healing. As I spent time in the Soul Room praying for the group of singles I was teaching, I suddenly heard God say to me, "Chuck, have you forgotten that I'm the Healer? But I can't heal people unless they're willing to be with Me." This God-given insight sparked ideas about the next steps of ministry I would take.

1. *What **message** would I share and continue to share?* Basically, I wanted to tantalize these remarkable and hurting people with the greatness and the grace of God. I said to them, "You are a people who stand in front of the mirror and let it define you. I want you to discover the excitement of standing in front of God and letting Him define you." Week after week I talked about the greatness of God and about how, when He impacts a life, He impacts a lifestyle. I shared that when He comes to live within us by the Holy Spirit, the lifestyle He calls us to is a lifestyle of abiding in Him, loving one another, and bearing witness to Him.

As I thought about this all-important message, I saw my time with these people (I ended up staying three-and-a-half years) as an opportunity to help them follow God more fully and develop a lifestyle where they could experience the nurture of their soul and the blessing of community. I also wanted them to be able to become church leaders and people who would impact their culture and the world for the Lord.

2. *What **opportunities** should we provide so that these singles could experience all this and more?* God led us to develop a Sunday-night group we called "Walkers," a name based on Genesis 17:1 where God says, "I am God Almighty; walk before me" (NASB). Walkers was designed to help people walk in the presence of God and to help those who were hungry for Him satisfy that hunger.

In Walkers, individuals signed a covenant to meet alone with God daily in Scripture and prayer as well as with a small group weekly for about eight weeks. We set the bar high at thirty minutes of time alone with the Lord daily. When we met, we began all together for a brief time of worship and prayer. Then we met in small groups to share what God had been showing us since our previous meeting, and we closed with sharing together in the large group.

What was the fruit of Walkers? Singles became rooted in the love of God through Scripture. Men began to grow in their love for Him, and He began to shape their attitudes, values, and schedules. Women began to discover God as Friend, Lord, and Companion. The cultural pressures of hunting for a mate moved to the background, and relationship with God came to the foreground. They began to see themselves and God differently. They saw the opposite sex differently. Out of this growing group of singles came numerous godly marriages. These couples are still growing as mates and now as parents.

But first there had to be a solid foundation. The foundation of abiding bore the fruit of such activities as mission trips, worship, teaching Sunday school, and other expressions of love for God. These Gen-X singles became intentional about creating space for God, and their intentionality enabled Lifestyle Leadership soil to develop.

3. *What **structure** would we develop so that these singles could grow in their understanding of God's great love for them and experience His*

healing touch in a community of His people? For too long we in the church have developed programs that tap into people's interests and skills, but we have not developed an accountability structure that nurtures their soul, heals their woundedness, or helps them develop a godly lifestyle characterized by abiding in Christ.

We saw Lifestyle Leaders begin to emerge from the Walkers. These individuals became people of influence who seasoned the whole group. At our Thursday night large group meeting, individuals from the Walkers groups reached out to newcomers, asked interactive questions, and shared the warm love of Christ. Their hunger for God, their communion with Him, and the community He was forming—all this began to change each ministry gathering as well as the entire culture. As one man observed, "The entire substance of our conversations at the restaurant after Thursday night is richer."

The change was occurring because of what God was given the freedom to do in the organism, not because of a better organizational approach to ministry. Whenever the organism experiences greater life, we must be thorough and effective in our organizational response, but we don't start with organization. Health and lasting fruit come only from organism. So people who had grown in Lifestyle Leadership soil were soon invited into Positional Leadership. As the Lifestyle Leadership soil became richer, Thursday night attendance grew from about 50 to over 250 each week.

In our last nine-week walk, 164 women and 158 men were involved in Walkers groups. We continued to share God's call to abide in Christ, to live as branches connected to the Vine, and to create space for God in our lives. The invitation to participate in Walkers was extended again and again, providing an opportunity for hungry singles to abide in Christ and eventually become Lifestyle Leaders.

And the fact that they were hungry for God was key to our ministry. In fact, we introduced Walkers by asking people, "Are you hungry for God?" People who have known Christ for ten years, seekers, and everyone in between can be hungry for God. About a year into the ministry, we began to see all kinds of people join Walkers because they were hungry for God. I'll share one story.

Our Thursday night gathering had ended when a young man walked over to me and asked if he should join Walkers. When I asked him, "Are you hungry for God?" he said yes, but that he wasn't a Christian. He had been raised Jewish. "Well, are you hungry for God?" I asked again. Before he could answer, I continued: "And to feed this hunger, are you willing to read the Bible and do the daily Bible studies?" He was. "And are you willing to be part of a men's group where you will share your discoveries?" He was. "Then I think it would be great for you to be in Walkers."

He joined for his first walk, and he continued to be in walk after walk, each time creating space for God and being in the Word. Enfolded by the brothers, he was a faithful participant on Thursday nights, and he sometimes attended Sunday-morning services, retreats, and informal gatherings. His hunger for God moved him to the birthing room eighteen months later at a Promise Keepers event in Los Angeles. As he responded to the invitation to receive Christ, between sixty and seventy men wanted to go forward with him to celebrate the birth of their new brother.

Today, over ten years later, he continues to be a follower of Christ. He leads a Pitcher/Cup…Saucer/Plate lifestyle, is married with three children, serves as an elder in a church, and is an influential leader in his workplace. By feeding his hunger for God in the Soul Room, he established a lifestyle that further flourished and continued when he came to the Savior. To God be the glory!

HAVING DREAMS FOR MINISTRY IS ONE THING.
BEING INTENTIONAL IN MINISTRY IS ANOTHER.

Father, Son, and Spirit, I'm so tempted to treat the Soul Room as a ministry consultation session instead of primarily as an intimate place of personal communion and refreshment. Your love, Your grace, and Your patience with me are so amazing. Forgive me when my relationship with You grows thin through life and ministry busyness. Ignite in me a tremendous passion to intentionally abide, love others, and bear witness—and from that Lifestyle Leadership soil, grow me into an effective leader.

Then, in my places of influence and leadership, show me how to design ministries where people who are hungry for God become the vital center from which the rest of the ministry grows. I ask this in the name of the Father, the excellent Gardener; in the name of the Son, the life-giving Vine; and in the name of the Spirit, the One who breathes His life into me. Amen.

Before You Take the Next Step

What insight from this chapter particularly resonated with you? What statement in this chapter affirmed you in some way? Explain.

What specific insight from these ministry stories challenged you? How will you respond?

What is one statement from this chapter that you will share with someone else in the next few days?

Are you currently rooted in Lifestyle Leadership soil? If so, cite some evidence, give God praise, and keep tending to your growth. If not, what steps might you take to become more rooted in Lifestyle Leadership soil? Be specific.

We live in the midst of challenging and often painful generational conflicts, yet God desires that "one generation would praise [His] works to another." How do we enable this to happen?

What Generational Changes
Are Shaping Our Culture and Its Values?

Building Bridges Between the Generations

- A professional pilot reports that American Airlines has spent one-quarter of a million dollars training pilots to understand generational differences. They invested that money because there was such generational conflict in the airplane cockpits. This mandatory training became necessary so that we passengers would have a healthier and safer cockpit crew when we fly American.

- A student in a seminary course shared the following: "I am manager of a local Container Store, and all the employees are Gen-Xers. We enjoy a great sense of teamwork and respect for one another, and the store is doing well. The problem we are facing is that a Baby Boomer has applied to work with us. We are struggling about whether to hire her because we Gen-Xers begin with relationship and then do the work, but our experience with Boomers is that they begin with task, and relationships are of secondary importance. We don't know if we want this dynamic in our store and our work environment. We have trouble trusting a person who is a Boomer."

The God-process moves us from *communion* with The Three to *community* among God's people. Now we look beyond the Soul Room to the Leadership Room of the world as we respond to Jesus' *commission* to us regarding how to live as His people among those who have yet to become followers of Christ. We are asking God to use us as a kingdom influence in the world—a world comprised of distinctly different generations. Before we enter the Leadership Room of the world, though, we must address essential issues in the Soul Room.

In chapters 15-18, we will gain insight and understanding about how to live among those we wish to engage with the good news of Christ. Often, Christians have used labels like "pre-Christian," "non-Christian," or even "pagans" and treated these people like a category rather than as individuals loved by God. In the coming chapters, we will simply talk about people without using these labels. First, we'll pray.

Father, Son, and Holy Spirit, because of *Your compassion for the world, I belong to You today. Whenever I meet with You in the Soul Room, please give me renewed excitement about the mission of living among the people of this world who don't yet know You—and an understanding of how to do that for Your truth and glory. Use my life for Your kingdom. For Your glory I pray this. Amen.*

THE DRIVING FORCES THAT SHAPE OUR CULTURE AND ITS VALUES

I believe that strong generational and societal forces continually shape our culture, impacting the church, our personal life, and our family life. Identifying and understanding those forces is therefore fundamental to effective ministry.

Understanding Generational Differences – The year you were born positions you in a specific generation, and that positioning is significant. In 1991, William Strauss and Neil Howe authored *Generations: The History of America's Future, 1584 to 2069*, a book that has greatly helped both the business community and the church better understand societal attitudes and changes. Consider their premise:

> We describe what we call the "peer personality" of your generation. You may share many of these attributes, some of them, or almost none of them. Every generation includes all kinds of people. Yet... you and your peers share the same "age location" in history, and your generation's collective mind-set cannot help but influence you—whether you agree with it or spend a lifetime battling against it.[1]

Before we look at specifics about the generations of our day, it is important to note two significant weaknesses in Strauss and Howe's theory. First is their cyclical view of history and, an outgrowth of this premise, their contention that history repeats itself every fifth generation. As Christians we believe that history is linear and is moving toward consummation in Christ's return. A second significant weakness of the *Generations* theory is its very American perspective. Most other cultures could not connect with the authors' viewpoint. Strauss and Howe nevertheless offer valuable insights about the people the church is both comprised of and reaching out to today.

Twentieth-Century Generations

Name	Birth Dates
G.I.	1901-1924
Silent	1925-1945
Boomers	1946-1964
Gen-X	1964-1984
Millennials	1984-2000?[2]

The G.I. Generation: 1901-1924 — Children born just after 1900 were America's first Boy Scouts and Girl Scouts and, years later, America's first "senior citizens."[3] They were young adults during the Great Depression and World War II, and the Boom Explosion came during their senior years. From this generation came seven presidents of our country and numerous well knowns such as Walt Disney, Bob Hope, John Wayne, Katherine Hepburn, Jimmy Stewart, Walter Cronkite, Billy Graham, and Lee Iaococca. They were totally impacted by the Second World War with its bloody battles, discouraging periods, military defeats, and eventual victory. They lived the American Dream of upward mobility, and homeownership reached the highest level of any generation.[4]

The Silent Generation: 1925 to 1945 — Children during the Great Depression, young people during World War II, and midlife adults during the Boom Awakening, members of the Silent Generation experienced VE-Day, VJ-Day, the Korean War, the Russians entering space, the establishment of the Peace Corps, the birth of the Civil Rights movement, the assassinations of John F. Kennedy, Bobby Kennedy, and Martin Luther King, Jr., the landing on the moon by Neil Armstrong,

Woodstock, and Watergate. The primary leaders of the feminist movement in the seventies also came from this generation.

Although no one from this generation has served as our president, members have played significant supporting roles to presidents as evidenced by Pierre Salinger (Kennedy), Bill Moyers (Johnson), Dick Cheney (Ford and Bush), James Baker III (Reagan), and John Sununu (Bush). Other notable members of the Silent Generation are Jackie Kennedy, Rosalynn Carter, and Barbara Bush as well as William F. Buckley, Jr., Sandra Day O'Connor, Clint Eastwood, Elvis Presley, Jack Nicholson, Ted Koppel, and Barbra Streisand.

This generation, caught between the get-it-done G.I. generation and the self-absorbed Boom generation, experienced great frustration. Yet they have been a calming influence in a G.I.-built world that could have splintered into pieces under the Baby Boomers' frontal attack.[5]

The Boomer Generation: 1946 to 1964 A huge baby boom followed World War II, and this new generation numbered 79 million whereas the Silent Generation had numbered only 49 million. Most Boomers were children as the war ended and TV was beginning. When they were young, Jonas Salk developed the polio vaccine, and the Sputnik lifted off. Their young adulthood was marked by their sit-ins, concerts, riots, flag burnings, Vietnam protests, and Woodstock. During the Boom Awakening or "Consciousness Revolution" (1967-1980), Boomers protested against the Vietnam War, napalm, the nuclear age, poverty, blind devotion to institutions, etc. and made it clear that their parents' values needed a major overhaul.[6] "The Boom ethos remained a deliberate antithesis to everything G.I.: spiritualism over science, gratification over patience, negativism over positivism, fractiousness over conformity, rage over friendliness, self over community."[7] Christopher Lasch views this quest for self as producing the "culture of narcissism" that has continued as the central theme throughout the Boomers' later adult years.[8]

The Gen-X Generation: 1965-1984 — For the most part, Gen-Xers were children during the Woodstock years of sit-ins, the Vietnam War, rallies against Vietnam, heavy drug use, the sexual revolution, flag burnings, and other expressions of anger and opposition to many of society's institutions.

Some of the well knowns of this generation include Brooke Shields, Mike Tyson, Lisa Bonet, Mary Lou Retton, and Gary Coleman. Strauss and Howe note the following:

> An awakening era that seemed euphoric to young adults was, to [younger Gen-Xers], a nightmare of self-immersed parents, disintegrated homes, schools with conflicting missions, confused leaders, a culture shifting from G to R ratings, new public-health dangers, and a "Me Decade" economy that tipped toward the organized old and away from the voiceless young. "Grow up fast" was the adult message.[9]

As one Baby Boomer observes, "As [my] generation went about trying to fulfill its needs, it dismantled the very institutions that made our childhoods secure."[10]

With those institutions gone, it's no surprise that Gen-Xers have been hit harder by divorce and consequently grown up in more complex families than any other American generation: they deal with "step-thises, half-that's, significant others, and strangers at the breakfast table beyond what any other child generation ever knew."[11] Furthermore, parents of Gen-Xers were more friends than parents, "always understanding; they never get very angry. There are no boundaries or limits set."[12] On top of all this, Gen-Xers are bearing the financial burdens of a greatly imbalanced trade deficit, an overwhelming national debt, and an inadequate Social Security system. It's hard for them to dream because of the emotional, financial, social, and moral climate of today's world.

The Millennial Generation or Gen-Y: 1984-2000? — The world Millennials are growing up in is quite different from the one in which the Gen X-ers were raised:

> First-wave Millennials are riding a powerful crest of protective concern, dating back to the early 1980s, over the American childhood environment. ...At dinner tables around the nation, 40-year-old parents are telling small children to stay away from drugs, alcohol, AIDS, teen pregnancy, profanity, TV ads, unchaperoned gatherings, and socially aggressive dress or manners.

> Grown-up Boomer radicals who once delighted in shocking their own moms and dads now surprise themselves with their own strictly perfectionist approach to child nurture. In growing numbers, fathers are demanding "daddy-track" work schedules that allow them more time at home to raise their young children.

> Where [Gen X-er] kids were best known as latchkeys, throwaways, boomerangs, and other terms implying that adults would just as soon have them disappear, Millennials have so far been perceived very differently—as kids whom adults wish to guard with dutiful care.[13]

Public education reflects this parental concern for their children's development and welfare. Kindergarten is more academic, elementary schools emphasize moral values (respect, cooperation, etc.), and high schools reward community service hours. Boomer parents are establishing firm rules for their children and paying careful attention to any violations of those rules—a sharp contrast to the way the Boomers' Silent parents would offer information and let Boomers make up their own minds.

Obviously, time will determine the well knowns of this generation, the oldest of whom is only twenty-three as I write this. Likewise, only time will reveal what this generation will be remembered for. Yet their adolescent years are not easy:

> We [adults] have evolved to the point where we believe driving is support, being active is love, and providing any and every opportunity is selfless nurture. We are a culture that has forgotten how to *be* together.[14]

Furthermore, family—which today is defined quite loosely—does not support young people the way it used to, and divorce is widespread. (In 1940, 2 percent of America's married population dealt with the tragedy of divorce; as of 2002, 43 percent of first-time marriages were ending in separation or divorce.[15]) The adolescent journey is getting longer because young people have no one helping them along the way. The seeds being sown by the Millennial Generation's abandonment of young people cannot bear good fruit for them or for society.[16]

OUR RESPONSE TO GENERATIONAL DIFFERENCES

In the remainder of this chapter, we'll look at various ways we can, in light of these very real generational differences, be bridge builders for our Lord. Our work begins in the Soul Room.

As we think about our own generation and identify the generations of the people in our lives, we may uncover some confusion and hurt. There is no better place to deal with that hurt than the Soul Room where you are always warmly welcomed and fully accepted by the Father, the Son, and the Holy Spirit. You are free to bleed, to rejoice, to repent, and to exchange old ideas for new ideas. You are free to be honest—and we must be honest about the existence of the generational walls, about the injuries we have sustained from people of other generations, and about the lack of compassion we often show to people of other generations. These walls—resulting from such factors as misunderstanding, judgmentalness, criticalness, hurt feelings, feeling superior, and emotional distance—hinder the work of God's Spirit in our lives and within His kingdom. We must also be honest about the hurting world, where hurts stem from family-of-origin experiences as well as generational hurts.

In the Soul Room we are not seeking a new program or a never-been-tried plan for evangelism. Instead, we are in the presence of the Father, Son, and Holy Spirit for a time of silence and prayer. We are reflective, listening, and responsive. Invite the Living God to meet with you and to pour Himself into the cup of your life. When the Spirit releases you, read on.

Celebrating the Good about Each Generation — For the next few minutes, give God thanks for your life and for the generation of which you are a part. Celebrate your time and place in His-story. Consider, too, the ways your good and wise God has grown you into His image because you are part of your particular generation.

Acknowledging Generational Walls and Injuries — You may be surprised to learn that seeing the world, living in the world, and engaging the world for the gospel will quickly cause generational issues to surface. We may, for instance, be too sensitive about loud music, sexy dress, a frozen demeanor, a lack of emotion, a display of emotion, someone making fun of another, tattoos, unique hairdos, noisy cars, bragging, being ignored, sarcasm, a person's dishonesty, a domineering style, crude speech, a judgmental air, or continual put-downs. We may be shocked by our own disgust, criticalness, or aloofness toward people who are different from us. We create "Them" and "Us" clubs. We arrogantly exude the superior attitude of missionary toward mission field.

But wait! We are sitting with the Father, the Son, and the Holy Spirit—and They gently remind us how we used to be. We are suddenly crushed by our fleshly "holier than thou" attitude. We are confronted by our ongoing need to be transformed into the character of the Lord Jesus. We are so unlike Him who lives in us. After all, He is immediately drawn to people from every generation. We are often repulsed by them; the Trinity always engages them. So we must pray: *God, forgive me for my critical nature. I am too often hostile or indifferent toward people who are different from me. I plead with You: by Your grace, continue to transform me. By the power of Your Spirit, make me embody the gospel and engage others with Your love and compassion.*

This kind of transformation happens in the Soul Room, and that transformation is to impact our lifestyle in the Leadership Room of the world and the culture. As I've said, the Soul Room is a place of community, of communion, of interaction, of relationship. It is a place for God's deep transforming work that enables us to think, live, and act as Jesus would. Dallas Willard describes the process this way:

> Spiritual formation for the Christian basically refers to the Spirit-driven process of forming the inner world of the human self in such a way that it becomes like the inner being of Christ himself. ... In the degree to which spiritual formation in Christ is successful, the outer life of the individual becomes a natural expression or outflow of the character and teachings of Jesus. Christian spiritual formation is focused entirely on Jesus. Its goal is an obedience or conformity to Christ that arises out of an inner transformation accomplished through purposive interaction with the grace of God in Christ. Obedience is an essential outcome of Christian spiritual formation (John 13:34,35;14:21)....
>
> We must understand that spiritual formation is not only formation of the spirit or inner being of the individual, though that is both the process and the outcome. It is also formation by the Spirit of God and by the spiritual riches of Christ's continuing incarnation in his people.[17]

We can build bridges between the generations when God—by His grace—transforms us. This God-process of inner formation results in the outer expression of His love in a hurting and "in need of Jesus" world. The Holy Spirit's aliveness in us and presence with us fuels this process: He shapes and reshapes our thoughts, attitudes, character, personality, and DNA so that Christlike patterns are the inevitable and often unconscious expression of the Spirit's work.

Remembering God's Heart for the Generations — In our desire to reach other generations with the good news of Jesus' love, we are to turn to our heavenly Father for guidance and help, confident that nothing is impossible for Him. Furthermore, God has a heart for the generations. Again and again throughout Scripture, He reminds us that He is faithful to all generations (Psalm 89:1, 100:5). Every generation is to remember God's faithfulness to earlier generations (Exodus 12:41-42), and every generation is to follow His commands (Exodus 27:20-28:1). In light of God's faithfulness to all generations, you can be confident that the Father, the Son, and the Holy Spirit join you as a team concerned about the generations you are reaching out to. In fact, the members of the Holy Trinity are excited to have you join Them. They have been waiting for you.

BUILDING BRIDGES: A STEP-BY-STEP PROCESS

Consider the following metaphor by John Stott, a pastor, theologian, and statesman whose heart beats for the entire globe:

> A bridge is a means of communication between two places which would otherwise be cut off from one another by a river or ravine. It makes possible a flow of traffic which without it would be impossible.... Throughout the history of the Church, Christians have tried to relate the biblical message to their particular culture.[18]

The church is indeed involved in the mission of bridge building, of building bridges between God's truth and widely varying cultural viewpoints and lifestyles. If we are to succeed in this effort, then "we have to take seriously both the biblical text and the contemporary scene... Only then shall we discern the connections between them and be able to speak the divine Word to the human situation with any degree of sensitivity and accuracy."[19] Michael Green adds this observation:

> While bridge building is the fundamental need for the church in contemporary society, a great many churches have not really begun. They have not even learned to build bridges within the church itself. The worshippers attend and then disperse. The pastor falls out with the organist. There is not much social interaction. The majority, I dare say, do not belong to any group that meets midweek. They simply keep up the tradition of Sunday churchgoing and may well not know the names of the people they sit next to in church. ... It may be likened to a body, but a church like this is a body with many detached limbs. Once there is some sort of bridge building within the church itself, it is much easier to build bridges to the people who live in the locality.[20]

I appreciate this honest and convicting description of the lack of bridge building—of relationship building across the generations—

within the local church today. Granted, I believe that bridge building must occur not only across the generations but within the generations. Developing and nurturing friendships is an essential for God's people, for people being transformed within by Christ and then living as leaders in His church and the world.

> Remembering what they shared is key to building relationships.

Now walk with me through this bridge-building process. First use it within your local congregation and then with people in your circle of influence—people at work and in your neighborhood, people you regularly see at the grocery store and at your kids' sporting events. May bridge building become a dynamic aspect of our response to God's call to unity in His church and a tangible response to His command to evangelize in the world.

So what exactly can you and I do to begin to build or strengthen bridges across the generations within the church—and beyond? Begin with yourself. Go to the Soul Room and enjoy the presence of the Father, the Son, and the Holy Spirit. Share your desire to be used to build bridges—to establish new friendships—between people of different generations within your church and outside your church. Then, still in the Soul Room, begin to abide for others (remember chapter 9?). Using the church directory or a list of people you want to reach, begin to pray for them by name and listen for any thoughts God might give you.

Next, led by the Holy Spirit, go from the Soul Room to the Leadership Room. Envision an event—worship, Bible study, a social gathering—for the people you want to meet. Then, when you attend the gathering, ask God to give you eyes to see the specific people He wants you to reach out to. Let Him lead you as you listen and ask questions about their family, their dog, their work, their vacation, their hobbies, their week, their…, their…, their…, their…. Show that you are genuinely interested in their lives. Allow the Holy Spirit to guide your conversations and be ready to obey if He nudges you to act ("Why don't we sit together in worship this Sunday?" or "Would you like to grab a cup of coffee this week?").

Later, when you are again in the Soul Room, give thanks to God for the particular people with whom you connected and pray for each person you met. Before you move on, file in your memory (and maybe on paper!) what you learned about people during your conversations with them. Remembering what they shared is key to building relationships. Before you see your new friends again, you might phone them. Let them know you enjoyed talking with them. Follow up on anything specific they shared earlier—and realize that some people will be warm and responsive; others, quieter and more hesitant about engaging in conversation. Find security in God's presence with you. Remember it takes time to develop the trust that is key to friendship. Some seeds of friendship will blossom and bloom rather soon, and others may not bloom for a long time. That's why this effort to build bridges is not a one-time exercise. Instead it will become—by God's grace as you spend time with Him in the Soul Room—a lifestyle fueled by the Holy Spirit.

The following six words offer guidelines for your daily bridge-building lifestyle. By God's grace, may this strategy—which I call "Being Sent into the World 2LAF" ("two laugh")—enable us to live more passionately for God's glory in our hurting world.

SENT INTO THE WORLD 2LAF

L... LISTEN *We are sent into the world to listen.*

Lord, may I listen not in order to respond, but to understand. May I listen not to find fault, but to gain insight. Father, enable me to listen with ears, eyes, facial expressions, and body language. Regardless of the speaker's generation and whether that person is among the abandoned, the disenfranchised, or the successful, he or she longs for someone to listen. By Your transforming grace, enable me to listen as the Lord Jesus has listened to me.

L... LOVE *We are sent into the world to love.*

Great Enabler, free me to love not with an agenda, but with no agenda. May I love not with ulterior motives, but with open heart and open arms. Lord , may I love not in hopes of a specific response, but regardless of the person's response. By Your transforming grace, enable me to love people unconditionally as the Lord Jesus has loved me.

A… ACCEPT *We are sent into the world to accept.*

Holy Spirit, enable me to accept people for who they are and where they are today. Prompt in me questions and compassionate curiosity so that I may get to know people as unique individuals. May I show my acceptance of them in my conversation and by the time I spend and invest in them. By Your transforming grace, enable me to accept people as You have accepted me in the Beloved, Your Son and my Savior, Jesus Christ.

A… APPRECIATE *We are sent into the world to appreciate.*

Holy Spirit, as You live within me, enable me to speak a word of appreciation for something specific about the people I meet. In this world that extends acceptance based on one's performance, may I extend Your acceptance that is based on a person's being wonderfully created by You. In generations reeling from broken homes and broken dreams, may I provide a smile, an embrace, a word of appreciation— and use it as a cup of cool water for a thirsty soul.

F… FORGIVE *We are sent into the world after receiving God's forgiveness.*

Lord God, I ask Your forgiveness. You know how I feel when I look at those who do not follow Jesus. You know when my heart is cold and when I feel disgusted. You know how often they annoy me and offend me. I know You can't use me in Your world with my heart like that. So, Father, please forgive my sinful attitudes, cleanse me so I can be an effective representative for You in the world. By Your transforming grace, enable me to realize that people are not the enemy; they are victims of the enemy.

F… FORGIVE *We are sent into the world to point people to forgiveness in Jesus.*

Lord God, having been forgiven by You, may I extend forgiveness and point others to the forgiveness available to them in Your Son. Use me to help people weighed down by failure, shame, and brokenness to discover that, in Your presence at the cross, they can find forgiveness and love through the blood of Christ. There they can receive from You a new beginning in life, a new dignity, a new direction, a new hope, and a new community. Enable me to live as one who knows Your forgiveness, forgives others, and heralds the news of forgiveness in Jesus Christ.

Sent Into the World 2LAF—
Listen, Love, Accept, Appreciate, Forgive, and Forgive

After we have spent time in the Soul Room, God's Spirit leads us into the Leadership Room where we find...

- trapped people enslaved in their God-rebellion and sin
- unique people positioned within a specific generation
- hurting people confined by generational walls resulting from misunderstanding and insecurity
- wounded people who need to see the wonders of God in their life

Regardless of your specific generation or mine, each of us is to go to all generations as an ambassador for Christ and the aroma of the Holy Spirit. We are sent into the world to enable people 2LAF.

WE WILL TELL THE NEXT GENERATION THE PRAISEWORTHY DEEDS OF THE LORD. (PSALM 78:4)

Dear Father, Creator of human life, I thank You for Your hand on my life. You are my personal God and the God of the generations. But You are not the God of the generational walls. Create in me not only a greater hunger for You, but also greater compassion for people. Enable me, Holy Spirit, to reach out with love to those in other generations as well as my own. And the world awaits, God, so send me. Lord God, go before me. Lord God, lead me. May You, the Pitcher, fill me to overflowing so that the Saucer of my relationships and the Plate of events will be rich with Your love and grace. I pray this in the transforming name of the Father, Son, and Holy Spirit. Amen.

Before You Take the Next Step

What specific thought in this chapter stimulated or challenged your thinking?

In which generation do you find yourself? How do you feel about your place among the other generations?

With which generation do you find it easiest to get along? Hardest? Why?

As you prepare 2LAF, who are some specific people God is putting on your heart? Write down their names so you will remember to pray for them.

*The philosophical shift from
the Enlightenment Era to the
Postmodern Era… will have
ramifications for us for at
least the next one hundred
years. It is vital that we
understand as much as we
can about this shift because it
will affect how we will do
ministry in the coming years.*
— Jimmy Long

What Major Paradigm Shift
Is Shaping Our Culture and Its Values?

Moving from Modernity to Postmodernity

Over the last fifty years, a major societal shift—a movement from the foundational philosophic paradigm of modernism to the paradigm of postmodernism—has been occurring in our culture and in the world at large. This change means that the way people think and live today is radically different from the way they thought and lived just fifty or so years ago. Like the generational changes we looked at in the previous chapter, these major societal changes compel us to rethink how we share the gospel with people who don't yet know Jesus.

In fact, the better we understand this shift from modernity to postmodernity, the more effectively we will be messengers in today's world. Toward that end, consider the following insightful picture of this shift offered by Dr. Millard Erickson in his book *The Postmodern World: Discerning the Times and the Spirit of Our Age*:

> **Gunsmoke** was a popular television series for approximately ten years… In spite of all the violence and even killing that took place, there was a moral quality to the program. Honesty, loyalty, and courage were all highly prized and regularly displayed. Right and wrong were objective. Good and evil were clearly contrasted. …
>
> A transitional program, in terms of modernism and postmodernism, is *L.A. Law*. Here we have the usual flexibility of moral standards…There

> seems to be an underlying assumption that there is a moral right and a moral wrong, and yet the determination or the interpretation of that right or wrong is based on a given community's standards. ...
>
> Contrast these programs with *Seinfeld*, perhaps the paradigmatic postmodern program of the 1990s. Not only do the characters not display moral fiber, they do not even think in terms of moral issues. There concerns are, from a moral standpoint, trivial. They are interested in pleasure, amusement, curiosity. ...Extremely seldom, if ever, are questions of moral rightness or wrongness of an action considered. Rather, personal convenience becomes a major factor.[1]

Dr. Erickson concludes that *Seinfeld* is "telling a story about the world. There is no objective right and wrong, only what forwards one's own cause, or helps or hurts one's own community."[2]

In this chapter, we will compare and contrast modernity (the mind-set of fifty years ago) and postmodernity (the mind-set of today). We will also consider the influence of postmodern philosophy on the way people think and live today as well as some of the myths of postmodernity. Finally, we will reflect on ways to build bridges to postmodern people who have yet to become followers of Christ so that we connect with them in their world.

Dear Father, Creator of the world and of all *humanity, create in me an eagerness to understand and relate to people who live and think differently than I do. Give me compassion to see them as Jesus does as well as energy for prayer and servanthood so that I may one day see them come to Jesus and grow as His disciples. Continue to form me into Your image so that I will be an effective tool in Your hands, a tool for engaging people of postmodernity thinking and living. I ask this in the name of the Father, the Son, and the Holy Spirit. Amen.*

SOCIETAL CHANGES: THE SITUATION

As discussed in the previous chapter, generational changes cause issues to develop between the generations. Societal changes, however, cause issues to occur within all generations. These issues—more far-reaching and significant than generational changes—influence the thinking and practices of an entire culture, and you and I are in the midst of a major cultural paradigm shift in how people think and live. Jimmy Long, the longtime director of InterVarsity Christian Fellowship's Blue Ridge Region, puts this current shift in historical context for us in his excellent book *Emerging Hope: A Strategy for Reaching Postmodern Generations*. He lists history's most significant paradigm shifts as follows:

1. Hellenistic/Roman (A.D. 300-600)
2. Medieval (A.D. 600-1500)
3. Enlightenment/Modern (A.D. 1500-2000)
4. Postmodern/Emerging (A.D. 1968-?)[3]

Although opinions differ as to the best labels and most accurate dates, these paradigm shifts nevertheless provide us with a framework for viewing not only our culture as it changes but also for seeing the events, forces, and ideas behind these changes.

In the past, major paradigm shifts have moved at glacial speeds, but with the globalization, communication, and transportation of our day, the changes have occurred more quickly, more broadly, and more deeply than in previous eras. It is therefore crucial that we who are God's people in this postmodern culture are aware of the changes in thought and lifestyle that are becoming the norm for the world in which we live. We must understand the people with whom we live and work, the people to whom we embody and tell the news of God's love, forgiveness, and transformation. In this discussion, I am going to use the terms *Enlightenment/Modern* and *Emerging/ Postmodern*. We'll begin by noting some of the distinctions between these two eras, starting with the significant change that has occurred in the perceived basis of our identities:

> Prior to the Enlightenment... people said, "I belong, therefore I am." Under the Enlightenment's influence, people said, "I think, therefore I am." Postmodern people now seem to be saying, "I feel, therefore I am," or "I shop, therefore I am," or "I look good, therefore I am," or "I disobey, therefore I am," or "I doubt, therefore I am" or "I am, so what?" We also observe the "retribalism" of much of the West—as peer groups, subculture, and ethnic groups produce an "I belong, therefore I am" source of identity once again.[4]

Dr. Jonathan Campbell, in his doctoral dissertation at Fuller Seminary's School of Intercultural Studies, discusses six aspects of the cultural shift from the modern to the postmodern eras—world view, philosophy, society, organization, strategy, and religion. Here are some of the forty-five differences he identifies:

- **Philosophy**: People of modernity operate from a base of reason, scientific empiricism, and pluralism while postmodernity people operate from a base of emotion, intuition, and relativism.

- **Society**: The modernity view regards progress as inevitable, and people's goals are security and success. Postmodernity people view progress as questionable, and they strive for pleasure and identity.

- **Religion**: People of modernity are religious/institutional and experience disenchantment, while postmodernity people are spiritual/relational and are experiencing re-enchantment. People of modernity build on truth and evidence/apologetic, while postmodernity people build on beliefs and experience/incarnational.[5]

We can view and experience such changes as either stressors and threats or as opportunities for personal growth as we herald the news of Christ in this era of emerging postmodernity.

Now, returning to Jimmy Long's discussion of the Enlightenment/Modern and the Emerging/Postmodern eras, we'll consider three of the primary shifts he identifies.

Moving from Objective Truth…to Subjective Truth

In the Enlightenment/Modern era, people accepted objective truth—truth that stands on its on own legs regardless of the situation, the time, or the people involved. Objective or absolute truth is what it is regardless of one's response to it. In the Postmodern/Emerging era, however, truth is subjective and relative to the situation and the individual.

As professor and writer Robert Webber observes, "Postmodernity rejects two main assumptions of modernity. The first is that the scientific method results in objective truth. The second is that truth is available through reason. Both of these assumptions lie behind twentieth-century evangelism.… Christianity was the verdict demanded by the evidence."[6] Do you see why the cultural shift cannot be ignored by the twenty-first-century church?

Now consider a postmodernity conversation and see what is

happening in our culture. Jazz musician Charlie Mingus says, "When I'm trying to play my music, I'm trying to play the truth of who I really am. The problem is that I'm changing all the time." To that scholar N. T. Wright responds, "Welcome to postmodernity—that's what it's like. And as for facts, all truth is somebody's truth."[7]

You can see that communication is greatly impacted by this Emerging Era view that truth is relative: you believe what you want to believe, and I'll believe what I want to believe. Furthermore, when you let the community in which you live and function shape most of what you believe, your beliefs may change if you leave one group for another. And that's not a problem for postmoderns who believe there is no universal truth for all of humanity for all of time. There are no eternal truths—like "You are created in God's image," "He is faithful and just to forgive us our sins," or "Jesus is coming again"—to provide definition or support in the particulars of life.

What does this postmodernity look like in classrooms? Marva Dawn, theologian, author, and educator, reports that "in university history departments, postmodernism leads to revisionist accounts of events. English teachers and visual artists who accept postmodern theories claim that there is no meaning in texts or paintings except what the reader or viewer brings to them."[8] Postmodernity offers people such slogans as "Life has no meaning. It's just a game"; "Every claim to truth is a power play and should be mistrusted"; and "You are the only one who cares about you."[9]

MOVING FROM THE INDIVIDUAL... TO THE COMMUNITY

In the era of Modernity, we elevated the individual. In fact in America, we admire the rugged individualist and are encouraged to become all that we can become as we pursue our own dream. In the process, however, we learned to love things and use people. The goal was to get ahead regardless of the cost in human relationships and community: I mattered.

For most of the Modernity Era, the family was the environment in which the individual was loved, nurtured, and encouraged. Since the 1960s, however, family life has been interrupted by technology and its values undermined by those of the media. In *The*

Shelter of Each Other: Rebuilding Our Families, Dr. Mary Pipher—a wife, mother, and psychologist specializing in families—writes that our culture is "at war with families."[10] She explains:

> The media forms our new community. The electronic village is our home-town…. Parents have no real community to back up the values that they try to teach to their children. Family members may be in the same house, but they are no longer truly interacting. They may be in the same room, but instead of making their own story, they are watching another family's story unfold.[11]

Our children are being raised by TVs, Walkmen, iPods, Xboxes, and the list goes on—and these surrogate parents aren't supporting the values, morals, or work ethic that have been the backbone of our society for generations. These appliances and the voices of the media instead foster as "our most central belief system … the importance of money…. Via media and advertising, our children are being educated to believe that products are what matter. This will hurt them and ultimately it will hurt us all."[12]

At one point, however, the media may have fostered the sense that America was a community in and of itself. Back in the 1950s, long before cable, satellite dishes, and movies we could rent and watch at home, the limited number of television channels offered Milton Berle, *I Love Lucy*, and *Ozzie and Harriet*. These shows helped us be together, laugh together, and enjoy—even value—being a family. Furthermore, these programs brought America together through a common experience. Today, with market segmentation and a much wider variety of viewing options, the American audience is divided, and national consensus or community is difficult to develop or sustain. As Long observes, "With the breakdown of the family and the loss of any national consensus, we are becoming a culture of homeless people who search continually for a place to belong."[13]

In this frightening shift from modernity to postmodernity, the stressed and confused American family has created an individual who longs to be in community, but these people are not turning to the community of family. Think about television programs like *Cheers*, *Friends*, and, as we saw earlier, *Seinfield*. We see these people in community, not in families. Being in community provides one with a sense of place, of belonging, and of identity—a role that family once played. Now it is in community that relationships are formed and personal development may occur. A postmodernity community is also the context for beliefs to develop and be deemed valid. The existence of a myriad of communities within our nation—within our culture—makes it difficult to have common beliefs, much less a consensus of beliefs, because each community has its own belief system. This cultural change in focus from the individual of the Modern Era to the community of Postmodernity is greatly affecting how we live.

MOVING FROM A METANARRATIVE OF SOCIETAL PROGRESS... TO A MICRONARRATIVE OF SOCIETAL CYNICISM

When you listen to people talk, read biographies, or revisit your own life, you discover that life is about stories. We love to hear what has happened to other people, and we love to tell our own life adventure. Whether a tale reflects an easy or a difficult journey, is pleasant or sad, uplifts or discourages, it breathes meaning and value into our lives. Stories often picture for others where we've come from, who we are, and why we do what we do.

During the Modern Era, many of our culture's stories were about how science was going to help us discover ways to make the world a better place. Our metanarrative—the culture's overarching (*meta*) story (*narrative*) that gave meaning to our personal stories— was essentially supported by the biblical account of the world and the human condition. With that solid foundation, people's dreams were large and positive. Everything about life was going to get better. Optimism was high. Societal progress was believed possible. But then came two world wars, the Depression, the spread of disease, the Atomic Age, the have-nots having less, and the haves having more. Fear, bitterness, and despair set in. The stories of hope dwindled. We have moved from an era of hope for progress to an era of societal cynicism.

As professor, leader in postmodern thought, and author Jean Francois Lyotard says, "It is very difficult to believe that there is one story about the world and the human condition that can be true."[14] Robert Webber discusses the consequences of that new reality:

This failure to have an overarching universal explanation of the world has led many to the hopeless conclusion that there is no meaning in this world other than the futile meaning each person can give to his or her life. All explanations of the world—scientific, religious, social—are of equal value and therefore of no value. Human existence cannot be explained and cannot be understood, and there is no one worldview that provides an ultimate explanation to this world and the life it sustains.… It is now politically incorrect to challenge another person's story.… A kind of eclecticism has occurred in society in which it is perfectly appropriate for each person to create his or her own story and defend it on the basis of feeling good about it. This is relativism.[15]

> *A person with a "get-ahead-at-any-cost" story experiences conflict with people who value honesty.*

As a people who have no big-story framework we believe is true, we listen to the news, read the blogs, hear the politicians, and grow more fearful and cynical every day. Why else would fewer and fewer people be voting? Why are suicides increasing? Why are people more and more angry and violent? Why do judges say, "This person in my court has no conscience"? Why is drug and alcohol use increasing? Why is it necessary to outlaw sex at high-school dances? Marva Dawn offers this answer:

> Manifestations of postmodern thinking… lead to a rejection of the truth, authority, meaning and hope. …Many of our children's friends and neighbors have no reference point, no guiding standard by which to access life… Having no larger story in which to place themselves, youth don't know who they are. … Without authorities in the postmodern world to guide the formation of their moral character, children today lack basic resources of principled disposition to know how to find joy in what is beautiful, to have compassion for those who suffer, to develop goals for their work and lives.[16]

As postmodernity rejects the modern metanarrative and moves to micronarratives, some people flounder in life, and others become defensive. Those who flounder do so because they want to be part of a bigger story, but they cannot find either the story or the door into a community where they might find an overarching story that gives meaning to life. Others become defensive because their story doesn't seem to be releasing their potential. They seem stuck in life; they're feeling less motivated; and they're experiencing a sense of defeat. Yet, when questioned, they argue that what they are doing is right for them.

For some individuals, their personal narrative—the micronarrative of one—begins to conflict with the micronarrative of another. A person using drugs, for instance, comes into conflict with one who doesn't especially when the user's story begins to involve lying, stealing, and injuring others. A person with a "get-ahead-at-any-cost" story experiences conflict with people who value honesty. I believe much of the tension in our society exists because of conflicting micronarratives and the loss of the metanarrative. And Jimmy Long concurs: "Lacking a common thread to hold us together, we grope around in the dark."[17]

Into this arena of micronarratives we who are Christ followers enter, bringing with us a listening ear, a heart of compassion, and a word of hope. We also humbly bring a remarkable story—a metanarrative—that I'll talk more about in the next two chapters. We need to be prepared and willing to share this metanarrative of the gospel.[18] We need to share the "large story… that the world is basically God's world, and it's a good world, but it's gone wrong, and evil has infected it in all sorts of ways which modernism really didn't want to take account of and which postmodernity has partly seen but then has wallowed in because it's got no answer."[19]

Our large biblical and Christian story, however, has the answer—not an answer, but *the* answer—to the problem of evil's existence: "The answer is that God the Creator has rescued the world from evil and is rescuing it from evil. That's why we need the death and resurrection of Jesus at the center of every Christian retelling, and every Christian challenge."[20] One more note about the value of the Christian's metanarrative, and this from Dr. N. T. Wright, one of the foremost New Testament scholars in the world: "Within postmodernity, people have tried to pay attention to the narrative [of the Bible] without paying attention to the fact that it's a true story."[21] The Bible is true; the metanarrative it offers is therefore key to a meaningful existence on this planet as well as to eternal life afterward.

In the true account of Revelation 5:9-10, God offers a glimpse of the glorious day when the people of God purchased with the blood of Christ—people from throughout history, people from every tribe and tongue and people and nation—celebrate the Lord's triumph over sin and Satan. On that day all creation will witness the grand results of obedience to Jesus' Great Commandment and Great Commission. And those results will reflect one's obedience to Christ's command to share His gospel. We can best do that when we clearly understand both the Good News and the group to whom we were going.

> *Often a segue to the gospel truth isn't hard to make. Consider the increased cultural attention being given to investing your life, not merely your money. This provides an easy transition to talk with people about their rationale for and their current stewardship of their energies, skills, monies, and time.*

Societal Changes: The Myths

Although well aware that we live in a secular culture, we can find ourselves taken aback when we hear people say, "There is no absolute truth. Truth is whatever you believe, whatever works for you."

Michael Green, author and senior research fellow at Wycliffe Hall, Oxford, has written a valuable book entitled *Sharing Your Faith with Friends and Family*. Drawing on insights from George Hunter in his book *How to Reach Secular People*, Green presents three common myths we often have about secular people.

- First of all, "secular people are not as irreligious as you might think: they just don't bring the Christian gospel within their purview. Instead, they deify the American dream, the New Age, football, or one of the many new cults."[22]

- Today's secular people "are not immoral, but are persuaded that one does not need God in order to lead a normal life."[23] People today have simply developed their own ethic of right and wrong.

- Third, "most of [today's secular people] are extraordinarily ignorant of what Christianity is all about. They have probably been exposed only to the echo of an echo of the gospel, if that....It is well to remember that most people even in universities, students and lecturers alike, are profoundly ignorant of Christian teaching."[24]

Let me add that I am amazed by how little contemporary people know or think about life after death. Hardly preoccupied with that eventuality, Green notes as well, "they are interested in making the most of life and finding meaning and pleasure in what they do know.

If evangelism used to be related mainly to the moment of dying, now it must be related to the matter of living."[25]

Did you hear that? We need to talk to people about the abundant living Jesus makes possible for us today! I am grateful that in the Resurrection we have the answer regarding death. But I am very excited about interacting with people about how they can have hope, their life can have rich meaning, and they can make a significant contribution to people and to the world in which they live. And often a segue to the gospel truth isn't hard to make. Consider the increased cultural attention being given to investing your life, not merely your money. This provides an easy transition to talk with people about their rationale for and their current stewardship of their energies, skills, monies, and time.

Michael Green offers another important insight about what not to talk to secular people about: "Secular people are more conscious of doubt than guilt (although they are guilty, just as people always have been), and so to begin talking to your friend about sin and guilt is likely to be unproductive. You are not scratching where they itch."[26] I can attest to the value of this insight, because I have found it helpful to share with a secular person an area of doubt, confusion, or struggle in my own life. Nonreligious people often assume that we who know Jesus have no doubts or struggles. We position ourselves above them when we act as though everything in our life and in the world is clear, straightforward, simple, black and white. Furthermore, when we live like this, we also communicate that Christianity is a system rather than a journey involving a dynamic relationship with Jesus, the Christ.

People today seek lasting meaning and purpose in marriage, or a rich and satisfying life through having children, or fulfillment in just the right job. Some assume that becoming people of significant influence and income will do it. Even as people take these steps and reach these goals, they feel something is still missing in their lives. We who know Jesus have discovered it is actually Someone who is missing from their lives. In order for us to share this discovery with people who don't yet know Christ, we need to ask God to provide for us meaningful relationships with them and to use our lives to display the work that He can do in a yielded life. But how do we develop these relationships?

BUILDING BRIDGES TO POSTMODERNITY PEOPLE

Develop a People Focus — Christ came to live and die for people. Too often in Christian leadership, we live and die for programs and ministries. As valuable as these events and outreaches are, they are merely vehicles for connecting with people. We must always remember that.

Now let me ask you a question: Who are the people for whom God is giving you a heart of concern? List their names, be sure to include people from the different aspects of your life (family, friends, co-workers, people you connect with through hobbies and recreational activities, and folks like the grocery story cashier whom you come into contact with regularly), and begin to pray for them.

As you choose to be more focused on people, be prepared for surprises from the Lord. Some people will thank you for your kindness; others may shy away. Some may stop and begin to converse with you, almost as though they had been waiting for someone to talk with. Also, read the Gospels and watch the way Jesus interacts with people. Then notice how He makes people of the marketplace feel cared about. May the Holy Spirit lead us to follow Christ's example in our postmodernity world.

Enter Their Community — Remember that, in our culture, community defines what postmoderns believe, provides them with a place of belonging, helps them write their micronarrative, and takes precedence over the individual. So it is invaluable to both see and be with people in their community. When you're invited, be certain to go. Realize what an honor it is for you and God to be invited into your friend's community.

Before you go, spend meaningful time in the Soul Room in listening prayer: Enjoy God's presence and learn from the insights He gives you. Share any concerns or anxieties with God so that the Pitcher will fill the cup of your life with His presence and His thoughts. Then go to your friend's community gathering to enjoy, to laugh, and to develop a closer friendship. Meet your friend's friends as well—and shortly after the gathering, affirm the people you met and be sure to say how much you enjoyed your time with them.

Empathize with Their Inner Person — Younger generations know well the experience of being hurt, and many have known abandonment. (Of course, older generations have known hurt, but they are usually better at concealing their pain.) This feeling of having no place to belong creates a deep, inner sense of alienation. Broken families, nameless neighbors, competitive co-workers, politicians who can't be trusted—the reasons for feeling alienated are many.

> We must ask God to both motivate us to pray and enable us to understand the twenty-first-century people among whom we live.

Furthermore, postmodernity people feel driven to distance themselves from even those closest to them; they avoid genuine relationships in order to protect themselves from greater hurt and disappointment. Their inner world of alienation causes them to have no emotional home and fuels not only an inner loneliness but often a poor self-image. Without any basis for acceptance and love, postmodernity people often experience a higher drive to achieve, but achievement doesn't provide any sense of genuine value or worth.

So how do we engage these postmodernity people? As always, we find a model in Jesus who understood the first-century people among whom He lived. We must ask God to both motivate us to pray and enable us to understand the twenty-first-century people among whom we live. We need to learn to understand and empathize with their inner person.

Connecting with postmodernity people by developing a people focus, joining them in their community when they invite us, and understanding and empathizing with their inner person will enable us to build bridges over which we can walk to them so that they might, in God's time, come to Jesus. Embodying the Lord Jesus and following His example, we engage them where they are—in their community. May we see it as an honor as well as a calling.

BECOME A FRIEND, ENTER THEIR COMMUNITY, BRING THEM HOPE.

Dear Lord, in a world that is hurting and has withdrawn from Your gospel truth, Your love, and Your ways, warm my heart to love; change my mind to understand; and motivate my feet to go and be among postmodernity people. Continue to form me so that I embody the truth I believe and the love of the Lord I know. Send me from the comfort I feel with my Christian friends and help me embrace the challenge of building meaningful friendships with postmodernity people. Father, lead me over the bridge that, in time, Your Spirit might lead them to Jesus. In the name of the Father, the Son, and the Holy Spirit I pray. Amen.

Before You Take the Next Step

What two or three thoughts caught your attention in this chapter? Why?

When you look at the foundation and values of your own life, are you more a modernity or postmodernity person? What might God want you to do to broaden your worldview?

Which postmodernity people in your network of friends and family might God want you to pray for? And how might He want you to care for these people?

*"Lord, forgive me that
I thought this
generation of young people
was looking for gimmicks. I
now see that they are looking
for relationship."
— Daphne Kirk
quoting a pastor's prayer
after meeting with a
multigenerational group*

How Do I Live Out
the Gospel in Today's World?

Following Christ's Example:

Impacting Your World by Your Lifestyle Witness

> The Word became flesh and blood,
> and moved into the neighborhood. —John 1:14[1]

Humanity hasn't been the same since Jesus walked the earth. What enabled Him to influence so significantly the people and culture in which He lived—and even us today? What attracted people to Him? Why was He able to make such a difference in people's lives? What we learn from the way Jesus lived will benefit us who are leaders trying to influence for Christ both the people around us and the culture in which we live. His example can help you and me become more effective difference-makers.

But first we need to address this fundamental issue: do we really believe that the everyday follower of Christ living out an everyday life is the key to the spread of the gospel? It more often seems that we believe that the kingdom spreads primarily through powerful speakers, well-planned events, and well-attended programs. But consider what pastor and writer John Stott learned when he asked his congregation two simple questions: "What first attracted you to Christ and the gospel?" and "What mainly or finally brought you to Christ?" Read Stott's description of their answers:

Over half referred to something they had seen for themselves in Christian people, their parents, pastors, teachers, colleagues or friends. As one put it, these "had something in their lives which I lacked but desperately longed for." In several cases it was "their external joy and inward peace." To a student nurse it was "the genuine and open friendship" offered by Christians; to an Oxford undergraduate studying law, their "sheer exuberance"; to a police constable, the "clear aim, purpose and idealism which Christian life offered" as seen in Christians; to a secretary in the BBC, "the reality of the warmth and inner resources which I observed in Christians"; and to a house surgeon, "the knowledge of Christ's working in another person's life."[2]

May God use this chapter to capture your heart with the exciting reality that you can indeed be a significant influence for the expansion of His kingdom in all the places He has planted you. You are not where you are by accident. Your life matters!

Jesus made a deep impact through lifestyle witness and through verbal witness. In the next chapter, I will talk about verbal witness. In this chapter, we will focus primarily on your personal lifestyle witness. We will learn from Christ about five dominant lifestyle postures, and I will offer suggestions and stories of how these lifestyle postures can be Spirit-shaped in our lives. I will also touch on the importance of godly community as being essential to your lifestyle expression of Jesus Christ for people in your circle of influence who have yet to become His followers.

Dear Father, Son, and Holy Spirit,

I long to receive Your love and Your insights so that I might significantly impact for Your kingdom the people in my circle of influence. Thank You for the record of the life of Your Son. Enable me to learn from Scripture how Jesus influenced the people around Him. Use this chapter to inspire me, renew me, and redirect me. My life is Yours. I pray this in the name of the Father who has a passion for the nations, for all peoples. Amen.

As a Leader, Christ Impacts People by His Presence

When Jesus moved into the neighborhood, He influenced the people around Him by simply being present with them. We call this the

Incarnation—the miracle of God-in-a-human-body living in our midst. Jesus came to be an influence right here among us. Are you excited about being an influence right where God has placed you—in your neighborhood, school, workplace, and community? Former U.S. Senate Chaplain Richard Halverson (now with the Lord) said, "We may as well trust that we are of the most use where we are. To quote another: 'We are certainly of no use where we are not!'"[3] May God's Spirit give us a holy excitement about where He has positioned us. May the lifestyle of Christ show us how we can influence people's lives and even world situations for God's kingdom by our presence.

As a Leader, Christ Impacts People by His *Awareness of Their Presence* Near Him

After John the Baptist explains that Jesus is the Lamb of God, two of his disciples suddenly begin to follow Christ. Sensing that someone is walking behind Him, Jesus turns around and asks, "What do you want?" They reply, "Where are you staying?" Their rabbi's response must have stunned them: "Come and see." The two accept this invitation, and as a result Andrew, one of the two, immediately invites his brother Simon (later called Peter) to come to the Christ. What might not have happened if Christ had been unaware of the two men walking a few steps behind Him? (See John 1:35-42.) Jesus led and influenced by being aware of people's presence.

* * *

The room is stuffy because of the crowd of people jammed inside to hear Jesus teach. Suddenly there is a noise above their heads. Something is happening on the roof. A hole slowly appears, and it grows larger and larger. Jesus stops teaching and looks up. A paralyzed man is lowered before Him, and Jesus responds to his needs. In one sense, though, Jesus responds to the committed passion of this man's friends: "*When Jesus saw their faith*, he said to the paralytic..." (Mark 2:5, emphasis added). Would you and I have seen only the paralyzed man and not noticed his committed friends? Christ's awareness of the people around Him enabled Him to honor the faith of the friends.

When Christ tells this paralyzed man that his sins are forgiven, He is also aware of what the Pharisees in the crowd are thinking. His awareness that these teachers of the law believed that only God could forgive sins prompts Him to address their concerns. Sensitive leaders have a growing level of awareness that influences the ways they touch people, speak to people, and connect with people. Sensitive leaders maintain a posture that notices what others may miss. (See Mark 2:1-12.)

* * *

Are there times when you and I are physically present in a situation, but our awareness antennae aren't tuned in? When we're in a leadership position, it is too easy to be more aware of program details than of the people around us. We may be present in body, but not present in heart. When this happens, we miss opportunities to be influencers for the kingdom.

A godly lifestyle, however, leads to a growing awareness of people, their concerns, and their needs, and God uses that people awareness to impact them with His love. Such people awareness and even environment awareness are formed and fueled prior to entering the Leadership Room. This awareness begins in the Soul Room with your intentional prayer for people who are not yet followers of Christ. As a result of such prayer, this awareness becomes authentically you and not merely a skill you develop. Healthy Saucer/Plate interactions are always the result of Pitcher/Cup Soul Room time when a cup is filled to overflowing with all that the Pitcher poured in!

As a Leader, Christ Impacts People with His *Curiosity* about and *Interest* in Them

Jesus' interactions with people show His curiosity and interest in those around Him. We also see Him spark their curiosity about the Father's kingdom by the questions He asks them and the observations He makes.

Picture Jesus walking through a large crowd. Many are bumping into one another, and countless conversations are swirling around Him. Suddenly He asks, "Who touched me?" With so many people jostling their Lord, the disciples find this a foolish question. But Jesus scans the crowd for the one who touched Him. Finally a woman, trembling with fear, comes forward and tells her story. Our Lord looks at her and says, "Daughter, your faith has healed you. Go in peace and be freed from your suffering" (Mark 5:34). Jesus' curiosity about what had happened around Him evokes a question and enables Jesus to affirm the faith of this suffering woman and physically heal her.

* * *

Remember when the Pharisees brought before Jesus a woman caught in the act of adultery? Jesus bends down and writes in the sand with His finger. Talk about raising curiosity! Have you ever wondered what Jesus drew or wrote in the sand? When He finally straightens up, He says to her accusers, "If any one of you is without sin, let him be the first to throw a stone at her" (John 8:7). What an unexpected and remarkable response! And consider how curiosity held the crowd's attention, created an opportunity for learning, and even opened the door for Jesus to give the woman hope. (See the complete account in John 8.) An intriguing statement or a meaningful question that stimulates curiosity can powerfully influence individuals and a community.

It is important to learn to ask meaningful questions—and to be sincerely curious and interested in the answers. Question asking must not be merely a handy technique but the fruit of an authentically caring heart formed by the Holy Spirit in the Soul Room. In the societal shift from modernity to postmodernity, your genuine concern about another person—your holy curiosity about that person's life and heart—is both a bridge to a trusting relationship and a significant step toward developing a lifestyle that attracts people to Jesus.

AS A LEADER, CHRIST IMPACTS PEOPLE WITH HIS COMPASSION

We see the compassion of Jesus revealed in a variety of actions and situations. He shows compassion when He sees a leper and heals him (Mark 1). We see Jesus' compassion as He looks out upon a lost humanity and is moved because they are like sheep without a shepherd (Matthew 9). We witness His compassion for the large and hungry crowd that has gathered. Jesus miraculously turns a few fish and a handful of loaves into a meal for these thousands—and He has plenty left over (Mark 6). We also see the depths of Jesus' compassion as He suffers on the cross. In these final and excruciatingly painful moments, He speaks to His mother and commissions John to care for her (John 19).

Such acts of kindness are tangible expressions of compassion and care. Such kindnesses indicate that the people you know are not just fixtures in your life or statistics in your ministry, but beloved creations of God in whom you are genuinely interested. We live in a harsh, cruel, I-couldn't-care-less-about-you culture. Any leaders who live out the genuine compassion of Christ among particular people—those they know as well as those they don't know—are of immense value and influence both in the world and for God's eternal kingdom. Probably every person you see today carries some pain or hurt, and few people they encounter will take time to show they care. In our love-things-and-use-people culture, compassion is such a rare quality that it stands out whenever it is encountered. May you and I be the eyes, ears, hands, feet, and mouth of God's compassion in Jesus' name.

> *The Soul Room ... was Jesus' place of preparation for living in the Leadership Room.*

As a Leader, Christ Impacts People by His *Preparation*

Jesus has called some men to follow Him and minister with Him, but just a few days later, they wake up and discover He is gone. Where could He be? Scripture teaches that Jesus was off, early in the morning, to be alone with His Father. He was an influential leader partly because He prepared Himself for the day by spending intimate time with His Father (Mark 1:35).

* * *

The time has come for Jesus to select an inner circle of followers from the larger group of His disciples. To prepare Himself to make these crucial decisions, Jesus goes out to a mountainside to pray and spends the night praying to God. The Soul Room—where the incarnate Son spent time with the Father and Spirit—was Jesus' place of preparation for living in the Leadership Room. And I believe that His people awareness, His holy curiosity, and His immeasurable compassion were formed and fueled in these places and during these times of preparation.

What Can I Do to Develop These Traits?

Christlike traits for effective kingdom influence are developed and strengthened in the Soul Room as we linger in God's presence, reflect on His life, and spend time in prayer. These character traits—formed over a lifetime—shape our lifestyle as well as our leadership. Such traits as the awareness of people, holy curiosity, and godly compassion are not leadership techniques we hone. They are the fruit of God's transforming work experienced through our prayers of preparation, prayer-in-the-midst, and reflective prayer afterward. Such prayers increase the impact of our kingdom influence in the world. Remember, we are in the world to live the lifestyle of Jesus Christ among people.

Lifestyle Leadership: *Accessible Presence* — Think about the coming week. In what everyday situations will you be with those who are not yet followers of Christ? Will you be buying groceries, making a deposit at the bank, or taking a walk? As you enter these places and are with these people, ask God to make you accessible to them. Be sensitive to create margins in your schedule that makes accessibility possible.

Lifestyle Leadership: *People Awareness* — Each time you enter a situation, practice being aware of the people around you. *What do you see?* What do you notice about the facial expressions of the people around you? about their interactions? *What do you hear?* What emotions do you hear in the conversations between people? What topics are being mentioned? *What do you sense about the group?* What is the prevailing mood? Do you sense competition or community? As you watch a group of people, ask God to show you how you can join Him in whatever is happening in that setting. Ask Him to guide you about whether to join the laughter, ask a question, reach out to someone on the fringes, provide insight, be a serving friend, offer to help, or simply listen with genuine interest. Later, remember that your influence is not easy to quantify. It reaches beyond what you could imagine.

* * *

The year was 1809. A man by the name of Edwin Dwight was walking through the campus of Yale University when he noticed a seventeen-year-old man sitting on the steps of Yale's main building and weeping. "His appearance was unpromising. He was clothed in a rough sailor's suit, was of a clumsy form, and his countenance dull and heavy."[4] Dwight almost walked past him, but instead he asked, "Do you wish to learn?" The young man's countenance immediately brightened. Moved by God's Spirit with concern for this young man, Dwight taught him to read and write. Later on he saw to it that this young man was cared for and tutored within the Christian community. Eventually, Edwin Dwight suggested that this young man go to live with his brother, Timothy Dwight, who was then president of Yale University and a dominant influence in America at the time. This young man ended up living with this family for many months.

Edwin Dwight and his brother eventually celebrated when this young Hawaiian Henry Obookiah came to faith in Jesus Christ. Out of this young man's conversion and passion came the founding of the Sandwich Island Mission, the organization that took the gospel throughout the Hawaiian Islands.[5] May our godly awareness of people's situations—the kind of awareness Edwin Dwight had when he almost walked past Henry Obookiah—lead us to gracious acts of kindness and gentle influence for God's kingdom. Person awareness and the enfolding of a stranger into the Christian community resulted in a significant chapter in the history of Christian missions.

* * *

Lifestyle Leadership: *Genuine Curiosity* — Asking questions is a valuable tool in our efforts to better know and understand people. Hearing the answers to our questions also enables us to both pray more insightfully and listen to God more effectively. So ask questions. Ask about where people have lived. Ask about their interests and free-time activities. Ask about family—the family in which they grew up and their current family. Ask about vocation and why they chose it. Ask about education. Ask about motivations and dreams.

* * *

A friend of mine is a lawyer in the field of chemical patents. In fact, he probably holds the chemical patent on some of the clothes you are wearing right now. He also teaches eleventh-grade Sunday school, and there he expresses a holy curiosity about the students in his class. Is school going well for them? What are they thinking about for their future? At one point, he casually suggested that these high-school students drop by his home on Friday nights. Little did he realize that, some thirty years later, high-school students would still be dropping by. Over the years, Paul and his wife Carolyn have gone through carpeting, refrigerators, ping-pong tables, windows, and chairs in their ministry to students. For many, their home has been the door to life in Christ—and their genuine curiosity about the lives of others increased their influence for the Lord.

* * *

Lifestyle Leadership: *Heartfelt Compassion* — When we work on developing an awareness of the people around us and on expressing genuine curiosity about their life and their heart, God's Spirit is able to direct us to care for, support, and encourage them—to live out godly compassion. You might make a phone call or send an e-mail. You might write a note, buy groceries for a family in which someone is sick, take a person to the airport, or ask people if you could pray for them.

* * *

I once walked into the office of a high-school guidance counselor. It was spring in the nation's capital—a time when students love to ditch school because the long, damp winter is finally over. It is also a time when antsy seniors can hardly wait to graduate. This counselor was the person in charge of disciplinary actions for the student body. I didn't really know him very well, but while we spoke in his office, I asked him how he was. For the next ten to fifteen minutes, I listened to his long list of frustrations, problems, and reasons for discouragement. While I listened, I prayed, asking God what He wanted me to do. I had no idea whether this man was a churchgoer or not.

Near the end of the conversation, though, the Spirit nudged me to ask this question: "In light of the heavy burdens you're carrying, would you mind if I prayed for you now?" His face lit up and he said, "Please do!" When I finished praying, he expressed his heartfelt gratitude for my prayer. You would have thought I had just handed him a

$100 bill. The Spirit may prompt us—as He did me in this situation—to extend the compassion of Christ by praying for the person we're with.

✳ ✳ ✳

> *I have seen that my leadership is strongest when my Soul Room time is richest.*

Lifestyle Leadership: *Ongoing Preparation—* This lifestyle of accessible presence, people awareness, genuine curiosity, and heartfelt compassion—this Lifestyle Leadership of Pitcher/Cup…Saucer/ Plate—is both sustained and stimulated by my ongoing preparation in the Soul Room. Granted, I have found leadership to be challenging, stretching, and fun as well as painful, draining, and confusing. I have also seen that my leadership is strongest when my Soul Room time is richest. During Soul Room time, I am reminded that the Sacred Three are truly my source of life and refreshment, of forgiveness and cleansing, of friendship and perspective.

Godly influence—expressed through presence, awareness, curiosity, and compassion—is the fruit of ongoing preparation and refocusing, and Jesus teaches this by His example. Early in His public ministry, the opportunities are great and the demands are high. People need to be reached with the gospel. The disciples need to be trained to serve. So what will be the lifestyle of Jesus Christ? How will He handle the demands placed on Him?

The Bible reports that "very early in the morning, while it was still dark, Jesus got up, left the house and went off to a solitary place, where he prayed" (Mark 1:35). He did this on other occasions as well. His life shows us that effective influence in the Leadership Room grows out of the preparation for leadership and life that occurs in the Soul Room. Consider now an eighteenth-century example of balancing Soul Room and Leadership Room, of integrating spiritual formation and leadership development.

William Wilberforce entered the British Parliament at the age of twenty-one. Six years later he came to faith in Christ. God soon kindled in his heart the passion to abolish the slave trade throughout the British Empire and to reform the spiritual, social, and moral life of the country. How would he continue to serve in Parliament and, at the same time, carry out this mission from God? Listen to this description of Wilberforce's lifestyle:

> He...spent several hours daily in earnest study of the Scripture. He also set aside time for self-examination, meditation and keeping the heart, that he might better perform "the duties of life." He believed that if he did not, "the most pressing claims will carry [my heart], not the strongest. " Wilberforce concluded: "The shortening of private devotions starves the soul, it grows lean and faint. This must not be."[6]

Wilberforce brought the concerns of the Leadership Room into the Soul Room where he presented his government co-workers to the Lord. Then, as he prepared to go out into the Leadership Room, "he often wrote down 'launchers,' a list of topics that might lead to deeper conversations about life in Christ." After his death, a list of friends he regularly prayed for was found among his papers. Included on this list were the czar of Russia, members of Parliament, and his neighbor's footman.[7]

A godly lifestyle that has a penetrating, gospel influence on people around us results from our ongoing preparation in the Soul Room. May you continually invest time in your place of preparation. Then may you—with increased passion and excitement—follow the Lord in our mission to the world that so desperately needs Jesus.

Impacting My World as Part of a Faith Community

Our world does need Jesus, but we aren't to meet that challenge as individuals. Being part of God's mission in the world must grow out of our being not only alone with God, but also our being part of a congregation that understands and lives out its God-given mission to the world. Yet hear this warning from missiologist David Watson: "The old order of the established and organized church, relying on its structures and traditions instead of the renewing of the Spirit of God, will not do.... Everything depends on our ability to catch a new vision of the church as it ought to be...and above all on our determination to keep our lives continually open to spiritual renewal."[8]

This essential role of community—"the church as it ought to be"—is nothing new. In fact—as with every other key truth of the Christian life—we can trace it back to our Lord. Jesus said, "Love one another. In the same way I loved you, you love one another. This is how everyone will recognize that you are my disciples—when they see the love you have for each other" (John 13:34-35, msg). In His leadership training of the Twelve, Jesus emphasizes the importance of community not only for the sake of fellowship and camaraderie, but also to enable other first-century people to see the validity of the gospel in the relational health and hope they lived out.

For too long, the modern church has been living more as a gathering of people committed to events rather than as a family of people committed to one another yet sent on a mission into the world. Because of the high value people of postmodernity place on community, being with our friends will be of higher importance than the topic of any meeting they attend with us. With the societal shift from modernity to postmodernity, vital community becomes the most essential dynamic for reaching the younger generations.

The dynamic for community is modeled by our Lord Jesus, who lives in the community of Father, Son, and Holy Spirit. While He walked this earth, Jesus lived and invested most of His time in a community of Twelve—and people noticed. Then, from Acts to Revelation, the dynamic community of Christ-followers was primary to the spread of the kingdom and the nurturing of the saints. The Christian community attracted the attention of the watching world. This lifestyle pattern was first a gathering for community, worship, and nurture and then a scattering for mission expression. It was and is not gathering *or* scattering; it is gathering *and* scattering.

BIBLICAL SUPPORT FOR COMMUNITY

Does healthy community really matter in the lifestyle and mission of the church? To find out God's answer to that question, I read the New Testament from Acts through Revelation and highlighted every verse that mentioned community—and I was blown away by what God showed me. Does healthy kingdom community matter in the lifestyle and mission of the church? The answer was a resounding yes, and I was awed by how central to personal kingdom growth and lifestyle outreach a healthy, growing body of believers is. Community is God's design; it is not an option.

And a healthy Christian community can have an impact because people of postmodernity—who feel rejected, abandoned, as if they don't matter, and who don't believe in objective truth—could come to trust and rely on community as a safe place of identity, hope, and protection. As we enter the world of these people, we treat them—by God's grace—with dignity and respect. Living authentic lives among them, we communicate that we don't have all of the answers to life, that we have struggles and fears, that we fail, that our feet are made of clay just as theirs are. We become people of influence in their lives because of our accessible presence, our people awareness, our genuine curiosity, and our heartfelt compassion. Our ongoing preparation in the Soul Room refreshes our soul and further motivates us to keep entering their world. In the Leadership Room of our faith community, we invite specific prayers for our friends. We also consider others who might walk over the bridge with us so that we can demonstrate community to them. Through our personal lifestyle and our Christian community, God enables us to be His presence in the postmodern culture and community—and we praise Him for that privilege.

THE GREAT POSTMODERN CHALLENGE: MAKING AN IMPACT

Throughout its history, God has called and positioned His church among diverse cultures as a people living and presenting the gospel of Jesus Christ. Today, we live among a people who are puzzled and hurting. They are hungry for community and for spiritual nourishment. Yet for the gospel to communicate its transforming power to these people, it must scale generational walls and bridge the gap caused by societal differences among us; the church must offer twenty-first-century people healthy, fresh, multigenerational communities of faith. God wants to use us to bring healing to the culture, to the church, and to families. May the Holy Spirit make us willing to leave our "holy huddles," our places of comfort and security, and empower us to go among people where we will build friendships for His glory and the spread of His kingdom.

THE OUTSTANDING POSTMODERN OPPORTUNITY:
MAKING AN IMPACT BY INVESTING YOUR LIFE

Many in the postmodern community were not raised in the Christian faith, and due to generational issues and societal issues, they are often living with great disillusionment and deep hurt. These people find themselves smiling on the outside but agonizing on the inside. They long for something more, but they are unable to place their finger on what the more is. You and I know what it is: they hunger for God. But they haven't seen or heard much of the authentic God named Jesus. They need to meet Him and, in Him, find a new foundation for life and a new outlook for their future. You and I have the virtually limitless opportunity to help them see themselves as beloved of God and invited into His kingdom family. Your response to God's call to be a light in a dark world—to be an individual grounded in and supported by godly community, to be committed to Lifestyle Leadership, to Pitcher/Cup... Saucer/Plate living—is definitely worthy of your life investment.

ARE YOU CONCERNED ABOUT THE PEOPLE IN YOUR WORLD?

ARE YOU WILLING TO INVEST YOUR LIFE IN SHARING THE GOSPEL WITH THEM?

Dear Lord, thank You for the different people You used to "live Jesus" in front of me, to tantalize me with the news of the gospel. Deepen my desire to move from the Soul Room into the Leadership Room of our culture and there be a person who is accessible, who is aware of people's needs and hurts, and who approaches relationships with holy curiosity and godly compassion. In Your name I pray. Amen.

Before You Take the Next Step

How do you feel about living among and sharing your faith with those who are not yet followers of Christ? Are you nervous, excited, unsure, confident, or something else? Explain.

Which lifestyle trait of Christ evident in His interaction with people is most compelling to you? Why?

Who are some particular friends for whom you are now praying that Christ would become real and meaningful in their lives? You might invite others to join you in praying.

*We communicate
the gospel to people by
listening to their story,
sharing our story, and
telling His story.*

How Do We Communicate
the Gospel to People?

Witnessing with Your Words: Telling Your Story

> Remember, our Message is not about ourselves; we're proclaiming Jesus Christ, the Master. All we are is messengers, errand runners from Jesus for you. It started when God said, "Light up the darkness!" and our lives filled up with light as we saw and understood God in the face of Christ, all bright and beautiful.—2 Corinthians 4:5-6 (MSG)

We've just talked about living out the gospel in today's world, and doing so can be a powerful witness to our Lord and Savior. But is communicating the values and priorities of Christ Jesus through a godly lifestyle an adequate witness? Some believers say, "I live the gospel. I let my life do my talking for me. I believe that my attitude, manner, and actions will cause people to see Jesus. After all, I'm not an evangelist."

In this chapter, however, we will examine why our witness to Christ must have a verbal, testimonial component. I will present three ingredients of verbal witness: hearing their story, telling your story, and telling His story. In light of the societal shift from metanarrative to micronarrative—the shift away from our culture having an all-encompassing story to an individual having only his or her own small story as a guide for life—the art of storytelling is essential to our Lifestyle Leadership.

Dear Father, *forgive me when I shy away from talking about You. Forgive me when I feel awkward and embarrassed when Your name comes up in a conversation. Enable me to speak freely and boldly of my relationship with You. Enable me to be confident in You. And, Lord, help me take a deeper and genuine interest in people who are not following You. Help me unlock and listen to their story. Use me to help people come to Christ and then grow in Him. In the name of the Father, Son, and Holy Spirit I pray. Amen.*

DO I REALLY HAVE TO TALK ABOUT JESUS?

I have no argument with those who declare that a godly lifestyle is essential to communicating the gospel. People will not see the difference Christ makes if our lives reflect the same values and patterns that theirs do. As one pastor wisely observed, "Christians are to *be* good news before they *share* the good news. The words of the gospel are to be incarnated before they are verbalized."[1] But the godliest life is unable to clarify the news of the Resurrection, God's plan for our forgiveness, and the foundation He provides for a new life of significance and love. Therefore, in the process of our living out a godly lifestyle, we must use words. Our witness must also be verbal. Elton Trueblood makes this very clear in *The Company of the Committed*:

> The spoken word is never really effective unless it is backed up by a life, but it is also true that the living deed is never adequate without the support which the spoken word can provide. This is because no life is ever good enough. The person who says naively, "I don't need to preach; I just let my life speak," is insufferably self-righteous. What one among us is so good that he can let his life speak and leave it at that?[2]

Samuel Shoemaker supports Trueblood's assertion: "I cannot by being good tell of Jesus' atoning death and resurrection, nor of my faith in His divinity. The emphasis is too much on me, and too little on Him."[3] Hear Trueblood finish making the case:

> We must use words because our faith must be in something vastly greater than ourselves. We make a witness by telling not *who* we are but *whose* we are. Though it would be ridiculous for me to try to make a witness by

telling of my own righteousness, which, after all, does not exist, it is not at all ridiculous for me to confess, with candor, to Whom I am committed. This is why the Vocation of Witness belongs necessarily to the Company of the Committed, rather than to the company of the good or the wise or the prudent.[4]

Acknowledging that our verbal testimony is essential to our mission to be God's light in this world, we need to ask ourselves some important questions: What components need to be included in our verbal witness? What can we do to connect with people who are not followers of Jesus—especially when we're afraid that they don't really want to listen to us in the first place? What do we say to them? Where do we begin?

HEAR THEIR STORY: WITNESS MUST BE INTERACTIONAL

Our verbal witness about Christ's purpose for coming to this earth is not usually the starting point of a conversation. Furthermore, prior to our verbal witness, we need to linger in the Soul Room in genuine, compassionate prayer for the person or people with whom we want to share the life-giving gospel truth. We labor before God for these precious folks He has created. We need to ask God to make us curious, even hungry, to get to know these people better.

Then, when we enter the Leadership Room, we must show heartfelt interest in the people we've been praying for. Remember, we are in their lives as servants and friends of Jesus Christ. We are to continually draw upon the Holy Spirit's presence to help us observe, listen, ask questions, and show genuine interest in the people we've been praying for. In a culture where we use people and love things, in a world where people feel hurt and abandoned, it is essential that we are enabled by the Spirit to show genuine interest in people. What interests them—sports, finance, entertainment, history, family of origin, whatever—must become of interest to you and me. Through our questions and sustained interest, we keep freeing them to tell their story. Our sincere interest in hearing and remembering their story means a great deal to them. Furthermore, they—rather than we—are the focus of the conversation, and that choice communicates that we care.

Now let me share a thought about how to truly listen. When people are telling me their stories, I use the following filter to gain deeper insights into their past as well as into who they are today. I call this filter, which comes from the field of psychology, the Basic Psychological Needs Filter. Let me explain.

Psychologists have discovered that all of humanity—male or female, young or old, regardless of ethnicity—have five basic appetites that must be satisfied. Every person will work toward this end, but without Christ, these essential needs for security, love, recognition, new experiences, and freedom from guilt are never *fully* met. This filter is helpful when you want to understand the person to whom you're listening and speaking because, regardless of their age, people do what they do in an attempt to meet one or more of these needs.

Satisfying the Appetite for *Security*: Feeling secure enriches a person's emotional and mental health—and consider for a moment the variety of humanity's attempts to be secure. We buy the latest and greatest. We get involved in relationships that may not be healthy. We marry. We pursue the hottest career opportunity. We dress to be "in." Some of these options for security may be enjoyable and even enriching. But have you ever had your source of security taken away? Have you ever had a person you relied on walk away? Listen to our Lord speak to our hunger for security: "I will never desert you, nor will I ever forsake you" (Hebrews 13:5, NASB). Those are not empty words. They are a reality, 24/7, now and through all eternity. You and I can rely on the faithful presence and steadfast love of Christ. He will never step away or turn His back on us. So, when you listen to the story of people, listen for what it is they are relying on to feel secure. After all, you have a better source of security to offer them.

Satisfying the Appetite for *Love*: We human beings need to be loved; we need loyal friends who accept us and care for us. But human love is so often fickle and untrustworthy. Our nation's high divorce rate is only one bit of evidence we can cite. Still, many people will do anything for love. God's people have this same appetite for love, but we belong to a God who, out of His love for us, sent His Son to the cross. As Paul said, "God demonstrates his own love for us in this: While we were still sinners, Christ died for us" (Romans 5:8).

You and I have an intimate relationship with Someone who knows everything we've ever thought, said, or done. Despite having that kind of file on us, God still loves us and is passionately committed to us. That truth is grace at its best. Like us, our friends as well as the people around us desperately need that grace. So, when you listen to someone's story, listen for where that person is trying to find love. Sometimes I can hardly wait to tell the person I'm talking with where I've found love—lasting, committed, life-giving love.

Satisfying the Appetite for *Recognition*: *He remembered my name.... She called me by name and seemed glad to see me.... He complimented me for my solo.... My husband thanked me for the good dinner.... The boss pulled me aside and praised me for my leadership....* Words of affirmation and encouragement are vital to our mental and emotional health, but such recognition can be fleeting. That's why I've seen capable and successful junior-high students enter senior high and get lost in the crowd. Two years later I see defeated young people standing before me. I've watched topflight seniors graduate from high school but never get their footing in the next chapter of life. I've watched men at the top of their profession lose their job and flounder with poor self-image and depression.

Where can we find recognition that is permanent, that becomes internalized and life-giving, that will sustain us for life? Where can we find recognition that is not based on our performance or how we compare to others? For an answer to these questions, read these words of Scripture:

> To all who received him, to those who believed in his name, he gave the right to become *children of God*—children born not of natural descent, nor of human decision or a husband's will, but *born of God*. (John 1:12-13, emphasis added)

> Do not let your hearts be troubled. Trust in God; trust also in me. In my Father's house are many rooms; if it were not so, I would have told you. *I am going there to prepare a place for you.* And if I go and prepare a place for you, I will come back and take you to be with me *that you also may be where I am.* You know the way to the place where I am going. (John 14:1-4, emphasis added)

> For you did not receive a spirit that makes you a slave again to fear, but you received *the Spirit of sonship*. And by him we cry, "Abba, Father." (Romans 8:15, emphasis added)

What amazing recognition we've received from the Creator of the universe and the Author of history! We are called children of God. We can anticipate living forever in the place that Jesus is now preparing for us. God offers us lasting recognition that steadies us through all of life. As a fellow believer put it, "My identity as Abba's child is not an abstraction or a tap dance into religiosity. It is the core truth of my existence."[5]

So, as I hear my friends' stories, I listen for their past and present recognition places—and together we celebrate those. I also look for opportunities to share some of my own recognition story. We may be recognized outwardly for achievements in music, sports, academics, job, or financial success. But the deeper, more permanent God-provided recognition is what transforms me now and what lasts forever.

Satisfying the Appetite for *New Experiences*: Think about the trouble we human beings get into—especially during our adolescent years—when life has grown routine, stale, and predictable, and we need new experiences. Where can we find new experiences that are healthy and fresh, that contribute to life and culture? If we listen and respond to God, His creativity will become evident in our lives and our ministry, and new experiences will be the norm.

Now for a minute imagine being on a planning retreat with the youth leadership team of Lake Avenue Congregational Church in Pasadena, California. Join me in the Soul Room with these committed and godly leaders. We've spent time in solitude with God and shared Scripture as well as our lives with one another. We are now praying by name for the almost three hundred high-school students who are part of the ministry. As we pray, we listen for what the Holy Spirit might be saying to us through the prayers of others and through our own thoughts. We are seeking program direction for the months of November through May.

As we sit and pray, we listen carefully. We note the names and concerns as well as any new ideas. We listen for recurring needs or interests, areas that suggest possibilities for future program events. As I listen and pray, I hear that we're stuck in a rut. The high-school students have so much, yet they seem bored and tired.

Then one member of the leadership team prays, "What is happening around us? Whom might we serve?" Suddenly I hear this prayer: "Lord, I wonder if we could serve others during the Christmas season by singing Christmas carols at LAX [Los Angeles International Airport]." My immediate internal response was "Lord God, You have to be kidding! How would we ever do this? We've never done this before." But others added their prayers of agreement with the LAX idea.

When we finished praying, we discussed the Christmas caroling idea. We realized that this event was valuable as a great new experience and a ministry adventure, but we had no idea where to start. Nevertheless, I agreed to look into the organizational side. First I located the person who oversees LAX (not a simple assignment!). When we finally connected, I made my request: "We have a wonderful group of high-school students who would love to bring encouragement to LAX Christmas travelers by singing Christmas carols throughout the airport."

I loved the response: "We've never had this request before. I'll have to talk with my superior and get back to you." Was I excited? Yes! Why? Because God's people were on the cutting edge of creativity in a culture place. We were reflecting the creative character of our Lord. After all, too often the church is seen as the least creative of America's institutions.

A few days before Christmas, four buses carrying two hundred high-school students and staff arrived at the international terminal at LAX. For the next four-and-a-half hours, we sang at various gates in all eight terminals and in every major waiting area throughout the entire airport. After singing for ten to fifteen minutes, the high-school students talked with the people in the crowd and shared God's love and blessing. Despite their frustration over late flights and their tired bodies, these travelers often joined us in singing the carols. Some even cried as we sang. We sensed God's Spirit allowing us to connect with hundreds of people in the midst of their day.

Now look again at this story. This remarkable Leadership Room experience didn't come out of a book of ideas for youth ministry. It was born in the Soul Room as the staff sat in the presence of God. As you know, we call it Pitcher/Cup—God pouring Himself into our lives, transforming our character, and increasing our compassion for people. Then we moved to Pitcher/Cup...*Saucer*: We began praying for our students by name (abiding for others). We shared with God the needs and hurts we were aware of, and we listened to Him for insights about these precious high-school students. The next step of this Pitcher/Cup...Saucer praying was our asking God for *Plate*—for an event that would touch the hearts and souls of our students, an event that God might be designing for His glory in order to bring people to Himself and to new places of growth in Him. During this stage of our praying, a wild idea about event, about Plate, came up. And you know the rest of the story. And that's how the spiritual formation of leaders happens: *Pitcher/Cup... Saucer/Plate*. And that's one way our creative God satisfies our human need for new experiences.

So think again about the people you know and some of the things they do to try to satisfy their thirst for new experiences. These options sometimes include destructive addictions like workaholism, drugs, alcohol, sexual promiscuity, gambling, pornography, or overspending. A unique journey results when we accept Jesus' invitations to "Come to Me" and "Come, follow Me," but every journey is filled with new and exciting experiences that are constructive, that nourish the soul, build community, bless others, and bless the heart of God. So, while interacting with people, tantalize them with how God is satisfying your appetite for that which is new, fresh, and meaningful.

Satisfying the Appetite for *Freedom from Guilt*: We hear of businesses paying millions of dollars to settle a lawsuit—and then read that "this company did not admit to any guilt in the matter." It is amazing the degree to which we have endeavored to remove guilt from corporate as well as individual dialogue.

Consider, for instance, a teenager I know who came to Christ. When her mother planned to get married, she asked if I would officiate at the wedding. While getting to know the mother, I ask about her previous marriage—and she explodes, "I don't want to hear about sin! I don't get near God because I don't want to hear all this about sin."

I feel grieved because the residue of the guilt within her is so deep, and she is rejecting the One who could bring cleansing and release from that guilt. You see, people have guilt whether they deny it or acknowledge it. The beauty is that God extends His grace and His forgiveness. Hear how the psalmist expressed this great news: "As high as the heavens are above the earth, so great is his love for those who fear him; as far as the east is from the west, so far has he removed our transgressions [sins] from us" (Psalm 103:11-12). Only in the Lord can we find freedom from guilt. That's definitely a message everyone needs to hear, so listen carefully to people's stories in order to determine where they are looking for that freedom.

Continue by Telling Your Story: Witness Must Be Testimonial

> The method of evangelism is inevitably the method of testimony.... The best way to reach another life is by saying, as simply as possible, "Whereas I was blind, now I see."[6]

You may know John 9 and the account of Jesus healing the man born blind. When the Pharisees confront him, the now-seeing man basically responds, "I know you may think He isn't from God since He gave me sight on the Sabbath; I know you are trying to make Him out to be a sinner."

The man's response the second time the Pharisees confront him is a classic testimonial: "I am unable to answer your questions, but I can tell you what happened to me. When I got up this morning, I couldn't see. I had to be led by another person. Yes, once I was blind, but now I can see. I see the blue of the sky and the white of the clouds. And I can see because Jesus touched my life."

Too often we are reluctant to share our own story of faith because we fear that we'll be asked questions we can't answer. Not knowing the answers, however, did not keep the blind man from confidently sharing his story about Jesus' impact on his life.

No one else can tell your story. No one else even *has* your story. No two testimonies are identical. The distinctiveness of your story of faith in Christ gives credibility to God's ability to draw diverse people to Himself in a variety of amazing ways. The testimonies of God's people reveal His creativity: each story is one-of-a-kind.

And let me point out that in this process of their story, your story, and then God's story, something huge and significant is happening. Remember that, in this postmodernity era, the micronarrative is the bottom line. What works for an individual is all that matters. The view is: "The only thing that matters in the world is *me*. I am the center of my own universe, and I determine my own existence, my own future."[7]

When you begin to share your story, however, you invite your listeners to compare their micronarrative. How does their hope compare to your hope? How does their inner fulfillment compare to your inner fulfillment? How does their life compare to your life? They hear you talk about your moving from "It's my life" to "It's God's life." They hear you talk about moving from being alone to living with One who resides in you. They hear not a micronarrative ("Life is all about me!") but a metanarrative ("I'm living my life with the living God, in His power, for His glory"). They hear you talk about living as part of His story. They see embodied in your life and they hear from your lips that life is more then they have experienced. Your story reveals a hurtful past that has been or is being healed. Your story contains accounts of broken relationships that have been restored. Your story speaks of a redeemed past that has gotten richer and healthier. Through God's Spirit, your listener's micronarrative begins to dwindle in significance, and your story of hope and healing begins to attract them to the Savior. God's Spirit begins to move them from being self-absorbed, from the selfishness of micronarrative, to the healing and hope of the metanarrative.

* * * * *

Over the years of telling my story, I have enjoyed watching people compare their story to my story as I placed my story within the context of God's story. A highly successful business person, a winning college coach, a popular, has-it-all-together high-school student, a winsome college student, a discouraged young person, parents feeling like failures, people defeated and adrift—the list goes on and on—and I have seen the Spirit draw these special people to Himself as they hear my story and begin to realize that Jesus provides forgiveness, hope, healing, vision, a community, surprises, and a future far grander than any ideas they had for their life. To be invited into the arms of God and into His story made their story seem rather small and insignificant.

One more point about telling your story: whenever you share your journey of faith in Christ, you help people understand that the Christian life is about both beginnings and, to coin a word, continuings. The Christian life is dynamic, not static. It zigs and zags; it has its definite ups and downs. It is not temporary, not a fad, not a "to do" list, not an insurance policy. It is past, present, and future. It is a lifelong, personal, growing relationship with the living Christ. When we believers tell our story, people hear about how one Christian journey began as well as about some of the steps along the way. They hear how the presence of Christ in your life enables you to cope with the challenges you face. Your sharing also helps others compare how you satisfy your appetites for security, love, recognition, new experiences, and freedom from guilt to how they are trying to do so.

CELEBRATE BY TELLING HIS STORY: WITNESS MUST BE SCRIPTURAL

When we listen to people's stories, we show our interest in them and in their journey. When we tell our own story, we share ourselves; we describe our own journey. We move from their story, to our story, to His Story. And God's story—for all humanity—provides a canopy over all human stories. In His Story He offers hope, forgiveness, health, community, and consummation to all of history. And when we tell Jesus' story, we reveal that we are part of something much greater than ourselves, and that is what the apostle Paul did when he stood before King Agrippa (Acts 26:28-29).

When told he could speak on his own behalf, Paul told the story of his coming to faith in Christ and the calling of God upon his life. He explained that he was part of something that is initiated by God and lived out by people. Paul's story is a clear account of God's doings. Listen to the apostle tell God's story:

> On one of these journeys I was going to Damascus with the authority and commission of the chief priests. About noon, O king, as I was on the road,

> I saw a light from heaven, brighter than the sun, blazing around me and my companions. We all fell to the ground, and I heard a voice saying to me in Aramaic, "Saul, Saul, why do you persecute me? It is hard for you to kick against the goads."
>
> Then I asked, "Who are you, Lord? "
>
> "I am Jesus, whom you are persecuting," the Lord replied. "Now get up and stand on your feet. I have appeared to you to appoint you as a servant and as a witness of what you have seen of me and what I will show you. I will rescue you from your own people and from the Gentiles. I am sending you to them to open their eyes and turn them from darkness to light, and from the power of Satan to God, so that they may receive forgiveness of sins and a place among those who are sanctified by faith in me."
>
> So then, King Agrippa, I was not disobedient to the vision from heaven. (Acts 26:12-19)

In Paul's encounter with God, Jesus made His story clear—and His story was clear in Paul's faithful testimony. The following four elements comprise the substance of Paul's God-story—and it is to be the substance of yours and mine:

- *Transformation into a New Condition* This transformation happens as God "open[s] their eyes and turn[s] them from darkness to light" (Acts 26:18). Once people acknowledge the truth about God, they will see things against the backdrop of the nature of God, who is light, instead of against the backdrop of our dark culture. This movement from darkness to light gives people a truer, more biblical perspective on themselves, on others, and on life in general.

- *Response to a New Influence* People turn "from the power of Satan to God" (Acts 26:18). The power of Satan is a self-centered, destructive power that uses people as impersonal tools in his schemes. God, however, embraces us as daughters and sons in His family. God's power gives us new life, eternal life, and a new life-power for His glory and our good.

- *Discovering a New Freedom* We experience this freedom when we accept the "forgiveness of sins" that Jesus offers (Acts 26:18). The ball and chain of guilt can keep us from new endeavors and new beginnings. Guilt about wrong things we've done, about ways we've hurt others, and about how we've disappointed God is cancerous, and it keeps us in Satan's grip. When the living God breaks into a life, the ball and chain of guilt is snapped, the soul is freed, and that person begins to soar in ways never before experienced or even imagined. This new freedom is a gift from God.

- *Living in a New Place* This happens as we experience a fresh start "among those who are sanctified by faith in [Christ]" (Acts 26:18). In this world we live among people who are competing for a place of belonging and significance. Our culture's high divorce rate leaves people confused, rootless, and often without a sense of family heritage. The place that once seemed secure is gone, but God's story gives us a heritage and permanent belonging. I learn that I am a vital person in His story, that I am essential to the unfolding of history.

So I listen to the story of others and I share my story, but it is His story that places both our stories in perspective. God's story, as Paul explained, gives new meaning and direction to our lives. Specifically, Jesus' revelation to Paul—"I have appeared to you to appoint you as a servant and as a witness..." (Acts 26:16)—was part of His storyline for all of history.

As I said earlier, my role as a follower of Christ is to be God's servant in every situation I find myself. I am a witness to my experience of God's love and grace to me in the past as well as His continuing love and grace in the present. I will also be a witness to the future work of grace that God will be doing in and through my life. As a witness, I will describe what I have seen and experienced. So, whenever I am communicating the gospel, I am actually sharing with a friend the news of another special Friend. In the process of living and speaking, I am merely endeavoring to tantalize my friends with the desire to meet my best Friend, the Lord Jesus Christ.

HEAR THEIR STORY,

SHARE YOUR STORY,

AND TELL HIS STORY.

Dear Lord Jesus, new life in You means I
am forgiven, and I have had a new beginning. Lord, I desire others to
have a dynamic relationship with You. I want them to experience the
new life You provide. Jesus, please increase my compassion for specific
people who have yet to embrace You. Through my love, my life, and
my conversation, may they be drawn to You and to Your story. Lord
God, free me to listen intently to the story that people want to tell
about themselves. Then free me to graciously and honestly tell both
my story and Your story. May I talk freely to people about You who
are my best Friend. And may my life in You bear the fruit of new
births into the kingdom of God. I pray this in the name of the Father
and the Son and the Holy Spirit. Amen.

Before You Take the Next Step

How has this chapter increased your confidence about being with people who
have yet to embrace Jesus?

Your Story: Take a few moments to remember your own "following Jesus" story
from the beginning until now. Enjoy a time of praise and worship as you
thank God for all that Jesus has done.

Their Story: As you talk with people, listen for their stories. Be attentive to what they share about how they're meeting their need for security, love, recognition, new experiences, and freedom from guilt.

His Story: May your time of abiding with Christ in Scripture help you see your story formed and enfolded by His story of love and redemption.

*The move from
thinking about being a
spiritually growing
leader to intentionally
choosing to live as one
blesses the Father's
heart, enriches the
kingdom, and fulfills
your life.*

From Reading a Book to Living a Book

From Gaining Information to Experiencing Continual Transformation

In a world of many books, what role will this book play in your life? Has it sharpened your understanding of godly leadership and described spiritual formation in helpful ways? Is the Pitcher/ Cup...Saucer/Plate metaphor fueling your desire to be alone with God? Have you gained some important new insights about the church? Have these chapters increased your understanding of and compassion for people in the culture in which you live?

Or will the book serve as more than a mere source of information and even inspiration? Will God use the truths between these covers to ignite in you a passion to grow in Him, a passion for spiritual formation that will shape and empower your leadership? Do you sense within you a holy resolve to enter into the God-process of being an apprentice of Jesus and "learning from him how to lead [your] life as he would lead [your] life if he were [you]"?[1]

Throughout this book I have commented about the crying need in our culture, in the home, and in the church for effective disciples and disciple-makers, for godly people whom the Lord can use as light and salt in this dark and hurting world. Why are such servant leaders so rare today?

Listen to a voice from the 1600s as well as a voice from the twenty-first century. First, in *A Serious Call to a Devout and Holy Life*, William Law addressed "why the generality of Christians fall so far short of the holiness and devotion of Christianity."[2] Law answers his question by saying it is simply the lack of a heartfelt intention to please God:

> If you will here stop and ask yourself why you are not as pious as the primitive Christians were, your own heart will tell you that it is neither through ignorance nor inability, but purely because you never thoroughly intended it.[3]

Do you find Law's point hard to argue with? Dallas Willard whole-heartedly agrees with Law:

> It could well prove a major turning point in our life if we would… ask ourselves if we really do intend to be life students of Jesus. Do we really intend to do and be all of the high things we profess to believe in? Have we decided to do them? When did we decide it? And how did we implement that decision?
>
> Intention and decision are absolutely fundamental in this matter of apprenticeship to Jesus.[4]

My prayer has been that God would use this book to grow in you the intention to be an apprentice of Jesus. Many of us read a book and walk away with little more than new information; I have frequently done that myself. New information can definitely be helpful, but my passion is that this book would become for you a source of guidance in your spiritual formation as a leader and a source of encouragement as you learn to integrate spiritual formation and leadership development. My prayer has been that God would use the truths in these pages to provide definition and ongoing help in the God process so that you can cooperate with Him as He makes you more like Christ and enables you to walk in His ways.

May this book bring you to a significant place of new or renewed intention and decision. May this book be more than words on a page. And may these words become flesh-and-blood, God-glorifying truth in your life. I invite you to join me—if you haven't already—in deciding to be a godly leader who intentionally lives out the God-process of Pitcher/Cup…Saucer/Plate.

WHERE WE'VE BEEN

In this chapter we will revisit some of the key questions I've asked as we've journeyed through this book. As we look again at the Pitcher/Cup...Saucer/Plate image, we will see both how it is designed to work and how it goes awry. We will, I pray, move toward a deeper understanding and greater excitement about the God-process of spiritual leadership development. Let us pray.

Lord, thank You for calling me to be Your child. I am privileged to call You "Abba, Father"; I am blessed that I am Your beloved. Thank You that, as I travel through this world of pressure and pain, the Prince of Peace resides in me. Thank You that, in a world that desperately needs godly leaders, I am "being transformed into [Christ's] likeness with ever-increasing glory, which comes from the Lord, who is the Spirit" (2 Corinthians 3:18). Almighty God, use this chapter to challenge my thinking, to open me up to Your transforming work in my character, and to further shape my lifestyle so that I honor and glorify You in all I say and do. I ask this in the powerful name of the Lord Jesus. Amen.

BIG IDEAS

Every time I teach in The Journey of The Leadership Institute (for more information, go to http://www.theleadershipinstitute.org/journey/), a friend of mine reminds me that I am presenting a *big idea*. She reminds me that *big ideas* take a long time to understand, process, and integrate into daily life. In light of that fact, I am going to summarize the *big ideas* of this book—the *big ideas* about the spiritual formation of leaders—that I have shared with you in these pages because I know that these ideas take awhile to embody in our leadership and our daily life. So, as I ask you several questions as a means of reviewing the material, beware of merely seeing the words on the pages. Instead, try to envision the truths shaping your speech, your manner, your attitudes, your relationships, your thinking, and your entire lifestyle, both private and public.

#1 Are your Christian life and your leadership style defined by a ministry model or by what I call a God-process of building leaders and ministries?

Ministry models provide helpful ideas and insights. Models offer program designs and guaranteed outcomes ("Do this and you'll get that"). God-process, however, offers no guaranteed outcomes, but it does offer you a guaranteed Companion. God Himself says, "I will be with you."

At the moment, which guarantee is more compelling to you—ministry outcomes or God's presence with you? Why? Which guarantee is having the greater impact on your life? Why?

#2 The God-process of spiritual formation involves two rooms. Which room do you frequent most often? Why? Are the two rooms each essential? Explain.

In America we have the two-room church, the Soul Room for spiritual formation and the Leadership Room for leadership development. People excited about spiritual formation use a particular vocabulary, read certain authors, and attend certain conferences. People excited about leadership development use a different vocabulary, read other authors, and attend other conferences. This Pick and Choose Club tragically hinders the holistic development of godly, spiritually growing, prayerful leaders in the American church. We have become either/or, but God process involves both rooms—the Soul Room *and* the Leadership Room.

Which room—the Soul Room or the Leadership Room—do you think is primary? Put differently, which one leads to the other? What does your schedule for the past month reveal about where you tend to spend your time?

#3 In a world flooded with information, where do you find wisdom? The Bible is to be the Christian's guidebook, the primary source for developing healthy leaders who are being transformed by God and leading His people as a result of His work in their lives.

Healthy leaders appreciate and approach the Bible as a book of Story, Message, and Way. Godly and growing leaders have learned that the Bible is a book of *stories* about pardon and process, not about performance and perfection. They recognize that the Bible is God's *message*—a message *from* Him and *about* Him—for all of humanity throughout all time. They also continue to discover that, from the first page of Genesis through the "amen" of Revelation 22:21, the Bible sets forth the ways of God.

The *story* of spiritually growing leaders, the micronarrative, reflects the story of God, the metanarrative. The *message* of God provides both the foundation for life on which healthy leaders stand and the heart of the life-saving, life-changing news they bring. The Bible as *way* inwardly transforms and outwardly guides the seeking leader in how to lead in the Jesus Way. As God's Spirit continues to transform us leaders, we read the Bible and live it out as an integration of story, message, and way.

Are you interacting with Scripture and living out the breadth of its truth and hope, its instruction and encouragement?

#4 God is a God of grace. In His love and grace, He continually extends two invitations to you. Have you accepted these invitations?

These invitations—which keep leaders energized and healthy—are from Jesus; they are not junk mail. So open His invitations to you—and do so every morning.

"Come unto Me all you who labor and are heavy laden" is the first invitation, and Jesus extends it because He knows your inner condition. He therefore invites you to know His strength and His peace, His comfort and His hope.

Jesus also issues the invitation "Come, follow Me, and I will make you fishers of men." Jesus knows our human proneness to do our own thing, to lead in our own way, to take the reins, to be in charge. But in God's kingdom, leadership is actually followership. And God transforms us through our followership, our apprenticeship in Christ, as well as through the finding, enfolding, and nurturing process of developing other healthy God followers. Talk about fulfilling!

Will you—a busy leader with lots to do, a leader with a resume—come? Will you, a take-charge leader, come and follow?

#5 So many voices! So many distractions! What really matters? You love Jesus' invitations to you, but how will they fit into the schedule and flow of your life?

That question is really a matter of identifying—and living according to—the priorities of a healthy and godly leader. We know that, in the Upper Room, Jesus taught that these priorities of life are abiding in Him, loving one another, and bearing witness. A godly and growing leader knows that the Vine is the Source of abundant life and daily energy. A godly and growing leader continually discovers that the source of life is the Vine. We are to first live out this Vine Life among kingdom people as we invest time and effort in loving one another (John 13:35). Our Vine Life further manifests itself in our bearing witness to Christ in a world of hurting people, a world that has rejected the Christ. These priorities provide definition and meaning to our schedule and to our relationships. We begin to follow the direction of God's Spirit rather than being moved along by the drivenness characteristic of our culture.

How well are you handling the tension that exists between pressures and priorities? Which tends to get most of your time, attention, and energy? What can you do to better listen for God's voice—and then ensure that you will follow Him?

#6 The story of God's pardon of our sins brings relief, cleansing, and freedom. But what else does the God process involve? What does He want to do in your life, for the rest of your days, so that you will continue growing in Him?

The Pitcher/Cup…Saucer/Plate process is God initiated and God sustained. As I've said, the *Pitcher* represents all that God is and longs to pour into the cup of your life. It represents His very essence, His Triune being as Father, Son, and Holy Spirit, and His desires for your life. The *Cup* represents your life—who you are today and all that God longs for you to become as He continually pours Himself into your life until it overflows with His character and grace. The *Saucer* represents your relationships, the network of people your life touches however frequently or infrequently. The divine overflow spills onto the saucer so that those people in your life get a taste of the Lord's goodness and love. Finally, the *Plate* represents the events, the places, and the organizations where God's gracious presence can flow through you and, at times, through your leadership roles.

Are you running directly from Pitcher to Plate in order to lead and minister? Linger with God and ask Him to help you answer that question.

#7 Who is in the Soul Room? Is it a safe place to go?

The remarkable welcoming committee of Father, Son, and Holy Spirit awaits you in the Soul Room. The Three are always glad to see you, and They always want you to feel at home and cherished. If you—as I too often do—enter the Soul Room in quest of a consultant, They will receive you as a friend. If you—as I do—enter wanting to know how to lead or manage something or someone, They will push aside your management concerns and draw you into Their circle of life-giving fellowship. As you get to know the Three more intimately, you'll discover Their desire for that same kind of intimacy with you that They enjoy with one another. The atmosphere in the Soul Room changes as you become a community of four. This experience is very mysterious and very transformational for every follower of Jesus. Moving from management to mystery is a miraculous component in the journey of a godly leader who is continuing to be transformed by God's grace. This communion with the Holy Trinity is indeed life changing.

> *Moving from management to mystery is a miraculous component in the journey of a godly leader.*

Do you regularly visit and frequently linger in the Soul Room? Or do you rush in and out so fast that you experience little sense of communion with the Trinity?

#8 How does the Soul Room become a special place for personal growth as well as leadership?

In communion with the Father, Son, and Holy Spirit, you will find yourself starting to relax and feel at home. You will be freer to give Them access to who you really are as well as to the areas of your life where your need Their wisdom and transforming work. You will find yourself coming to the Soul Room to abide for yourself, not just for the ministry or for other people. Keenly aware that you are the clay, you will find yourself wanting the Potter's workmanship to be evident in your life.

Furthermore, as you abide for yourself, you will start to realize that the Soul Room is the place to interact with the Three about your leadership and ministry responsibilities. You will find yourself asking for insight about how to love and minister to the people under your care. Father, Son, and Spirit will help you dream about what these people—by divine grace—can become. The Three also grow in you the desire to pray for others. So the Soul Room becomes a place where you abide for others as well as for yourself.

In what specific ways has the Soul Room been meaningful to you in the last month? When will you enter the Soul Room in the coming week?

#9 The church—populated as it is by sinners and existing counter-culturally as it does—gets good press and bad in this fallen world. What exactly is the church? And how is it to function effectively?

The church is people, and this body of people is God's "show and tell" vehicle for displaying the work He does to transform lives both individually and collectively. Yet too often we regard church as events to which we go, not a community of people to whom we belong. I can't emphasize enough that the church is people purchased by the blood of Christ and learning to live in committed communities—a design that is not easy to live out, a design that requires God's transforming work in every one of us who follows Christ.

Put differently, the church is an organism that breathes because of the life of Christ within it. Yet the church can too easily become primarily an organization with jobs and responsibilities, tasks and duties. This dynamic tension between organism and organization is unavoidable, and we in the church too often try to solve a problem organizationally when the real problem lies in the health and lifestyle of the organism. The church often spends more time doing organizational tasks than it does gathering to worship the Lord, nurture their relationship with Him, enjoy fellowship with one another, and be scattered in mission.

Who are the people in the church who are touching your life? Be specific—and thankful. Who are the people in the church you are touching? Ask God to direct your steps and to use you to love with His love.

#10 The church has so many opportunities to be salt and light, a source of love and hope and healing, in this dark and hurting world.

How do we know what really matters, how do godly leaders grow a healthy church, and how do we develop leaders who are continuing to grow spiritually?

Local churches and their leaders know the enormous opportunities and constant demands of ministry today. In light of that reality, every church and ministry must be intentional about sequentially cultivating two radically different soils. The first soil is *Lifestyle Leadership soil*, the soil of invitation ("Come unto Me" and "Come, follow Me"); the soil of the Upper Room (abiding, loving one another, and bearing witness). Too often this Lifestyle Leadership soil is the source of nurture and growth for only a highly committed few when it is intended to be the norm for every follower of Christ. This soil of organism, of spiritual nurture that grows godly leaders, is to be primary and central in the church. The second soil that every church and ministry needs is *Positional Leadership soil*. People who have organizational and ministry responsibility are planted here, but too often it bears the fruit of tiredness and burnout. To avoid that bitter fruit, leaders must stay firmly rooted in the first soil even as they send their roots into the second soil. Together—and as the people of God adopt the seven intentional leader behaviors discussed in chapter 13—these two soils grow healthy leaders and effective ministries.

What are you doing in your life and ministry to stay rooted in Lifestyle Leadership soil and to extend your roots into Positional Leadership soil? Pray through the seven behaviors and listen for God's word to you.

#11 What can you do to better understand—and, for the Lord's sake, engage more fully with—our rapidly changing world?

We live in a world where the emotional and experiential distance between the generations continues to increase, and walls of protection—walls resulting from misunderstanding—have resulted. We who are the people of God must begin to overcome and tear down these intergenerational walls. As we do so and as we discover the precious people of other generations, may we follow the Spirit's leading, experience His empowering, and engage people from generations other than our own. After all, God sends us beyond the church gathered on His mission of love and forgiveness to all the generations.

In addition to dealing with generational differences, we in the twenty-first-century church must also deal with significant societal changes. Specifically, the culture has shifted from a modern to a post-modernity mind-set, and people are thinking and living differently. The postmodernity view maintains that there is no objective truth; this view offers no overarching story to give meaning and purpose to life; and the community is more important than the individual. No wonder postmoderns experience a sense of loss and bewilderment about life. May we who know Jesus—His unshakable truth, His story that gives us purpose, and His personal love for us—cross over the bridge from our comfort zone, enter the community of postmoderns, and be listening friends who are making new friends in Jesus' name.

What generational walls are still standing in your life—and what will you do about them? Who are the postmodernity people with whom you are establishing and/or strengthening friendships?

#12 Christ's people are so different from our culture's postmodern people. Can God really impact the world through people like you—and if so, how?

Jesus lived in a neighborhood, worked with wood, was familiar with fishing, and embodied the character of God, for He was God. In essence, "Christ is the visible expression of the invisible God" (Colossians 2:15, PHILLIPS). Our invisible God lives within us so that we too can embody His character and, by the power of His Spirit, impact people through our lifestyle and our verbal communication. When people see an honest character in us and experience an engaging friendship with us, they both enjoy our company and respect us, and those are key to the development of mutual friend-ships where they can share their story and their life. We followers of Jesus are to keenly listen to their story and look for the opportunity to share our own story and His story.

Are you comfortable living beyond your circle of friends who follow Jesus Christ? Why or why not? Who are some specific people outside that circle for whom you are praying and with whom you are attempting to develop a friendship?

DIFFERENT CONFIGURATIONS OF THE GOD-PROCESS

God's plan for our spiritual formation is a plan that results in godly, growing individuals and healthy and effective ministry. We've talked about that plan—about the God-process—with the Pitcher/Cup... Saucer/Plate metaphor. This divine design is perfect, but too often we mess it up.

Drained and Driven

These leaders see themselves as in charge. The motto "Leaders Lead" describes them, and "followership" is not a prominent word in their vocabulary. These leaders tend to grow impatient when things don't go their way on their timetable, they feel the pressures mount, and their personality style compels them to charge ahead. They often feel and even lead as if God is late. They empty their cup—their life—as they lead, but love and power overflowing from the Lord aren't fueling their leadership.

Lord, draw me to Yourself, to You who are the Pitcher and the Source of life.

My Cup Has a Crack

These leaders are faithful and busy, but tired and struggling. Their primary commitment to Saucer/Plate leaves them little, if any, intentional time for Pitcher/Cup, and any measure of blessing or fruit from Saucer and Plate may cause them to long for the Pitcher less and less. The pattern is to keep leading… and to be spiritually formed and renewed less and less. These leaders are positioned for burnout.

Lord, create in my heart the desire to be more intentional about my Pitcher/Cup time.

Thriving on Events

The Pitcher/*Plate*… Saucer/Cup leader is often motivated by exciting programs and dynamic events. Every event needs to be bigger and better than the last, and the program-centered leader needs people to make these events happen. Too often these dear volunteers become tools in the leader's hand rather than people with a story who touch the leader's heart.

Leadership that begins with an outward focus on events also tends to keep us from receiving God's grace and experiencing His transforming touch in our life. We pray more often for programs than for people, including ourselves.

Lord, restructure my leadership so that it is ordered Pitcher/Cup…Saucer/Plate and therefore can be fully blessed by You.

Thriving on Being with People

The Pitcher/*Saucer*...Plate/Cup leader enjoys and is energized by being with people. Events are regarded as a source of frustration or even an interruption in life and ministry. Such leaders run from person to person, and at the end of the day they are tired but somewhat fulfilled. These people-centered leaders usually do pray for others—often before praying for themselves—but they tend to have a hard time dealing with the plank in their own eye before the speck in a brother's eye. Co-dependents (folks who need affirmation regardless of the damage receiving such affirmation does to their own boundaries) often live out this pattern of ministry.

Lord, may I let You love and transform me so that You can touch people through me.

I Love the Soul Room

The Pitcher/Cup leader is captivated by an inward and vertical focus on the Lord. These leaders know that the Soul Room is a place they can experience deep personal healing, restoration, and comfort. They treasure the greater intimacy with God they develop here. But in the Soul Room, these people stand alone, and they are reluctant to let God broaden their vision to Saucer/Plate. Their spirituality is characterized by isolation, not integration; their leadership is not influenced by their Pitcher/Cup time. They easily become leaders of the one-room church: the Soul Room is the focus, and the Leadership Room is assumed. This is not God-process.

Lord, excite me about what You can do when the Pitcher/Cup of my life flows over into my Saucer and Plate relationships.

God's Process for Being Effective Spiritual Leaders

Pitcher, Cup, Saucer, and Plate represent the dynamic ingredients in God's process for your spiritual transformation and godly leadership. As the Pitcher—the infinite Source of energy, direction, passion, love, and everything else you need for ministry—pours Himself into the Cup of your life, overflow is inevitable. By God's grace, this ongoing overflow spills onto the Saucer and Plate of your life, into the relationships and the ministries God has called you to. Your leadership then is an overflow of God's love, His character, and His power—of all of Himself that He is pouring into the Cup of your life. Leading from overflow like this is God-process: you receive that transforming and empowering overflow in the Soul Room, and it spills over into the Leadership Room. Leadership from such godly overflow and the resulting inner transformation of your heart enables long-lasting leadership and a fruitful ministry, and in those God is honored, the community is kept healthy, and His kingdom grows. To God be the glory!

With that vision in mind, I repeat what I said at the beginning of this chapter: May this book bring you to a significant place of intention and decision to be a godly leader who responds to Jesus' invitations "Come unto Me" and "Come, follow Me," a godly leader who intentionally lives out the God-process of Pitcher/Cup... Saucer/Plate. May you join and share with others who have this same intention.

I close with words from the apostle Paul who expresses well my desire for your life and for mine:

**May the God of hope fill you with all joy and peace
as you trust in him, so that you may overflow with hope
by the power of the Holy Spirit.**

—Romans 15:13

**May the grace of the Lord Jesus Christ,
and the love of God,
and the fellowship of the Holy Spirit
be with you all.**

—2 Corinthians 13:14

Notes

Introduction

1. John Stott, "Make Disciples, Not Just Converts," *Christianity Today* (October 25, 1999), 28-29.

2. Robert Webber, *Ancient-Future Evangelism: Making Your Church a Faith-Forming Community* (Grand Rapids: Baker, 2003), 13.

3. J. Oswald Sanders, *Spiritual Leadership: Principles of Excellence for Every Believer* (Chicago: Moody Press, 1967), 16.

4. Stephen R. Covey, *The 7 Habits of Highly Effective People: Powerful Lessons in Personal Change* (New York: Simon & Schuster, 1989), 18-19.

Chapter 1

1. Michael H. Hart, *The 100: A Ranking of the Most Influential Persons in History* (New York: Hart Publishing Company, 1978), 79.

2. Eugene H. Peterson, *Under the Unpredictable Plant: An Exploration of Vocational Holiness* (Grand Rapids: Eerdmans, 1992), 127.

Chapter 2

1. Consider this quote from Sirach 51: 26, a book from the Roman Catholic Old Testament: "Put your neck under the yoke and let your soul receive instruction" (Wycliffe Bible Commentary, Electronic Database, 1962, Moody Press).

2. Dietrich Bonhoeffer, *The Cost of Discipleship* (New York: Touchstone, 1995), 37-38.

3. R. P. G. Tasker, *The Gospel According to Matthew* (Grand Rapids: Eerdmans, 1961), 122.

4. *Theological Dictionary of the New Testament*, ed. Gerhard Kittle, Volume 4, trans. Geoffrey W. Bromiley (Grand Rapids: Eerdmans, 1967), 441.

5. Drawn from John Ortberg, *The Life You've Always Wanted: Spiritual Disciplines for Ordinary People* (Grand Rapids: Zondervan, 2002), 11-26.

6. John R. W. Stott, *Authentic Christianity*, ed. Timothy Dudley-Smith (Downers Grove, IL: InterVarsity, 1995), 168.

7. Eugene H. Peterson, *A Long Obedience in the Same Direction: Discipleship in an Instant Society* (Downers Grove, IL: InterVarsity, 1980), 17.

Chapter 3

1. Eugene H. Peterson, *Subversive Spirituality: Discovering the Secret of a Man's Soul* (Grand Rapids: Eerdmans, 1994), 5.

2. John Eldredge, *Wild at Heart* (Nashville Thomas Nelson, 2001), 210

3. Eugene H. Peterson, *The Jesus Way: A Conversation on the Ways That Jesus Is the Way* (Grand Rapids: Eerdmans, 2007), 6-7.

Chapter 4

1. The original language of Mark 1:17 makes clear that "it would be a slow and long process, but Jesus could and would do it. He would undertake to make fishers of men out of fishermen" (A. T. Robertson, *New Testament Word Pictures* on the software program *PCStudy Bible* under "Commentaries").

Chapter 5

1. InterVarsity Press Commentary (from Internet commentary).

2. Richard Foster, *Meditative Prayer* (Downers Grove, IL: InterVarsity, 1983), 6.

3. J. I. Packer, *A Quest for Godliness: The Puritan Vision of the Christian Life* (Wheaton, IL: Crossway, 1990), 215-216.

4. Andrew Murray, *Abide in Christ* (Fort Washington, PA: Christian Literature Crusade, 2000), 13.

5. Thomas Merton as quoted by Brennan Manning, *Abba's Child: The Cry of the Heart for Intimate Belonging* (Colorado Springs: NavPress, 1994), 27.

Chapter 6

1. Peter van Breemen in Brennan Manning, *The Ragamuffin Gospel: Good News for the Bedraggled, Beat-Up, and Burnt Out* (Sisters, OR: Multnomah, 1990), 39.

2. Richard Foster, *Prayer: Finding the Heart's True Home* (San Francisco: Harper, 1992), 85.

3. Kallistos Ware, "Ways of Prayer and Contemplation," in *Christian Spirituality: Origins to the Twelfth Century*, eds. Bernard McGinn and John Meyendorff (NY: Crossroads, 1985), 398, quoted in Diogenes Allen, *Spiritual Theology* (Boston: Cowley Publications, 1997), 12.

4. Klaus Issler, *Wasting Time with God: A Christian Spirituality of Friendship with God* (Downers Grove: InterVarsity, 2001), 159.

5. Brennan Manning, *Abba's Child: The Cry of the Heart for Intimate Belonging* (Colorado Springs: NavPress, 1994), 66.

6. Eugene H. Peterson, *Christ Plays in Ten Thousand Places: A Conversation in Spiritual Theology* (Grand Rapids: Eerdmans, 2005), 7.

Chapter 7

1. Klaus Issler, *Wasting Time with God: A Christian Spirituality of Friendship with God* (Downers Grove: InterVarsity, 2001), 155-56.

2. Dallas Willard in Klaus Issler, *Wasting Time*, 155.

3. Simon Chan, *Spiritual Theology: A Systematic Study of the Christian Life* (Downers Grove: InterVarsity, 1998), 65.

4. Henri J. M. Nouwen, *Life of the Beloved: Spiritual Living in a Secular Wrold* (New York: Crossroads, 1992), 34.

5. Henry Cloud, *Changes That Heal: How to Understand the Past to Ensure a Healthier Future* (Grand Rapids: Zondervan, 1990, 1992), 28.

6. Cloud, 28.

7. Cloud, 25.

8. Chan, p. 71.

9. Howard Hendricks in *Graduation Moments: Wisdom and Inspiration from the Best Commencement Speeches Ever* (Colorado Springs: Honor Books, 2004), 99.

10. J. I. Packer, *A Quest for Godliness: The Puritan Vision of the Christian Life* (Wheaton, IL: Crossway, 1990), 203.

11. James Torrance in Chan, 62.

Chapter 8

1. Robert Mulholland, *Shaped by the Word: The Power of Scripture in Spiritual Formation* (Nashville: Upper Room Press, 1985), 21.
2. Mulholland, 22.
3. Mulholland, 23.
4. Simon Chan, *Spiritual Theology: A Systematic Study of the Christian Life* (Downers Grove: InterVarsity, 1998), 160.

Chapter 9

1. Andrew Murray, *The Secret of Intercession* (Fort Washington, PA: Christian Literature Crusade, 1998), 13.
2. Oswald Chambers, *My Utmost from His Highest: An Updated Edition in Today's Language*, ed. James Reimann (Grand Rapids: Discovery House, 1992), April 1.
3. Chambers, *My Utmost*, April 1.
4. John Calvin quoted in Richard Foster, *Prayer: Finding the Heart's True Home* (San Francisco: HarperSanFrancisco, 1992), 197.
5. Foster, 191.

Chapter 10

1. This Richard Halverson quote undoubtedly came from one of his "Perspective" letters, but we have been unable to locate the issue.
2. Julie Gorman, *Community That Is Christian: A Handbook on Small Groups* (Wheaton, IL: Victor Books, 1993), 16-17.
3. Charles Colson, *The Body* (Dallas, TX: Word, 1992), 65-66.
4. John R. W. Stott, *Ephesians: Building Community in Christ* (Downers Grove, IL: InterVarsity, 1998), 3.

Chapter 11

1. Eugene H. Peterson, *Under the Unpredictable Plant: An Exploration of Vocational Holiness* (Grand Rapids, MI: Eerdmans, 1992), 35-36.
2. Jim Peterson, *Church Without Walls: Moving Beyond Traditional Boundaries* (Colorado Springs: Nav Press,1992), 115.
3. Richard Halverson in Peterson, *Church Without Walls*, 116.
4. Ronald A. Heifitz and Marty Linsky, *Leadership On the Line: Staying Alive through the Dangers of Leading* (Boston, MA: Harvard Business School Press, 2002), 212.
5. Eugene H. Peterson, *Leap Over a Wall: Earthy Spirituality for Everyday Christians* (San Francisco: HarperSanFrancisco, 1997), 138.
6. Richard Halverson, *How I Changed My Thinking About the Church* (Grand Rapids: Zondervan, 1972), 42.
7. Halverson, 42.
8. Peterson, *Leap Over,* 138.
9. Peter Drucker, *The Effective Executive: The Definitive Guide to Getting the Right Things Done* (New York: Harper & Row, 1966), 15.
10. Ray C. Stedman, *Body Life* (Glendale, CA: Regal, 1972), 26.
11. Parker Palmer, *The Courage to Teach: Exploring the Inner Landscape of a Teacher's Life* (San Francisco: Jossey-Bass, 1998), 62.
12. Palmer, 62-63.
13. Palmer, 65-66.

Chapter 13

1. Lois E. LeBar, *Education That Is Christian* (Colorado Springs: Cook Communications, 1989), 64.

Chapter 15

1. Neil Howe and William Strauss, *Generations: The History of America's Future, 1584 to 2069* (New York: Vintage, 1991), 8-9.

2. Jimmy Long, *Emerging Hope: A Strategy for Reaching Postmodern Generations* (Downers Grove, IL: InterVarsity, 2004), 26.

3. Howe and Strauss, 263.

In this section and in the subsequent sections on generations, I am sharing insights from Strauss and Howe unless otherwise noted.

4. Howe and Strauss, 279-285.

5. Howe and Strauss, 295-307.

6. Howe and Strauss, 302.

7. Christopher Lasch, *The Culture of Narcissism: American Life in an Age of Diminishing Expectations* (New York: Norton, 1979), 23, 30.

8. Howe and Strauss, 321.

9. Long, 39.

10. Howe and Strauss, 329.

11. Howe and Strauss, 329.

12. Howe and Strauss, 339-340.

13. Howe and Strauss, 339-340.

14. Chap Clark, *Hurt* (Grand Rapids: Baker Academic, 2004), 46.

15. Clark, 34.

16. Clark, 34, 44-53.

17. Dallas Willard, *Renovation of the Heart: Putting On the Character of Christ* (Colorado Springs: NavPress, 2002), 22-24.

18. John Stott, *Between Two Worlds: The Challenge of Preaching Today* (Grand Rapids: Eerdmans, 1982), 137, 138.

19. Stott, 180

20. Michael Green, *Sharing Your Faith with Friends and Family: Talking about Jesus Without Offending* (Grand Rapids: Baker, 2005), 29-30.

Chapter 16

1. Millard J. Erickson, *The Postmodern World: Discerning the Times and the Spirit of Our Age* (Wheaton, IL: Crossway, 2002), 18-20.

2. Erickson, 23.

3. Jimmy Long, *Emerging Hope: A Strategy for Reaching Postmodern Generations* (Downers Grove, IL: InterVarsity, 2004), 64.

4. George G. Hunter, *The Celtic Way of Evangelism: How Christianity Can Reach the West Again* (Nashville: Abingdon, 2000), 97.

5. Jonathan Campbell quoted in Paul Jensen, *The Collapse of Space and Time and The Spirituality of the Postmodern Generations* MP534 READER (Pasadena, CA: Fuller Theological Seminary's School of World Mission, 2003), 8.

6. Robert E. Webber, *Ancient-Future Evangelism: Making Your Church a Faith-Forming Community* (Grand Rapids: Baker, 2003), 62.

7. N. T. Wright, "The Christian Challenge in the Postmodern World," May 18, 2005, Lecture at the Church Leaders' Forum, Seattle Pacific University, http://www.spu.edu.depts/uc/response/summer2k5/features/postmodern.asp.

8. Marva J. Dawn, *Is It a Lost Cause?: Having the Heart of God for the Church's Children* (Grand Rapids: Eerdmans, 1997), 22.

9. Dawn, 23.

10. Mary Pipher, *The Shelter of Each Other: Rebuilding Our Families* (New York: Ballantine, 1996), 9.

11. Pipher, *Shelter of Each Other*, 13-14.

12. Pipher, *Shelter of Each Other*, 16.

13. Long, 76.

14. Webber, 123.

14. Webber, 124.

15. Dawn, 22,23,26,27.

16. Long, 79-80.

17. Back in the late seventies, sensing the need for Christians as well as people not yet following Jesus to understand God's story—this metanarrative—I wrote an overview of the Bible entitled *Getting to Know the Book of the Christian: A Historical Biographical Overview*. It contains thirty-six Bible studies that range from Genesis to Revelation (twenty-four studies in the Old Testament and twelve studies in the New).It may be beneficial for you to purchase this book for yourself and for those to whom you are ministering. You can do so online at TheLeadershipInstitute.org under "Books."

18. Wright, "The Christian Challenge."

19. Wright, "The Christian Challenge."

20. N. T. Wright, "Mere Mission", www.christianitytoday.com/ct/2007/january/22.38.html22

21. Michael Green, *Sharing Your Faith with Friends and Family: Talking about Jesus Without Offending* (Grand Rapids: Baker Books, 2005), 27.

22. Green, 28.

23. Green, 28.

24. Green, 28.

25. Green, 28.

Chapter 17

1. Eugene H. Peterson, *The Message: The Bible in Contemporary Language* (Colorado Springs: NavPress, 1995), 219.

2. John R. W. Stott in *Authentic Christianity*, ed. Timothy Dudley-Smith (Downers Grove: InterVarsity, 1995), 191.

3. Richard C. Halverson, *Wisdom on Life* (Gresham, OR: Vision House, 1994), section 44.

4. Edwin Dwight, *The Memoirs of Henry Obookiah* (Honolulu: Woman's Board of Missions for the Pacific Islands, the Hawaii Conference, the United Church of Christ, 1968), 14.

5. Dwight, 100.

6. Kevin Belmonte, *Hero for Humanity: A Biography of William Wilberforce* (Colorado Springs: NavPress, 2002), 89.

7. Paul Jensen, "The Spirituality and Mission of William Wilberforce and the Clapham Sect" (Orange, CA: an unpublished paper, 2000), 23.

8. David Watson, *I Believe in the Church* (Grand Rapids: Eerdmans, 1979), 37-38.

Chapter 18

1. Joseph C. Aldrich, *Life-Style Evangelism: Crossing Traditional Boundaries to Reach the Unbelieving World* (Portland: Multnomah, 1981), 20.
2. Elton Trueblood, *The Company of the Committed* (San Francisco: Harper & Row, 1980), 53.
3. Samuel M. Shoemaker as quoted in Trueblood, 54.
4. Trueblood, 54.
5. Brennan Manning, *Abba's Child: The Cry of the Heart for Intimate Belonging* (Colorado Springs: NavPress, 1994), 71.
6. Trueblood, 55.
7. Robert E. Webber, *Ancient-Future Evangelism: Making Your Church a Faith-Forming Community* (Grand Rapids: Baker, 2003), 124.

Chapter 19

1. Dallas Willard, *The Divine Conspiracy: Rediscovering Our Hidden Life in God* (San Francisco: HarperCollins, 1998), 285.
2. William Law, *A Serious Call to a Devout and Holy Life* (New York: Paulist Press, 1978), 57.
3. Law, 57.
4. Willard, 299.

For information regarding Chuck Miller speaking, teaching, training, or consulting, contact him at: cchuckm@cox.net or Barnabas Inc., PO Box 1358, Lake Forest, CA 92609.

Printed in the United States
153485LV00002B/6/A

9 781604 773132